Mastering the Java Virtual Machine

An in-depth guide to JVM internals and
performance optimization

Otavio Santana

Mastering the Java Virtual Machine

Group Product Manager: Kunal Sawant
Publishing Product Manager: Samriddhi Murarka
Book Project Manager: Manisha Singh
Senior Editor: Nisha Cleetus
Technical Editor: Vidhisha Patidar
Copy Editor: Safis Editing
Indexer: Rekha Nair
Production Designer: Aparna Bhagat
DevRel Marketing Coordinator: Shrinidhi Manoharan

First published: February 2024

Production reference: 2070324

Published by Packt Publishing Ltd.
Grosvenor House
11 St Paul's Square
Birmingham
B3 1RB, UK

ISBN 978-1-83546-796-1

www.packtpub.com

To my wife, Poliana Santana, for being my loving partner throughout our joint life journey as God's biggest blessing.

– Otavio Santana

Contributors

About the author

Otavio Santana is a passionate architect and software engineer focused on cloud and Java technologies. He has deep expertise in polyglot persistence and high-performance applications in finance, social media, and e-commerce.

Otavio has contributed to the Java and the open source ecosystem in several ways, such as helping the direction and objectives of the Java platform since Java 8 as a **Java Community Process (JCP)** executive member, besides being a committer and leader in several open source products and specifications.

Otavio is recognized for his open-source contributions and has received many awards, including all JCP Award categories and the Duke's Choice Award, to name a few. Otavio is also a distinguished Java Champion and Oracle ACE program member.

About the reviewers

Frank Delporte is a Java Champion and works as a senior technical writer at Azul, the largest company that is 100% focused on Java and the **Java Virtual Machine (JVM)**. He's the author of *Getting Started with Java on the Raspberry Pi* (webtechie.be/books) and a contributor to pi4j.com. Frank speaks at conferences and blogs (on webtechie.be and foojay.io) about Java, JavaFX, and experiments with electronics. For Foojay (the website for friends of OpenJDK), he also produces a podcast, with several episodes per month, covering a wide range of Java-related topics.

Artur Skowroński is head of Java/Kotlin engineering at VirtusLab and a trainer, conference speaker, and editor of the *JVM Weekly* newsletter, where he constantly covers the new advancements in the JVM world. With more than 10 years in the industry, he has had the opportunity to work in diverse roles, such as software engineer, tech lead, engineering manager, solution architect, and even technical product manager for the vived.io project. However, he always considers himself an engineer first and foremost.

Table of Contents

Part 2: Memory Management and Execution

4

Execution Engine   65

5

Memory Management   77

6

Garbage Collection and Memory Profiling   99

Part 3: Alternative JVMs

7

GraalVM   121

8

The JVM Ecosystem and Alternative JVMs   133

Part 4: Advanced Java Topics

9

Java Framework Principles   149

Preface

Mastering the Java Virtual Machine is your gateway to unlocking the mysteries of the **Java Virtual Machine (JVM)**, from its fundamental architecture to advanced Java concepts. In the dynamic world of Java development, understanding the intricacies of the JVM is paramount for crafting robust and high-performance applications. This book is crafted to cater to a spectrum of skill levels, whether you're a seasoned Java developer seeking to deepen your expertise or a newcomer eager to grasp the essentials.

Our goal is to empower you with comprehensive knowledge and practical insights that transcend the typical boundaries of JVM understanding. From the basics of class file structures to the nuances of memory management, execution engines, and garbage collection algorithms, each chapter builds upon the last, forming a cohesive narrative that guides you from foundational concepts to advanced Java topics.

As you traverse these pages, you'll explore the role of the JVM in executing Java applications and gain proficiency in optimizing performance through just-in-time compilation. We'll navigate the complexities of dynamic class loading, memory profiling, and alternative JVMs, including the intriguing landscape of GraalVM.

The exploration extends into Java framework principles, reflection, and the application of Java annotation processors. Each topic is accompanied by practical examples and real-world insights, ensuring that you grasp the theoretical concepts and learn how to apply them effectively in your projects.

Whether you're looking to fine-tune your Java applications, make informed decisions about JVM implementations, or enhance your understanding of Java development, this book is your comprehensive guide. The journey concludes with a thoughtful reflection on the covered material and recommendations for further exploration.

Embark on this odyssey into the heart of Java's powerhouse, and let *Mastering the Java Virtual Machine* be your compass. The knowledge within these pages empowers you to confidently navigate JVM's complexities and elevate your Java development skills to new heights.

Who this book is for

This book caters to a broad audience of Java developers, ranging from newcomers to seasoned professionals. It is ideal for those just starting in Java development, offering foundational insights into the language and its underlying processes. Intermediate Java programmers will find value in bridging the gap between basic and advanced development, gaining a deeper understanding of JVM intricacies to optimize their code effectively. For experienced software engineers, the book provides cutting-edge insights into dynamic class loading, memory management, and alternative JVMs, ensuring that their knowledge remains at the forefront of Java development. Technical managers and architects can use the book to make informed decisions about JVM implementations and overall Java development best practices. Computer science students and educators will also find the structured approach to JVM concepts suitable for educational purposes. Whether aiming to optimize Java application performance, deepen understanding of JVM internals, or stay abreast of the latest developments, this book is a comprehensive resource for a diverse audience, presenting content progressively for a seamless learning experience.

What this book covers

Mastering the Java Virtual Machine is a comprehensive guide designed to deepen your understanding of the **Java Virtual Machine (JVM)** and empower you to optimize Java application performance. Whether you're a seasoned Java developer seeking to enhance your skills or a novice looking to delve into the intricacies of JVM internals, this book is crafted to provide valuable insights and practical knowledge to elevate your Java development journey. Through detailed explanations, real-world examples, and hands-on exercises, you'll embark on a trip to master the inner workings of the JVM and explore advanced Java topics that will enrich your expertise in Java programming.

Chapter 1, Introduction to the Java Virtual Machine, offers a foundational overview of the JVM, elucidating its pivotal role in executing Java applications. You'll gain insights into the fundamental architecture of the JVM, exploring its key components and their functions in Java code execution.

Chapter 2, Class File Structure, delves into the structure of Java class files, understanding bytecode representation, constant pools, and the processes of class loading and verification within the JVM.

Chapter 3, Understanding Bytecodes, explores the bytecode instructions the JVM uses, enabling you to comprehend the low-level execution of Java applications and analyze bytecode instructions effectively.

Chapter 4, Execution Engine, dives into the JVM's execution engine, where you'll learn how bytecode is interpreted and optimized through **just-in-time compilation (JIT)**, enhancing your ability to fine-tune performance in Java applications.

Chapter 5, Memory Management, explores memory management concepts in the JVM, covering essential topics such as heap and stack management, garbage collection fundamentals, and memory allocation strategies for optimizing Java application memory usage.

Chapter 6, Garbage Collection and Memory Profiling, gains in-depth knowledge of garbage collection algorithms and memory profiling techniques employed by the JVM, equipping you with skills to optimize memory usage and identify performance bottlenecks effectively.

Chapter 7, GraalVM, embarks on exploring GraalVM, an innovative alternative JVM, and understands its unique features and potential use cases compared to traditional JVM implementations.

Chapter 8, JVM Ecosystem and Alternative JVMs, explores the broader JVM ecosystem, including alternative JVM implementations like OpenJ9 and GraalVM, and understand their distinctions and applications in Java development.

Chapter 9, Java Framework Principles, delves into the principles underlying the design of Java frameworks, offering insights into trade-offs, metadata usage, and annotation principles for effective framework design and utilization.

Chapter 10, Reflection, gains a comprehensive understanding of the reflection API in Java, exploring its capabilities for dynamic behavior, field access, method invocation, and proxy usage in Java applications.

Chapter 11, Java Annotation Processor, explores using Java Annotation Processors to read metadata at build time and generate code dynamically, enhancing your ability to streamline development tasks and improve code quality.

Chapter 12: Final Considerations explores the evolving landscape of Java development, discussing emerging trends and technologies such as Reactive Programming with Java. You'll grasp the fundamental principles of Reactive Programming, understand its role in designing responsive and scalable applications, and discover the usage of libraries like Reactor and RxJava for implementing reactive patterns. This chapter is a gateway to future exploration and growth in your Java development journey.

To get the most out of this book

Before you begin reading this book and diving into the software requirements, it is crucial to understand the following technologies: Java 17, Maven, Git, and Docker. Familiarity with Java 17 is assumed, including knowledge of its syntax, object-oriented programming concepts, and familiarity with core libraries and frameworks. Understanding Maven will be beneficial, as it is a popular build automation tool for managing dependencies and building Java projects. Proficiency in Git, a version control system, is necessary to track and manage source code changes effectively. Lastly, knowledge of Docker, a containerization platform, will help understand how to package and deploy software applications in isolated environments.

Software/hardware covered in the book	Operating system requirements
Java 17	Windows, OSx, or Linux
Maven	Windows, OSx, or Linux
Git	Windows, OSx, or Linux
Docker	Windows, OSx, or Linux

If you are using the digital version of this book, we advise you to type the code yourself or access the code from the book's GitHub repository (a link is available in the next section). Doing so will help you avoid any potential errors related to the copying and pasting of code.

Download the example code files

You can download the example code files for this book from GitHub at `https://github.com/PacktPublishing/Mastering-the-Java-Virtual-Machine`. If there's an update to the code, it will be updated in the GitHub repository.

We also have other code bundles from our rich catalog of books and videos available at `https://github.com/PacktPublishing/`. Check them out!

Conventions used

There are a number of text conventions used throughout this book.

`Code in text`: Indicates code words in text, database table names, folder names, filenames, file extensions, pathnames, dummy URLs, user input, and Twitter handles. Here is an example: "`ACC_PUBLIC (0x0001)` indicates that the class is public and can be accessed from other packages."

A block of code is set as follows:

```
public final class AccessSample {
    private int value;

    public AccessSample(int value) {
        this.value = value;
    }
}
```

When we wish to draw your attention to a particular part of a code block, the relevant lines or items are set in bold:

```
public class ConstantPoolSample {
    private String message = "Hello, Java!"; // String literal stored
                                             // in the constant pool
    public static void main(String[] args) {
        ConstantPoolSample sample = new ConstantPoolSample();
        System.out.println(sample.message); // Accessing the field
                                             // with a symbolic reference
    }
}
```

Any command-line input or output is written as follows:

```
javac Animal.java
javap -verbose Animal
```

Bold: Indicates a new term, an important word, or words that you see onscreen. For instance, words in menus or dialog boxes appear in **bold**. Here is an example: "It's worth mentioning that alternatives such as **InstantOn from Open Liberty** also exist"

> **Tips or important notes**
> Appear like this.

Get in touch

Feedback from our readers is always welcome.

General feedback: If you have questions about any aspect of this book, email us at `customercare@packtpub.com` and mention the book title in the subject of your message.

Errata: Although we have taken every care to ensure the accuracy of our content, mistakes do happen. If you have found a mistake in this book, we would be grateful if you would report this to us. Please visit `www.packtpub.com/support/errata` and fill in the form.

Piracy: If you come across any illegal copies of our works in any form on the internet, we would be grateful if you would provide us with the location address or website name. Please contact us at `copyright@packt.com` with a link to the material.

If you are interested in becoming an author: If there is a topic that you have expertise in and you are interested in either writing or contributing to a book, please visit `authors.packtpub.com`.

Share Your Thoughts

Once you've read *Mastering the Java Virtual Machine*, we'd love to hear your thoughts! Scan the QR code below to go straight to the Amazon review page for this book and share your feedback.

`https://packt.link/r/1835467962`

Your review is important to us and the tech community and will help us make sure we're delivering excellent quality content.

Download a free PDF copy of this book

Thanks for purchasing this book!

Do you like to read on the go but are unable to carry your print books everywhere?

Is your eBook purchase not compatible with the device of your choice?

Don't worry, now with every Packt book you get a DRM-free PDF version of that book at no cost.

Read anywhere, any place, on any device. Search, copy, and paste code from your favorite technical books directly into your application.

The perks don't stop there, you can get exclusive access to discounts, newsletters, and great free content in your inbox daily

Follow these simple steps to get the benefits:

1. Scan the QR code or visit the link below

https://packt.link/free-ebook/9781835467961

2. Submit your proof of purchase
3. That's it! We'll send your free PDF and other benefits to your email directly

Part 1: Understanding the JVM

Embarking on our journey, we unravel the fundamental workings of the **Java Virtual Machine** (**JVM**) and its pivotal role in executing Java applications. We then explore the intricate structure of Java class files, delving into bytecode, constant pools, and class loading processes. Transitioning further, our focus turns to decoding the language of the JVM, and its impact on the execution of Java programs. These introductory chapters set the stage for a progressive exploration into the depths of JVM intricacies, laying a solid foundation for mastering the JVM.

This part has the following chapters:

- *Chapter 1, Introduction to the Java Virtual Machine*
- *Chapter 2, Class File Structure*
- *Chapter 3, Understanding Bytecodes*

1

Introduction to the Java Virtual Machine

In the ever-expanding software development universe, Java is a shining star known for its versatility, cross-platform capabilities, and robust performance. At the heart of Java's exceptional capabilities lies the **Java Virtual Machine** (**JVM**), a sophisticated technology that serves as the backbone of the Java ecosystem. In this chapter, we embark on an enlightening journey to demystify the inner workings of the JVM, delving deep into its internals to unveil the secrets of its operation.

In this chapter, we will delve deeper into the historical evolution of the JVM, explore its architecture, and understand its role in executing Java applications. Furthermore, we'll cover essential topics, such as bytecode, class loading, memory management, and the execution engine, which form the foundation of the JVM's functioning. By the end of this chapter, you will possess the foundational knowledge needed to unravel the intricate inner workings of the JVM. So, let's begin our exploration of this marvel of technology as we journey into the heart of the JVM.

In this chapter, we'll explore more about those topics:

- A brief history of Java
- Introduction to the JVM
- How the JVM works

Technical requirements

This chapter's GitHub repository, found at - `https://github.com/PacktPublishing/Mastering-the-Java-Virtual-Machine/tree/main/chapter-01`

Exploring the evolution of Java

The Java programming language, along with its robust platform, has a storied history characterized by its unique and innovative features. A central figure in this narrative is the JVM, a crucial component that has left an indelible mark on Java's evolution and enduring significance. The JVM plays a pivotal role in making Java what it is today, and its importance to Java's history cannot be overstated.

The JVM is the linchpin that enables Java's *Write Once, Run Anywhere* promise to become a reality. This promise, which redefined software development, directly responded to the challenges of creating software for networked consumer devices such as set-top boxes, routers, and other multimedia devices. By design, the JVM allows compiled Java code to be transported across networks, operate seamlessly on various client machines, and provide safety assurance. The JVM's architecture and execution model ensures that Java programs behave consistently, regardless of their origin or the host machine they run on. This evolution from small, networked devices to large-scale servers showcases Java's versatility and enduring impact on the world of software development.

This capability became even more compelling with the rise of the World Wide Web. The ability to download and run Java programs within web browsers while guaranteeing safety was a game-changer. It provided unprecedented extensibility, allowing dynamic content to be added to web pages securely. This extensibility, demonstrated by the HotJava browser, showcased the JVM's role in shaping the web as we know it today.

However, it's worth noting that as the web evolved, technologies like Flash and Java browser plugins gradually disappeared due to security concerns and the emergence of more modern web standards. Despite these changes, the JVM's influence persisted in various domains, from enterprise server applications to Android mobile development, underscoring its enduring significance in the broader software landscape.

In essence, the JVM is the technological backbone that makes Java adaptable, secure, and platform independent. Its importance to Java's history lies in its ability to deliver on Java's promise, making it a foundational technology for web and software development. The enduring success and relevance of Java can be directly attributed to the JVM's role in its evolution, solidifying its place in the annals of computing history.

The historical journey of the JVM we've embarked upon not only sheds light on the rich tapestry of the Java platform's development but also underscores the pivotal role played by the JVM in shaping the platform's unique identity. From its inception as a response to the challenges of networked consumer devices to its transformative influence on web-based content and its extensibility, the JVM stands as the cornerstone of the Java ecosystem. This journey provides a fitting context for exploring the JVM's inner workings, as introduced in the next section.

Furthermore, it's worth noting that the JVM's influence extends beyond Java itself. It is the engine for many other languages such as Kotlin, Scala, Groovy, and more. Understanding the JVM's history allows us to appreciate how it has evolved to deliver on Java's promise of platform independence, its adaptability to various programming languages, and its enduring relevance in software development across multiple languages and applications.

An overview of the JVM

The JVM is the bedrock upon which the entire Java platform stands. It serves as the silent but omnipresent guardian of Java, facilitating its unique attributes. The JVM is responsible for the platform's independence from specific hardware and operating systems, the compact size of compiled Java code, and its formidable ability to safeguard users against malicious programs.

In essence, the JVM is an abstract computing machine, not unlike a tangible computer you might find on your desk. It boasts an instruction set and manipulates various memory areas by executing code at runtime. Implementing a programming language using a virtual machine is not new, with one of the most prominent examples being the P-Code machine of UCSD Pascal. This foundation allows the JVM to transcend physical hardware and provide a consistent environment for Java applications.

The journey of the JVM, however, began with a prototype implementation at Sun Microsystems, Inc., where it was hosted on a handheld device reminiscent of a contemporary **personal digital assistant (PDA)**. Today, Oracle's implementations have expanded the reach of the JVM to mobile, desktop, and server devices. Notably, the JVM doesn't tether itself to any particular implementation technology, host hardware, or operating system. It is a versatile entity that can be realized through interpretation, compilation, microcode, or direct silicon implementation.

What's unique about the JVM is that it knows nothing about the specifics of the Java programming language. Instead, it is intimately familiar with a particular binary format—the class file format. These class files encapsulate JVM instructions, also known as bytecodes, along with a symbol table and supplementary information.

To ensure security, the JVM enforces robust syntactic and structural constraints on the code contained within class files. However, this is where the JVM's inclusive nature shines. Any programming language with functionality that can be expressed in terms of a valid class file can find a hospitable home within the JVM. This inclusivity allows implementers of various languages to leverage the JVM as a delivery vehicle for their software, thanks to its machine-independent platform.

The JVM operates at the operating system layer, serving as a critical bridge between Java applications and the underlying hardware and operating system. It plays a crucial role in executing Java code while abstracting hardware complexities and providing a secure and consistent environment for Java applications.

It also acts as an interpreter for Java bytecode, transforming high-level Java code into low-level instructions that the underlying hardware can understand. It manages memory, handles multithreading, and provides various runtime services, allowing Java applications to run seamlessly across different platforms and operating systems.

A runtime instance of the JVM has a specific and well-defined life cycle. Its mission is clear—to run a single Java application. Here's a breakdown of the JVM life cycle:

1. **Instance birth**: When a Java application is launched, a runtime instance of the JVM is created. This instance is responsible for executing the application's bytecode and managing its runtime environment.

2. **Execution**: The JVM instance starts running the Java application by invoking the `main()` method of a designated initial class. This `main()` method serves as the entry point for the application and must meet specific criteria: it should be public, static, return `void`, and accept a single parameter, which is an array of strings, (`String[]`). As of the time of writing, it's important to note that the criteria for the `main()` method may evolve, as a preview version in Java 21 suggests potential simplifications. Therefore, developers should stay informed about the latest language updates and evolving best practices regarding the `main()` method's signature. Any class with such a `main()` method can serve as the starting point for a Java application.

3. **Application execution**: The JVM executes the Java application, processing its instructions and managing memory, threads, and other resources as needed.

4. **Application completion**: Once the Java application is executed, the JVM instance is no longer needed. At this point, the JVM instance dies.

It's important to note that the JVM follows a *one application per instance* model. Suppose you start multiple Java applications concurrently on the same computer, using the same concrete implementation of the JVM. In that case, you'll have multiple JVM instances, each dedicated to running its respective Java application. These JVM instances are isolated from each other, ensuring the independence and security of each Java application.

In concluding this comprehensive JVM overview, we've journeyed through the foundational elements that make Java a versatile and platform-independent programming language. The JVM, the linchpin of Java's execution environment, orchestrates the seamless integration of diverse code across operating systems and architectures. As we transition to the next section, our understanding of the JVM's inner workings primes us to explore the dynamic processes that unfold when Java code comes to life more deeply. This exploration will unravel the intricate steps taken by the JVM in executing Java applications, shedding light on the magic that happens behind the scenes. Join us as we embark on the journey to uncover the execution intricacies of Java code within the JVM.

How the JVM executes Java code

The JVM is a remarkable technology that plays a central role in executing Java applications. It's designed to make Java platform-independent, allowing you to write once, and run anywhere. However, understanding how the JVM works involves not only Java but also the integration of native code to interact with specific hardware and operating systems.

The JVM executes Java applications, which are written in the Java programming language and compiled into bytecode. Bytecode is a low-level representation of Java code that is platform-independent. When a Java application is executed, the JVM interprets or compiles this bytecode into machine code for the host system's hardware.

To interact with the host system and leverage platform-specific features, the JVM can use native methods. These native methods are written in languages such as C or C++ and are dynamically linked to the specific platform on which the JVM is running. These methods provide a bridge between the platform-independent Java code and the native code specific to the host system.

Native methods are beneficial when Java applications need to access information from the operating system or utilize system resources that are not easily accessible through pure Java code. For example, when working with filesystems, directories, or other platform-specific features, native methods can provide a direct interface to the underlying operating system.

It's crucial to understand that despite the Java programming language's commitment to platform independence, the JVM is inherently platform-specific. It signifies that a tailored virtual machine implementation exists for every distinct platform. This virtual machine implementation is a specific instantiation of the JVM designed to adapt seamlessly to the peculiarities of the host system's hardware architecture and operating system. This platform-specific adaptation ensures optimal compatibility and performance, emphasizing the JVM's dynamic nature as it tailors its execution environment to the unique characteristics of each underlying platform.

In the captivating visual of *Figure 1.1*, we witness the seamless execution of a unique Java program across three distinct platforms: Windows, macOS, and Linux, all thanks to the JVM. Each venue boasts its dedicated JVM instance, tailored to its specific hardware and operating system. The beauty of this scene lies in the uniformity of the program itself – it remains unaltered, a testament to the *Write Once, Run Anywhere* promise of Java. As we observe, the program's functionality remains consistent across the trio of operating systems, emphasizing the platform independence that the JVM bestows. It's a striking demonstration of the JVM's adaptability, ensuring that the same Java program can thrive harmoniously in the diverse landscapes of Windows, macOS, and Linux, embodying the essence of cross-platform compatibility.

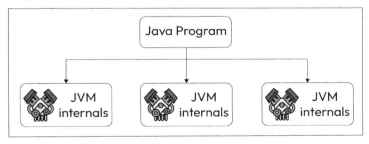

Figure 1.1: The JVM across multi-platforms

The JVM serves a singular yet vital purpose: to execute Java applications. Its life cycle is straightforward, giving birth to a new instance when an application begins and gracefully concluding its existence when the application completes. Each application, when launched, triggers the creation of its dedicated JVM instance. It means that running the same code three times on the same machine initiates three independent JVMs.

While the JVM may operate quietly in the background, numerous concurrent processes ensure its continuous availability. These processes are the unsung heroes that keep the JVM running seamlessly. These are as follows:

- **Timers**: Timers are the clockwork of the JVM, orchestrating events that occur periodically, such as interruptions and repetitive processes. They play a crucial role in maintaining the synchrony of the JVM's operations.

- **Garbage collector processes**: The garbage collector processes manage memory within the JVM. They execute the essential task of cleaning up memory by identifying and disposing of objects that are no longer in use, ensuring efficient memory utilization.

- **Compilers**: Compilers within the JVM take on the transformative role of converting bytecode, the low-level representation of Java code, into native code that the host system's hardware can understand. This process, known as **just-in-time** (**JIT**) compilation, enhances the performance of Java applications.

- **Listeners**: Listeners serve as the attentive ears of the JVM, ready to receive signals and information. Their primary function is to relay this information to the appropriate processes within the JVM, ensuring that critical data reaches its intended destination.

Diving deeper into the parallel processes or threads within the JVM, it's essential to recognize that the JVM allows concurrently executing multiple threads. These threads run in parallel and enable Java applications to perform tasks simultaneously. This concurrency in Java is closely linked to native threads, the fundamental units of parallel execution at the operating system level. Additionally, it's worth noting that, as of Java 21, virtual threads have become a new feature. Virtual threads introduce a lightweight form of concurrency that can be managed more efficiently, potentially altering the landscape of parallel execution in Java. Developers should consider this while considering thread management strategies for their applications.

When a parallel process or thread in Java is born, it undergoes a series of initial steps to prepare for its execution:

1. **Memory allocation**: The JVM allocates memory resources to the thread, including a dedicated portion of the heap for storing its objects and data. Each thread has its own memory space, ensuring isolation from other threads.

2. **Object synchronization**: Thread synchronization mechanisms, such as locks and monitors, are established to coordinate access to shared resources. Synchronization ensures that threads do not interfere with each other's execution and helps prevent data corruption in multi-threaded applications.

3. **Creation of specific registers**: The thread is equipped with specific registers, which are part of the thread's execution context. These registers hold data and execution state information, allowing the thread to operate efficiently.

4. **Allocation of the native thread**: A native thread, managed by the operating system, is allocated to support the Java thread's execution. The native thread is responsible for executing the Java code and interacting with the underlying hardware and operating system.

If an exception occurs during the execution of a thread, the native part of the JVM promptly communicates this information back to the JVM itself. The JVM is responsible for handling the exception, making necessary adjustments, and ensuring the thread's safety and integrity. If the exception is not recoverable, the JVM closes the thread.

When a thread completes its execution, it releases all the specific resources associated with it. It includes the resources managed by the Java part of the JVM, such as memory and objects, and the resources allocated by the native part, including the native thread. These resources are efficiently reclaimed and returned to the JVM, ensuring that the JVM remains responsive and resource efficient.

In essence, thread management in the JVM is a complex and highly orchestrated process, allowing for concurrently executing multiple threads, each with its own memory space and specific resources.

In the realm of data, the JVM operates with two fundamental categories:

- **Primitives**: Primitives are basic data types that include numeric types, Boolean values, and return addresses. These types do not require extensive type checking or verification at runtime. They operate with specific instructions tailored to their respective data types. For example, instructions such as `iadd`, `ladd`, `fadd`, and `dadd` handle integer, long, float, and double values, respectively.

- **Reference values**: The JVM supports objects that are either instances of dynamically allocated classes or arrays. These values fall under the reference type, and their operation closely resembles that of languages such as C/C++. Reference values represent complex data structures, and the JVM performs runtime type checking and verification to ensure the integrity and compatibility of these data structures.

In the realm of primitive types, the JVM encompasses numeric types, which cover both integers and floating-point values. The ability to handle simple data types and complex, reference-based data structures allows the JVM to support various applications and scenarios.

The JVM's capacity to gracefully handle exceptions, manage the life cycle of threads, and operate on both primitive and reference data types reflects its robust and versatile nature, making it a cornerstone of the Java platform.

The JVM is a versatile and powerful platform that supports various primitive data types, each serving distinct roles in Java programming. These primitive data types are fundamental building blocks for defining variables and handling basic data operations within the JVM. From numeric types such as integers and floating-point values to Boolean values and the unique `returnAddress` type, these data types play a critical role in the efficient and precise execution of Java programs.

Figure 1.2 shows the JVM types split by primitives and reference values.

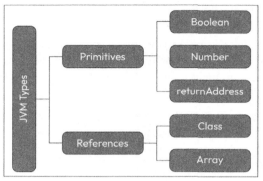

Figure 1.2: The JVM types

Each type also has a size and range. *Table 1.1* provides a comprehensive overview of the JVM's primitive data types, including their names, sizes, variations, default values, and types. It offers a valuable reference for Java developers and enthusiasts to understand the core data types at the heart of the JVM.

Type Name	Size (bits)	Variation	Default Value	Type
byte	8	-128 to 127	0	Numeric
short	16	-32,768 to 32,767	0	Numeric
int	32	-2,147,483,648 to 2,147,483,647	0	Numeric
long	64	-9,223,372,036,854,775,808 to 9,223,372,036,854,775,807	0	Numeric
float	32	IEEE 754 single precision	0.0	Numeric
double	64	IEEE 754 double precision	0.0	Numeric
char	16	0 to 65,535	'\u0000'	Numeric
boolean	N/A	N/A	false	Boolean
returnAddress	N/A	N/A	N/A	returnAddress

Table 1.1: JVM's primitive data types, including their names, sizes, variations, default values, and types

These primitive types in the JVM encompass various numeric types, Booleans, and the particular `returnAddress` type, each with its own characteristics and default values. This table is a quick reference for understanding these primitive data types within the JVM.

The `returnAddress` type in the JVM represents a particular data type critical in method invocation and return. This type is internal to the JVM and is not directly accessible or utilized by the Java programming language. Here's an explanation of the importance and reason behind the `returnAddress` type:

- **Method invocation and return**: The `returnAddress` type is used by the JVM to manage method invocations and returns efficiently. When a method is invoked, the JVM needs to keep track of where to return once it completes its execution. This is crucial for maintaining the flow of control in a program and ensuring that the execution context is correctly restored after a method call.

- **Call stack management**: In the JVM, the call stack is a critical data structure that keeps track of method calls and returns. It maintains a stack of `returnAddress` values, each representing the address to which control should return when a method completes. This stack is known as the method call stack or execution stack.

- **Recursion**: The `returnAddress` type is essential in handling recursive method calls. When a method invokes itself or another method multiple times, the JVM relies on `returnAddress` values to ensure that control returns to the correct calling point, preserving the recursive state.

The `returnAddress` type is an internal mechanism the JVM uses to manage method invocation and return at a low level. It is not part of the Java programming language specification, and Java code does not directly interact with or access `returnAddress` values. This design decision aligns with Java's goals of providing a high-level, platform-independent, and secure language.

The JVM handles the management of `returnAddress` values transparently, ensuring that method calls and returns within Java code are seamless and reliable. By abstracting this lower-level functionality from the Java language, Java programs can focus on high-level logic and application development without the need to manage the intricacies of the call stack and `returnAddress` values.

The `returnAddress` type is a crucial part of the JVM's internal mechanisms for managing method invocations and returns. While it is significant for the JVM's operation, it remains hidden from the Java language itself, as the JVM handles it transparently to ensure the integrity and reliability of method calls and returns in Java programs.

In the JVM, the boolean type has limited native support. Unlike other programming languages where boolean values are represented as a distinct data type, in the JVM, boolean values are managed using the `int` type. This design choice simplifies the implementation of the JVM and also has historical reasons tied to the bytecode instruction set.

Here are some key aspects of how boolean values are treated in the JVM:

- **Boolean as integers**: The JVM represents boolean values as integers, with 1 typically denoting `true` and 0 representing `false`. This means that boolean values are essentially treated as a subset of integers.

- **Instructions**: In JVM bytecode instructions, there are no specific instructions for boolean operations. Instead, operations on boolean values are carried out using integer instructions. For example, comparisons or logical operations involving boolean values are performed using integer instructions such as `if_icmpne` (if int comparison not equal), `if_icmpeq` (if int comparison equal), and so on.

- **Boolean arrays**: When working with arrays of boolean values, such as `boolean[]`, the JVM often treats them as byte arrays. The JVM uses bytes (8 bits) to represent boolean values, which align with the `byte` data type.

- **Efficiency and simplicity**: The choice to represent boolean values as integers simplifies the JVM's design and makes it more efficient. It reduces the need for additional instructions and data types, which helps keep the JVM implementation straightforward.

While this approach may seem somewhat unconventional, it is a part of the JVM's design philosophy that aims to maintain efficiency and simplicity while supporting boolean values within Java programs. It's worth noting that while boolean values are represented as integers in the JVM bytecode, Java developers can work with boolean values using the familiar `true` and `false` literals in their Java source code, and the JVM takes care of the necessary conversions during execution.

In the JVM, reference values are pivotal in managing complex data structures and objects. These reference values represent and interact with three main types: classes, arrays, and interfaces. Here's a closer look at these reference types in the JVM:

- **Classes**: The foundation of object-oriented programming in Java. They define the blueprint for creating objects and encapsulating data and behavior. In the JVM, reference values for classes are used to point to instances of these classes. When you create an object of a class, you create an instance of that class, and the reference value points to this instance.

- **Arrays**: Arrays in Java provide a way to store collections of elements of the same data type. In the JVM, reference values for arrays are used to reference these arrays. Arrays can be of primitive data types or objects, and the reference value helps access and manipulate the array's elements.

- **Interfaces**: Interfaces are a fundamental concept in Java, allowing for the definition of contracts that classes must adhere to. Reference values for interfaces are used to point to objects that implement these interfaces. When you work with interfaces in Java, you use reference values to interact with objects that fulfill the interface's requirements.

One common characteristic of reference values in the JVM is their initial state, which is always set to `null`. The `null` state represents the absence of an object or a reference to an object. It is not a defined type but a universal indicator of an uninitialized reference value. Reference values can be cast to `null`, regardless of their specific type.

Setting reference values to `null` is particularly useful when you need to release resources, indicate that an object is no longer in use, or simply initialize a reference without pointing it to a specific object. Handling `null` references is a crucial aspect of Java programming used for various purposes, including memory management and program logic.

Reference values in the JVM are essential for managing classes, arrays, and interfaces. They provide a means to work with complex data structures and objects in Java. Initializing reference values as `null` allows flexibility and precision when working with objects, making it a fundamental aspect of Java's reference handling.

In the JVM, `null` is a special reference value that represents the absence of an object or the lack of a reference to an object. It is not a defined type but indicates that a reference value does not currently point to any object. When a reference is set to `null`, it effectively means it is not referencing any valid object in memory.

The concept of `null` serves several important purposes in the Java language and the JVM:

- **Initialization:** When you declare a reference variable but do not assign it to an object, the default initial value for that reference is `null`. This default value is essential for scenarios where you want to declare a reference but not immediately associate it with an object. This practice allows you to declare a reference variable and assign it to an object when needed, giving you flexibility in your program's structure.

- **Absence of value:** `null` indicates no valid object associated with a particular reference. It is useful for cases where you need to represent that no meaningful data or object is available at a certain point in your program.

- **Resource release:** While setting references to `null` can help indicate to the JVM that an object is no longer needed, it's essential to clarify that the primary responsibility for memory management and resource cleanup lies with the Java **Garbage Collector** (**GC**). The GC automatically identifies and reclaims memory occupied by no longer-reachable objects, effectively managing memory resources. Developers typically do not need to set references to `null` for memory cleanup explicitly; it's a task handled by the GC.

While `null` is a valuable concept in Java and the JVM, its usage comes with trade-offs and considerations:

- **NullPointerException:** One of the main trade-offs is the risk of `NullPointerException`. If you attempt to perform operations on a reference set to `null`, it can lead to a runtime exception. Therefore, it's crucial to handle `null` references properly to avoid unexpected program crashes.

- **Defensive programming**: Programmers need to be diligent in checking for `null` references before using them to prevent `NullPointerException`. It can lead to additional code for `null` checks and make it more complex.

- **Resource management**: While setting references to `null` can help release resources, it's not a guaranteed method for resource management. Some resources may require explicit cleanup or disposal, and relying solely on setting references to `null` may not be sufficient.

- **Design considerations**: When designing classes and APIs, it's important to provide clear guidance on how references are meant to be used and under what circumstances they can be set to `null`.

In summary, in the JVM, `null` is a valuable tool for representing the absence of objects and for resource management. However, it requires careful handling to avoid `NullPointerException` and ensure proper program behavior. Proper design and coding practices can help mitigate the trade-offs associated with using `null`.

In this comprehensive overview of the JVM, we've explored the inner workings and critical components that make Java a powerful and versatile programming platform. The JVM serves as the backbone of the Java ecosystem, providing the ability to run Java applications across diverse operating systems and hardware architectures. We've delved into its support for primitive and reference data types, its handling of `null` concerns, and its role in managing classes, arrays, and interfaces.

Through the JVM, Java achieves its *Write Once, Run Anywhere* promise, enabling developers to create platform-independent applications. However, understanding the JVM's intricacies, including how it manages threads, memory, and resources, is essential for optimizing Java applications and ensuring their reliability.

The JVM's design choices, such as representing boolean values as integers, reflect a balance between simplicity and efficiency. We've also touched on the importance of `returnAddress` for managing method invocations and returns.

The JVM is a remarkable and intricate technology that empowers Java developers to build robust, secure, and platform-agnostic software. With its unique features and capabilities, the JVM is a cornerstone of Java's enduring success in software development.

Summary

In this chapter, you have comprehensively understood the JVM, unraveling its critical role in executing Java applications. We explored the platform-specific nature of the JVM, emphasizing that, despite the Java language's platform independence, each platform requires a distinct virtual machine implementation for optimal compatibility and performance.

The information provided in this chapter is invaluable for several reasons. Firstly, it demystifies the underlying workings of the JVM, shedding light on its role in making Java's *Write Once, Run Anywhere* promise a reality. Understanding the JVM's platform-specific adaptation is crucial for developers and practitioners in ensuring their Java applications perform optimally across diverse hardware and operating system environments.

Looking ahead to the next chapter, *How the JVM Executes Java Code*, you can expect a deeper dive into the dynamic processes that occur when Java code is executed within the JVM. This exploration will provide practical insights into the inner workings of the JVM during code execution, equipping you with essential knowledge applicable to real-life workplace scenarios. As developers encounter various platform environments, the insights gained from this chapter will empower you to navigate the intricacies of the JVM, optimize Java code for diverse computing landscapes, and enhance your problem-solving capabilities in real-world Java development scenarios.

As we conclude our exploration of the JVM, we're now poised to venture further into the heart of Java's core by diving into the intricate world of *class file structures* in the next chapter. Understanding the structure of class files is pivotal in comprehending how Java code is organized, compiled, and executed within the JVM. So, let's move forward and explore the building blocks that make Java's class files come to life, bridging our journey from the JVM to the fascinating realm of Java's class structures.

Questions

Answer the following questions to test your knowledge of this chapter:

1.   What is the primary purpose of the JVM?

    A.   To write Java code

    B.   To compile Java code

    C.   To run Java applications

    D.   To debug Java code

2.   How does the JVM handle boolean values?

    A.   As a distinct data type

    B.   As an array of bytes

    C.   As an integer type

    D.   As a floating-point type

3.   What is the initial state of a reference value in the JVM?

    A.   Undefined

    B.   Zero

    C.   Null

    D.   True

4. Which of the following is not a type of reference in the JVM?

    A. Classes

    B. Arrays

    C. Interfaces

    D. Primitives

5. What is the primary role of the `returnAddress` type in the JVM?

    A. Representing boolean values

    B. Managing method invocations and returns

    C. Handling exceptions

    D. Storing reference values

Answers

Here are the answers to this chapter's questions:

1. C. To run Java applications

2. C. As an integer type

3. C. Null

4. D. Primitives

5. B. Managing method invocations and returns

2

Class File Structure

Within the intricate tapestry of **Java virtual machine** (**JVM**) internals, the class file structure is a vital guide, leading us through the intricate dance of bytecode, constant pools, and class loading. As we delve into this chapter, our focus sharpens on unraveling the binary intricacies encoded within Java class files, shedding light on the mechanisms orchestrating the seamless execution of Java applications.

At its core, bytecode serves as the silent conductor, translating the high-level language of Java into a form understandable to the JVM. This chapter dissects the bytecode architecture, exploring how it encapsulates program logic and bridges the semantic gap between developers and the JVM. Parallelly, we unveil the symbolic repository known as the constant pool, delving into its role as a keeper of constants, strings, and other symbolic elements. Additionally, we explore class loading, the dynamic gateway shaping the runtime environment, and its pivotal role in bringing Java classes to life within the JVM. This chapter will teach you the components of a class file so that you have all the knowledge to convert Java files to class files in the next chapter.

In this chapter, we'll explore the following topics:

- Decoding class files
- Understanding the headers of class file
- Fields and data repositories
- Methods of the Java class file

Technical requirements

For this chapter, you will require the following:

- Java 21
- Git
- Maven
- Any preferred IDE

- This chapter's GitHub repository, found at - `https://github.com/PacktPublishing/Mastering-the-Java-Virtual-Machine/tree/main/chapter-02`

Decoding class files

The class file structure is the linchpin in the symbiotic relationship between compiled Java code and the JVM. In JVM execution, where platform independence is paramount, the class file format emerges as a standardized, hardware-agnostic binary representation of compiled Java code. This format is a pivotal bridge, allowing developers to express their intent through high-level Java code (and even other languages such as Kotlin) while ensuring the JVM can understand and execute it seamlessly across diverse hardware and operating systems.

This structured format is not merely a binary translation of Java source code; it is a meticulous blueprint that the JVM relies upon to navigate the intricacies of bytecode, constant pools, and class loading. By adhering to the class file structure, the JVM gains a universal understanding of how to interpret and execute Java programs. Moreover, the class file format encapsulates critical details, such as byte ordering, which might vary in platform-specific object file formats. This precision becomes indispensable in guaranteeing consistent execution, irrespective of the underlying hardware or operating system, emphasizing the pivotal role of the class file structure in upholding the cross-platform compatibility foundational to Java's promise of "*write once, run anywhere.*" The class file structure is the Rosetta Stone that ensures the harmonious translation of Java's high-level abstractions into the language comprehensible to the JVM, fostering a realm where Java's portability and versatility come to life.

Java class files, the binary blueprints of compiled Java code, adhere to a structured format crucial for the JVM to interpret and execute programs seamlessly. Each element uniquely encapsulates the information necessary for the JVM to execute Java programs, from headers to fields and methods. This section provides an overarching view of the class file structure, laying the foundation for a deeper understanding of its components.

Figure 2.1 vividly illustrates the transformative journey of a Java file into its corresponding class file structure. The process initiates with a pristine Java file, symbolized by a clear and concise code snippet. This raw representation encapsulates the developer's logic, intentions, and functionalities, serving as the blueprint for a Java program.

The next phase unfolds as a compilation stage, where a compiler, depicted as a dynamic conversion engine, translates the human-readable Java code into an intermediate form known as bytecode. This bytecode, represented in a series of compact, platform-independent instructions, mirrors the abstract operations of the original Java code.

The figure further evolves to showcase the assembly of the class file structure. Here, the bytecode is meticulously organized, encapsulating the compiled instructions and metadata, such as method signatures, access modifiers, and data structures. These elements collectively construct the intricate framework of the class file, a binary representation optimized for execution within the JVM.

As the visual journey concludes, the transition from Java code to class file structure becomes a testament to the cross-platform capabilities of Java. This process ensures that the compiled Java program can seamlessly execute in diverse environments, maintaining the essence of the developer's logic while adhering to the platform-independent nature of the JVM. *Figure 2.1* encapsulates the elegance and efficiency of the compilation process, where the abstract ideas coded in Java materialize into a structured and executable form within the Java class file. Let us look at the following figure to understand this:

Java Source   Java Compiler   Class file

Figure 2.1: The process of converting Java source code into a class file

The elegant structure of the JVM class file is precisely defined. It begins with the **magic** number and minor and major version details and then moves on to the constant pool, a linguistic repository essential for runtime interpretation. The access flags, class hierarchy, and interfaces are then listed, paving the way for fields and methods to encapsulate data and behavior. This streamlined structure ensures the seamless execution of Java applications, where each component is a vital note in the symphony of bytecode transformation within the JVM. The following code block shows the overall picture of bytecode transformation:

```
ClassFile {
    u4              magic;
    u2              minor_version;
    u2              major_version;
    u2              constant_pool_count;
    cp_info         constant_pool[constant_pool_count-1];
    u2              access_flags;
    u2              this_class;
    u2              super_class;
    u2              interfaces_count;
    u2              interfaces[interfaces_count];
    u2              fields_count;
    field_info      fields[fields_count];
    u2              methods_count;
    method_info     methods[methods_count];
    u2              attributes_count;
    attribute_info  attributes[attributes_count];
}
```

In our quest to unravel the inner workings of Java class files, a crucial juncture emerges as we focus on the examination of headers, fields, and methods. These elements constitute the fabric of the class file structure, each playing a distinct role in shaping the landscape through which the JVM navigates.

The journey begins with exploring class file headers, akin to the preamble setting the stage for a performance. Headers harbor essential metadata, providing the JVM with crucial information to orchestrate the execution of Java programs. Following this, we delve into fields and data repositories within class files. Understanding the organization and types of fields illuminates the data architecture that underlies Java classes. Finally, our odyssey concludes with examining methods and the engines that drive program execution. Here, we dissect how methods encode the logic of Java programs, enabling their dynamic and seamless interpretation by the JVM. This exploration promises to demystify the intricate relation between headers, fields, and methods, unlocking the gateway to a deeper comprehension of Java class files.

In unraveling the intricate layers of Java class files, we've navigated through the architectural nuances that define the heart of Java programs. From the distinctive magic signature to the orchestrated dance of fields and methods, each component plays a pivotal role in shaping the functionality and structure of a class. As we conclude this session, the journey seamlessly extends into the next, where we will delve into the headers of class files. Understanding these headers is akin to deciphering the preamble to execution, unlocking the foundational elements that guide the JVM in interpreting and executing code. Join us in the next session as we explore the vital information encapsulated in class file headers, bridging the gap between high-level Java code and the dynamic realm of the JVM.

Understanding the headers of class file

Headers serve as the introductory notes, containing metadata crucial for the JVM. This section explores the header's role in setting the stage for Java program execution. The class file header serves as the gatekeeper, guiding the JVM through the intricacies of the bytecode that follows. It houses details such as the Java version compatibility defining the language features the class file relies upon. Additionally, the header declares the class' constant pool, a symbolic repository that references strings, types, and other constants, further shaping the semantic landscape for program interpretation. A nuanced understanding of class file headers is essential for developers, as it forms the basis for the JVM's decisions during the loading and execution phases, ensuring the harmonious translation of high-level Java code into the binary language comprehensible to the virtual machine. As we navigate this pivotal section, we will unravel the significance of each byte within the header, unlocking the door to a deeper appreciation of how class files lay the groundwork for the seamless execution of Java programs within the JVM.

Within the class file header, a trove of vital information is meticulously encoded, serving as the cornerstone for the JVM's understanding and execution of Java programs. Let's delve into the critical elements housed within this preamble:

- **Magic number**: At the very outset of the header lies the magic number, a distinctive set of bytes that uniquely identifies a file as a Java class file. With the hexadecimal value of 0xCAFEBABE, this cryptographic signature is the JVM's first verification step, ensuring it deals with a valid class file. The presence of this magic number is akin to a secret handshake, allowing the JVM to confidently proceed with the interpretation and execution of the associated bytecode. It is an unmistakable mark, signaling the file's legitimacy and setting the foundation for a secure and accurate runtime environment within the JVM.

- **Java version compatibility**: The declaration of Java version compatibility within the class file header is a pivotal piece of information. This section indicates the language features and specifications the class file adheres to, allowing the JVM to interpret bytecode correctly. The compatibility is expressed through two integral components—`minor_version` and `major_version`:

  - `minor_version`: This represents the minor version of the Java compiler that generated the class file. It reflects incremental changes or updates to the compiler that don't introduce significant modifications.

  - `major_version`: This signifies the primary version of the compiler. A change in the major version indicates significant alterations or the introduction of new language features.

Navigating the rich tapestry of Java class files, the declaration of Java version compatibility within the class file header serves as a crucial compass, guiding the JVM to interpret bytecode precisely. The interplay between `minor_version` and `major_version` delineates incremental changes in the compiler and signifies major milestones in Java's evolution. To illuminate this journey, the following table unfolds the correlation between `major_version` and the corresponding Java SE releases, spanning from the inception of JDK 1.1 to the latest innovations in Java SE 21. This comprehensive roadmap encapsulates the symbiotic relationship between class files and Java versions, showcasing how the JVM dynamically adapts to the nuanced evolution of the Java language, ensuring seamless compatibility and execution across a spectrum of releases:

major_version	Java release
45	JDK 1.1
46	JDK 1.2
47	JDK 1.3
48	JDK 1.4
49	J2SE 5.0
50	Java SE 6
51	Java SE 7
52	Java SE 8
53	Java SE 9
54	Java SE 10

major_version	Java release
55	Java SE 11
56	Java SE 12
57	Java SE 13
58	Java SE 14
59	Java SE 15
60	Java SE 16
61	Java SE 17
62	Java SE 18
63	Java SE 19
64	Java SE 20
65	Java SE 21

Table 2.1: The class file version

By analyzing these version numbers, the JVM ensures it interprets the bytecode with the appropriate language specifications, fostering compatibility between the Java class file and the runtime environment. This nuanced versioning system allows for the seamless evolution of Java, ensuring backward compatibility while accommodating new language enhancements introduced in successive releases.

- **Constant pool reference**: Nestled within the intricate tapestry of the class file structure, the constant pool emerges as a symbolic treasure trove, encompassing references to strings, classes, field names, method names, and other pivotal constants crucial for the interpretation and execution of Java programs. In specifying that the class file header *references the start of the constant pool*, we denote that this header contains vital information indicating the initiation point of the constant pool within the overall class file architecture. This nuanced detail is a guiding beacon for the JVM, directing it to the dynamic repository of symbolic information. It's akin to a map, ensuring the JVM efficiently navigates and interprets the constant pool, unlocking the foundational elements essential for accurately executing Java code.

This reference is a crucial link that connects the class file's binary representation to the rich semantic world of the Java programming language. Each entry in the constant pool serves as a linguistic building block, enabling the JVM to comprehend and execute the bytecode accurately.

Let's take a simple Java class as an example to illustrate the constant pool reference:

```
public class SampleClass {
    public static void main(String[] args) {
        String greeting = "Hello, Java!";
        System.out.println(greeting);
    }
}
```

In this snippet, the constant pool would include entries for the following:

- `SampleClass`: A symbolic representation of the class itself
- `main`: A reference to the method name
- `String`: A reference to the `String` class
- `"Hello, Java!"`: A reference to the string literal

The constant pool reference in the class file header points to the beginning of this pool, allowing the JVM to access and utilize these symbolic entities efficiently during program execution. Understanding this linkage sheds light on how the JVM translates high-level Java constructs into the binary language encapsulated within class files.

- **Access flags**: Encoded within the class file header, access flags are a set of binary values that convey essential information about the accessibility and nature of a Java class. These flags define the class' characteristics, such as whether it is public, final, abstract, or possesses other attributes. Access flags serve as blueprints for the JVM to enforce access control and comprehend the structural nuances of the class during program execution.

The following are some common access flags:

- `ACC_PUBLIC (0x0001)`: Indicates that the class is public and can be accessed from other packages
- `ACC_FINAL (0x0010)`: Denotes that the class cannot be subclassed, providing a level of restriction to its inheritance
- `ACC_SUPER (0x0020)`: Historically used to indicate that the `invokespecial` instruction should be used rather than `invokevirtual` when invoking methods on the superclass
- `ACC_INTERFACE (0x0200)`: Signals that the class is an interface rather than a regular class
- `ACC_ABSTRACT (0x0400)`: Marks the class as abstract, implying that it cannot be instantiated independently
- `ACC_SYNTHETIC (0x1000)`: Indicates that a compiler generated the class and is not in the source code

- `ACC_ANNOTATION (0x2000)`: Denotes that the class is an annotation type
- `ACC_ENUM (0x4000)`: Marks the class as an enumerated type

    Consider the following Java class as an example:

    ```java
    public final class AccessSample {
        private int value;

        public AccessSample(int value) {
            this.value = value;
        }

        public int getValue() {
            return value;
        }

        public static void main(String[] args) {
            AccessSample sample = new AccessSample(42);
            System.out.println("Sample Value: " + sample.
            getValue());
        }
    }
    ```

In this illustrative example, we have the following:

- `ACC_PUBLIC`: Signals the class' declaration as public, allowing its accessibility from other classes
- `ACC_FINAL`: Imposes finality on the class, inhibiting inheritance and ensuring its structure remains unaltered
- `ACC_SUPER`: Automatically configured by the compiler, this flag ensures the invocation of superclass methods is performed efficiently
- `ACC_SYNTHETIC`: Indicates the absence of synthetic elements in this straightforward class, providing transparency in code understanding

While shedding light on the intricacies of the code undoubtedly holds value, it is paramount to embark on a more comprehensive exploration. It entails going beyond surface-level explanations and explicitly articulating the invaluable advantages that come with a deep understanding of each class' distinctive characteristics. By delving deeper into the significance of these access modifiers, we illuminate what is happening in the code and why it matters. Understanding the nature of each class and its associated flags fosters a more transparent comprehension of the codebase, promoting effective collaboration among developers and ensuring robust, maintainable, and transparent software development practices.

Understanding these flags provides insights into the nature of the class but also enables the JVM to enforce access control and execute the Java program with precision.

- **This class and superclass information**: The header includes indices pointing to the constant pool entries representing the current class and its superclass. This information establishes the class hierarchy, allowing the JVM to navigate the inheritance structure during execution.
- **Interfaces, fields, and methods counts**: Counts of interfaces, fields, and methods declared in the class follow in the header. These values provide the JVM with a blueprint of the class structure, enabling efficient memory allocation and execution planning.

Understanding these details encoded within the header is akin to deciphering the DNA of a Java class file. It forms the basis for the JVM's decisions during class loading, verification, and execution, ensuring a seamless and accurate translation of high-level Java code into executable bytecode. The header, therefore, stands not just as a preamble but as a critical guidepost, steering the JVM through the intricate landscape of class file interpretation and execution.

In exploring the Java class file header, we've decoded the essential elements that initiate the JVM's journey into the binary world of bytecode. From the unmistakable magic number affirming the file's legitimacy to the nuanced details of Java version compatibility and access flags, the header serves as the preamble to execution, guiding the JVM through the intricacies of class file interpretation. The constant pool reference acts as a symbolic gateway, connecting the binary representation to the rich semantic world of Java.

As we conclude our exploration into the headers of Java class files, let's take a moment to recap the insights gained thus far. We've deciphered the symbolic treasure trove encapsulated within the constant pool, understanding its pivotal role in referencing strings, classes, field names, and method names, which are essential for the interpretation and execution of Java programs. Recognizing the dynamic nature of this repository, we've examined how the class file header serves as a guiding beacon, referencing the commencement of the constant pool within the overall class file structure.

The knowledge acquired in this chapter unveils the intricate architecture of Java class files and lays the foundation for a more profound comprehension of the code's execution. Understanding the headers is akin to decoding the preamble to execution, providing crucial insights into the initiation and navigation of the constant pool, a fundamental aspect of Java's dynamic behavior.

As we transition into the next section, we carry with us the awareness of a class file's symbolic foundation and its significance in ensuring the accurate execution of Java programs. Join us in the upcoming exploration, where we will delve into the nuanced details of access flags, interfaces, fields, and methods, further enriching our understanding of Java's class file structure.

Fields and data repositories

In the unfolding exploration of class file intricacies, we now delve into the section dedicated to fields and data repositories. This pivotal section dissects the dynamic nexus where code and data converge within Java classes. Fields, the information custodians, transcend the realm of mere variables, encapsulating the very essence of data storage. As we navigate this section, we will unravel the diversity of field types, from instance variables to class variables, and decode their role in shaping the architecture of Java classes. Join us in uncovering the harmonious interplay between fields and the constant pool, where symbolic references enrich the language and contribute to the dynamic layer of data representation within the class files. This session serves as a gateway to the beating heart of Java programs, showcasing how fields become the dynamic vessels through which code transforms into executable realities within the JVM.

The declaration of a field involves specifying its data type, a unique identifier, and optional modifiers that define its visibility, accessibility, and behavior. By dissecting the syntax of field declarations, developers gain insight into how these containers store and organize data, creating a symbiotic link between the high-level code and the binary representation within class files. This nuanced understanding allows for effective utilization of fields, enhancing the clarity and efficiency of data management in Java programs.

Beyond their syntax, fields exhibit diversity through various types, each serving distinct roles within Java classes. Two primary categories are instance variables and class variables:

- **Instance variables**: These fields are associated with an instance of a class and have a unique set of values for each object. Instance variables encapsulate the state of individual objects, defining their characteristics and attributes. Understanding the distinctions and nuances of instance variables is crucial for modeling the dynamic properties of objects within the broader class structure.

- **Class variables**: Unlike instance variables, class variables are shared among all class instances. These fields are denoted with the `static` keyword, indicating that they belong to the class rather than individual instances. Class variables are well suited for representing characteristics or properties common to all objects instantiated from the class. Navigating the scopes and distinctions between instance and class variables lays a foundational understanding for effective data management, influencing the behavior of Java programs.

Developers can architect robust and adaptable class structures by comprehending the intricacies of field declarations and the diversity of field types. This foundational knowledge empowers them to design Java programs that elegantly balance the dynamic nature of data with the structured code, ensuring efficient and purposeful data management within the JVM.

Within the intricate architecture of Java class files, the connection between fields and the constant pool is a symbiotic link that enriches the language's capacity for dynamic and symbolic data representation. The constant pool is a repository for symbolic references, encompassing strings, class names, method signatures, and other constants essential for Java program interpretation.

In the context of fields, the constant pool becomes a reservoir of references, enhancing the versatility of data representation within class files. When a field is declared, its name and type are stored as entries in the constant pool. It allows for efficient and symbolic referencing of field names and types during runtime, enabling the JVM to interpret and manage data dynamically.

A practical example becomes invaluable to grasping the significance of the constant pool connection. Consider a scenario where a class includes a field with a complex data type, such as a custom object or a string literal. The constant pool stores the reference to the field and efficiently manages the relations to the field's data type, as shown in the following code:

```
public class ConstantPoolSample {
    private String message = "Hello, Java!"; // String literal stored
                                             // in the constant pool
    public static void main(String[] args) {
        ConstantPoolSample sample = new ConstantPoolSample();
        System.out.println(sample.message); // Accessing the field
                                            // with a symbolic reference
    }
}
```

In this example, the string literal `"Hello, Java!"` is stored in the constant pool, and the field `message` references this constant. This linkage facilitates streamlined access and interpretation of data during program execution. Through this sample, developers witness how the constant pool serves as a dynamic repository, enhancing the efficiency and interpretability of Java class files.

Understanding this connection is pivotal for developers aiming to optimize data storage and access within their Java programs. It not only ensures the seamless execution of code but also exemplifies the elegance with which Java leverages symbolic references for dynamic data representation.

Fields within Java class files serve as dynamic repositories, seamlessly bridging the realms of code and data. Our exploration has unveiled the syntax and semantics of field declarations, emphasizing their role in encapsulating variables and attributes. The nuanced understanding of field types, from instance to class variables, forms a cornerstone for effective data management in Java programs. This connection between fields and the constant pool enriches the language's capacity for dynamic interpretation, showcasing the synergy that enhances the versatility of data representation within class files.

Building upon this foundation, our journey continues with the exploration of **methods**. Just as fields encapsulate data, methods encapsulate behavior within Java classes. Join us in the next segment to unravel the intricacies of method declarations, parameter passing, and the dynamic execution of code. Together, we will deepen our understanding of how methods contribute to the functional essence of Java programs within the JVM.

Methods in the class file

Let's embark on an in-depth exploration of the heart of Java class files—methods. These dynamic components serve as the architects of behavior within classes, shaping the very essence of Java programs and orchestrating the precise execution of code within the JVM. In this session, we'll peel back the layers to unravel the intricacies of method declarations, parameter passing, and the dynamic execution of code. We aim to provide you with a solid foundational understanding of how methods fundamentally contribute to Java classes' structural integrity and functionality.

Within class files, a method's return type is key to understanding the nature of the data generated during execution. This critical element acts as a guiding beacon for the JVM, enabling it to anticipate the expected outcomes of each method. Whether a method yields an `int`, `String`, or any other data type, the return type encapsulates this vital information, enriching our grasp of how methods fit into the broader program structure.

We will delve even deeper into the nuances of methods in the following chapters, providing you with a more comprehensive understanding of their role and significance in the world of Java programming.

Summary

In exploring methods within the intricate landscape of Java class files, we've uncovered their pivotal role as the architects of program behavior. The class file structure encapsulates crucial information about return types, access modifiers, and parameters, guiding the JVM in executing code dynamically and efficiently.

As we conclude this part of our exploration, the journey through class file intricacies continues into the next chapter. The upcoming topic delves into the essence of bytecode, serving as the intermediary language that bridges high-level Java code with the platform-independent execution environment of the JVM. Together, we will unravel the bytecode layer, understanding how it transforms method logic into executable instructions, ensuring the portability and universality of Java programs. This exploration into bytecodes promises to deepen our understanding of Java's cross-platform capabilities, providing insights into the magic that enables Java code to run seamlessly across diverse environments.

Questions

Answer the following questions to test your knowledge of this chapter:

1. What is the purpose of the "Magic" number in the Java class file header?

    A. It identifies the developer who wrote the code

    B. It identifies the file as being a Java class file

    C. It marks the end of the constant pool

    D. It determines the class hierarchy

2. Which section of the class file structure stores symbolic references, strings, and constants?

   A. Fields

   B. Access flags

   C. Constant pool

   D. Methods

3. What does the `interfaces_count` field in the class file structure represent?

   A. The number of methods in the class

   B. The number of interfaces implemented by the class

   C. The access flags for interfaces

   D. The total size of the constant pool

4. What do fields and methods represent in the context of class files?

   A. Variables and attributes

   B. Linguistic repositories

   C. Cryptographic seals

   D. Access modifiers

5. What is the primary purpose of the attributes section in the class file structure?

   A. Determines the class version

   B. Stores symbolic references

   C. Manages bytecode execution

   D. Provides additional information about the class

Answers

Here are the answers to this chapter's questions:

1. B. It identifies the file as being a Java class file
2. C. Constant pool
3. B. The number of interfaces implemented by the class
4. A. Variables and attributes
5. D. Provides additional information about the class

3
Understanding Bytecodes

In the intricate world of the JVM, bytecode serves as the intermediary language that enables Java programs to transcend the boundaries of platform-specific hardware and operating systems. As we delve into the heart of JVM internals, this chapter focuses on deciphering the bytecode, a fundamental component in executing Java applications. Bytecode, represented as a set of instructions, acts as the bridge between high-level Java code and the machine-specific language of the underlying hardware. By comprehending bytecode, developers gain insights into the inner workings of the JVM, empowering them to optimize code performance and troubleshoot intricate issues.

At the core of bytecode lies a diverse set of instructions that dictate the low-level operations performed by the JVM. This chapter unravels the nuances of arithmetic operations, shedding light on how the JVM handles mathematical calculations. From essential addition and subtraction to more complex procedures, we explore the bytecode instructions that govern these processes. Furthermore, we delve into value conversions, demystifying how the JVM transforms data between different types. Understanding these low-level operations is paramount for developers seeking to fine-tune their applications for optimal performance and efficiency. Join us on a journey into the bytecode realm, where the intricacies of arithmetic operations and value conversions pave the way for mastering the JVM.

In this chapter, we'll explore the following topics:

- Bytecode unveiled
- Arithmetic operations
- Value conversions
- Object manipulation
- Conditional instructions

Technical requirements

For this chapter, you will require the following:

- Java 21
- Git

- Maven

- Any preferred IDE

- This chapter's GitHub repository, found at - `https://github.com/PacktPublishing/ Mastering-the-Java-Virtual-Machine/tree/main/chapter-03`

Bytecode unveiled

Bytecode, a pivotal concept in Java programming, is the intermediary language that facilitates the cross-platform compatibility and execution of Java applications on the JVM. This session aims to demystify bytecode, providing a comprehensive overview of its significance, purpose, and the spectrum of operations it enables within the JVM.

At its core, bytecode acts as a bridge between high-level Java code and the machine-specific language of the underlying hardware. When a Java program is compiled, the source code is transformed into bytecode, a set of instructions comprehensible to the JVM. This platform-independent bytecode allows Java applications to execute seamlessly across diverse environments, a fundamental tenet of Java's *Write Once, Run Anywhere* mantra.

Why do we have bytecode? The answer lies in the portability and versatility it brings to Java applications. By introducing an intermediate step between the high-level source code and machine code, Java programs can run on any device equipped with a JVM, irrespective of its architecture or operating system. This abstraction shields developers from the intricacies of hardware-specific details, fostering a more universal and accessible programming environment.

Now, let's delve into the operations encoded within bytecode. Bytecode instructions cover a myriad of functionalities, ranging from basic load and save operations to intricate arithmetic calculations. The JVM's stack-based architecture governs these operations, where values are pushed and popped onto and off the stack, forming the basis for data manipulation. Arithmetic operations, encompassing addition, subtraction, multiplication, and more, are executed through specific bytecode instructions, allowing developers to understand and optimize the mathematical underpinnings of their code.

Value conversion, another facet of bytecode operations, involves transforming data between different types. Whether converting integers to floating point numbers or managing other type transitions, bytecode instructions provide the foundation for these operations. This flexibility is crucial for developers crafting code and seamlessly handling diverse data types within the Java ecosystem.

Beyond this, bytecode orchestrates the creation and manipulation of objects, governs conditional statements, and manages the invocation and return of methods. Each bytecode instruction contributes to the overall execution flow of a Java program, and understanding these operations empowers developers to craft efficient, performant, and reliable applications.

Indeed, understanding the bytecode behavior is crucial for navigating the intricacies of the JVM. Bytecode instructions are designed to operate on specific types of values, and recognizing the type being operated upon is fundamental to writing efficient and correct Java code. The initial letter of each bytecode mnemonic often serves as a valuable hint for discerning the type of operation being performed.

Let's delve into this tip for recognizing the type of operation based on the initial letter of the bytecode mnemonic:

- **i for integer operations**: Bytecodes starting with i, such as iload (load integer), iadd (add integer), or isub (subtract integer), signify operations involving integer values. These bytecode instructions manipulate data stored as 32-bit signed integers.

- **l for long operations**: The l prefix, as seen in lload (load long) or lmul (multiply long), indicates operations on 64-bit signed long integers.

- **s for short operations**: Bytecodes beginning with s, for instance, sload (load short), are associated with operations on 16-bit signed short integers.

- **b for byte operations**: The b prefix, found in bytecode instructions such as bload (load byte), denotes operations on 8-bit signed byte integers.

- **c for char operations**: Operations on 16-bit Unicode characters are represented by bytecode instructions starting with c, such as caload (the load array of char).

- **f for float operations**: The f prefix, seen in bytecode mnemonics such as fload (load float) or fadd (add float), signals operations involving 32-bit single-precision floating point numbers.

- **d for double operations**: Double-precision floating point numbers (64-bit) are the focus of bytecode instructions starting with d, such as dload (load double) or dmul (multiply double).

- **a for reference operations**: Operations involving object references are represented by bytecode instructions starting with a, such as aload (load reference) or areturn (return reference).

This systematic naming convention helps developers quickly identify the type of data being manipulated by a bytecode instruction. By recognizing the initial letter and associating it with a specific data type, developers can write more informed and precise code, ensuring that the bytecode operations align with the intended data types and behaviors within the JVM. This understanding is fundamental for mastering bytecode and optimizing Java applications for performance and reliability.

In Java bytecode, Boolean values are typically represented using integers (0 for false and 1 for true). However, it's essential to note that Boolean values do not have dedicated bytecode instructions; instead, the standard integer arithmetic and logical instructions are used. For instance:

- iadd, isub, imul, idiv, and similar instructions work seamlessly with Boolean values

- Logical operations such as *and* (iand), *or* (ior), and *xor* (ixor) can be used for Boolean logic

The key takeaway is that Boolean values are treated as integers in bytecode, allowing developers to use the same arithmetic and logical instructions for both numerical and Boolean computations.

Bytecode provides the groundwork for arithmetic operations, shaping the mathematical core of Java programs. Our journey continues in the next section, where we'll delve into the intricate world of arithmetic operations in bytecode. We'll dissect the instructions governing addition, subtraction, multiplication, and more, unraveling the bytecode sequences defining Java applications' mathematical essence.

By understanding the arithmetic operations encoded in bytecode, developers gain insights into the inner workings of their code, enabling them to optimize performance and enhance efficiency. Join us in the next section to uncover the secrets behind arithmetic operations and pave the way for mastering the intricacies of the JVM.

Arithmetic operations

In this section, we embark on a focused exploration of one of the cornerstone aspects of bytecode: arithmetic operations. These operations are the mathematical underpinnings that breathe life into Java programs, shaping the numerical landscape of computations within the JVM.

Bytecode arithmetic operations follow a fundamental principle: they operate on the first two values on the `operand` stack, performing the specified operation and returning the result to the stack. This session delves into the intricacies of bytecode arithmetic, shedding light on its nuances, behavior, and impact on program execution.

The arithmetic operations in bytecode are subdivided into two major categories: those involving floating point numbers and those dealing with integers. Each category exhibits distinct behaviors, and understanding these differences is crucial for Java developers seeking precision and reliability in their numerical computations.

As we navigate the bytecode arithmetic terrain, we explore the instructions governing addition, subtraction, multiplication, and division for floats and integers. We dissect the bytecode sequences encapsulating these operations, clarifying their implementation and performance implications.

Addition, subtraction, multiplication, and division

The fundamental arithmetic operations are the building blocks of numerical computations in Java. From adding integers (`iadd`) to dividing doubles (`ddiv`), each bytecode instruction is meticulously designed to handle specific data types. Uncover the nuances of adding, subtracting, multiplying, and dividing integers, longs, floats, and doubles:

- **Addition**:

    - `iadd`: Adds two integers

    - `ladd`: Adds two longs

    - `fadd`: Adds two floats

    - `dadd`: Adds two doubles

- **Subtraction**:

  - `isub`: Subtracts the second integer from the first
  - `lsub`: Subtracts the second long from the first
  - `fsub`: Subtracts the second float from the first
  - `dsub`: Subtracts the second double from the first

- **Multiplication**:

  - `imul`: Multiplies two integers
  - `lmul`: Multiplies two longs
  - `fmul`: Multiplies two floats
  - `dmul`: Multiplies two doubles

- **Division**:

  - `idiv`: Divides the first integer by the second
  - `ldiv`: Divides the first long by the second
  - `fdiv`: Divides the first float by the second
  - `ddiv`: Divides the first double by the second

Remainder and negation

- **Remainder (remainder)**:

  - `irem`: Computes the remainder of dividing the first integer by the second
  - `lrem`: Computes the remainder of dividing the first long by the second
  - `frem`: Computes the remainder of dividing the first float by the second
  - `drem`: Computes the remainder of dividing the first double by the second

- **Negation (negation)**:

  - `ineg`: Negates (changes the sign of) the integer
  - `lneg`: Negates the long
  - `fneg`: Negates the float
  - `dneg`: Negates the double

Shift and bitwise operations

Dive into the world of bitwise operations (`ior`, `iand`, `ixor`, `lor`, `land`, `lxor`) and shift operations (`ishl`, `ishr`, `iushr`, `lshl`, `lshr`, `lushr`). Discover how these operations manipulate individual bits, offering powerful tools for advanced computations and optimizations:

- **Shift operations (shift)**:
  - `ishl`, `ishr`, `iushr`: Shifts the bits of an integer to the left, right (with sign extension), or right (without sign extension)
  - `lshl`, `lshr`, `lushr`: Shifts the bits of a long to the left, right (with sign extension), or right (without sign extension)

- **Bitwise operations**:
  - `ior`, `lor`: Bitwise *or* for integers and longs
  - `iand`, `land`: Bitwise *and* for integers and longs
  - `ixor`, `lxor`: Bitwise exclusive *or* for integers and longs

Local variable increment

Unlock the potential of the `iinc` instruction, a subtle yet powerful operation that increments a local variable by a constant value. Learn how this bytecode instruction can enhance code readability and efficiency in specific scenarios:

- **Local variable increment** (`iinc`): `iinc` increments a local variable by a constant value

Comparison operations

Delve into the world of comparing values with instructions such as `cmpg`, `dcmpl`, `fcmpg`, `fcmpl`, and `lcmp`. Uncover the subtleties of yielding results such as 1, -1, or 0, indicating greater, less, or equal comparisons for doubles, floats, and longs:

- **Comparison**:
  - `dcmpg`, `dcmpl`: Compares two doubles, yielding 1, -1, or 0 (greater, less, or equal)
  - `fcmpg`, `fcmpl`: Compares two floats, yielding 1, -1, or 0 (greater, less, or equal)
  - `lcmp`: Compares two longs, yielding 1, -1, or 0 (greater, less, or equal)

In the world of bytecode comparison, instructions such as `dcmpg` and `dcmpl` effectively compare double-precision floating point numbers, yielding 1, -1, or 0 to signify greater, lesser, or equal comparisons. Similarly, `fcmpg` and `fcmpl` handle single-precision floats. However, when it comes to long integers, `lcmp` simplifies things by providing a single result of 1, -1, or 0, indicating greater, lesser, or equal comparisons. This streamlined approach optimizes long integer comparisons in bytecode.

These bytecode instructions form the backbone of arithmetic and logical operations in Java programs. It's crucial to note that the behavior of these operations may differ for integers and floating point numbers, especially when dealing with edge cases such as division by zero or overflow conditions. Understanding these bytecode instructions provides developers with the tools to craft precise and robust numerical computations in their Java applications.

After explaining the concept of bytecode and showcasing some arithmetic operations, we will delve deeper into the world of bytecode arithmetic within the JVM by examining a practical example. Our focus will be on understanding the process by analyzing a simple Java code snippet, which performs a basic arithmetic operation, i.e., adding two integers. This hands-on exploration aims to unravel the intricate workings of bytecode arithmetic.

Consider the following Java code snippet:

```
public class ArithmeticExample {
    public static void main(String[] args) {
        int a = 5;
        int b = 7;
        int result = a + b;
        System.out.println("Result: " + result);
    }
}
```

Save the code in a file named `ArithmeticExample.java` and compile it using the following command:

javac ArithmeticExample.java

Now, let's use the `javap` command to disassemble the bytecode:

javap -c ArithmeticExample.class

After executing the command, it will generate the output of the bytecode:

public static void main(java.lang.String[]);

The code is as follows:

```
    . . .
    5: iload_1          // Load the value of 'a' onto the stack
    6: iload_2          // Load the value of 'b' onto the stack
    7: iadd             // Add the top two values on the stack
                        (a and b)
    8: istore_3         // Store the result into the local variable
'result'
    . . .
```

The following takes place in these bytecode instructions:

- `iload_1`: Loads the value of the local variable a onto the stack
- `iload_2`: Loads the value of the local variable b onto the stack
- `iadd`: Adds the top two values on the stack (which are a and b)
- `istore_3`: Stores the result of the addition back into the local variable result

These bytecode instructions precisely reflect the arithmetic operation int result = a + b; in the Java code. The `iadd` instruction performs the addition of the loaded values, and the `istore_3` instruction stores the result back into a local variable for further use. Understanding this bytecode provides a detailed look at how the JVM executes a simple arithmetic operation in a Java program.

In our journey through bytecode arithmetic, we've dissected the seemingly mundane yet profoundly impactful process of adding two integers in a Java program. The bytecode instructions unveiled a hidden layer of intricacy, showcasing how high-level operations transform into machine-executable code within the **Java virtual machine (JVM)**.

As we close this section, our next destination awaits: the realm of value conversions. Understanding how different data types interact in bytecode is pivotal for crafting robust and efficient Java applications. In the upcoming section, let us delve into the intricacies of value conversions, unraveling the nuances of transforming data within the JVM. The journey continues, and each bytecode instruction brings us one step closer to mastering the depths of Java bytecode.

Value conversions

In this section, we immerse ourselves in the intricate realm of value conversions within the JVM. These conversions serve as the chameleons of the bytecode landscape, enabling variables to transform their types gracefully by allowing integers to stretch into longs and floats to transcend into doubles without compromising the fidelity of their original values. The bytecode instructions that facilitate these metamorphoses are crucial in maintaining precision, preventing data loss, and ensuring the seamless integration of different data types. Join us as we dissect these instructions, uncovering the symphony of elegance and accuracy that underpins Java programming:

- **Integer to long (i2l):** Explore how the `i2l` instruction promotes an integer variable to a long, preserving the original value's precision
- **Integer to float (i2f):** Delve into the world of `i2f`, where an integer gracefully transforms into a float without sacrificing precision
- **Integer to double (i2d):** Witness the precision-preserving journey from integer to double through the `i2d` instruction
- **Long to float (l2f) and long to double (l2d):** Examine the elegance of `l2f` and `l2d`, where long values seamlessly transition to float and double, respectively

- **Float to Double (f2d):** Explore the f2d instruction, showcasing the promotion of float to double while maintaining precision

As we navigate the intricacies of bytecode, we encounter a critical segment devoted to managing shortening—a delicate process marked by potential loss and overflow considerations. In this exploration, we delve into the bytecode instructions that transform variables into shorter data types, acknowledging the nuanced challenges associated with precision loss and overflow risks. Let us now explore this set of instructions:

- **Integer to byte (i2b), integer to short (i2s), integer to char (i2c):** Investigate the potential precision loss as integers transform into byte, short, and char types through i2b, i2s, and i2c instructions

- **Long to integer (l2i):** Examine the considerations involved in converting long to integer using the l2i instruction, acknowledging the possibility of overflow

- **Float to integer (f2i), float to long (f2l):** Uncover the challenges of converting float to integer and long through f2i and f2l, taking note of precision and overflow concerns

- **Double to integer (d2i), double to long (d2l), double to float (d2f):** Navigate through the d2i, d2l, and d2f instructions, understanding the delicate balance of precision and potential overflow in converting double to integer, long, and float

In the realm of bytecode intricacies, the following best practices serve as a compass guiding us through practical considerations. Here, we bridge theory and application, exploring the tangible implications of bytecode instructions on real-world Java programming scenarios. From preserving precision in complex arithmetic operations to navigating the flexibility of object-oriented design, these practical considerations illuminate the significance of understanding and mastering bytecode in the development landscape.

- **Preserving precision in arithmetic:** Connect the dots between value conversions and arithmetic operations, ensuring precision is maintained in complex calculations

- **Handling object references:** Explore how value conversions contribute to the flexibility of object-oriented programming, allowing smooth transitions between classes and interfaces

As we decipher the bytecode instructions governing value conversions, the preceding points equip you with the insights needed to navigate the subtleties of transforming variable types within the JVM.

In the following illustrative Java code sample, we spotlight value conversions, explicitly focusing on conventions that transform variable types within the JVM. The code snippet demonstrates the subtle dance of promotions and considerations for precision loss or overflow. As we traverse the bytecode results, our attention remains steadfast on the instructions that bring these conventions to life:

```
public class ValueConversionsExample {
    public static void main(String[] args) {
```

```
// Promotion: Enlargement of Types
int intValue = 42;
long longValue = intValue; // Promotion: int to long

float floatValue = 3.14f;
double doubleValue = floatValue; // Promotion: float to double

// Shortening: Considerations for Loss and Overflow
short shortValue = 32767;
byte byteValue = (byte) shortValue; // Shortening: short to
                                    // byte

double largeDouble = 1.7e308;
int intFromDouble = (int) largeDouble; // Shortening: double
                                       // to int
```

The results are displayed as follows:

```
System.out.println("Promotion Results: " + longValue + ", " +
    doubleValue);
System.out.println("Shortening Results: " + byteValue + ", " +
    intFromDouble);
    }
}
```

Save the provided Java code in a file named ValueConversionsExample.java. Open your terminal or command prompt and navigate to the directory where the file is saved. Then, use the following command to compile the code:

```
javac ValueConversionsExample.java
```

After compiling, you can use the javap command to disassemble the bytecode and display the relevant parts. Execute the following command in the terminal or command prompt:

```
javap -c ValueConversionsExample.class
```

In this analysis, we focus on specific segments of bytecode to explore how Java code transforms into machine-executable instructions within the JVM. Our attention centers on selected bytecode parts, revealing the intricacies of promotions, precision considerations, and shortening in the realm of Java programming. Follow along as we decipher the language of the JVM, offering a visual narrative of the conventions that shape Java bytecode.

```
 0: bipush        42
 2: istore_1
 3: iload_1
 4: i2l
```

```
 5: lstore_2
 8: ldc               3.14
10: fstore_4
11: fload             4
13: dstore            5
17: ldc               32767
19: istore            7
21: iload             7
23: i2b
24: istore            8
27: ldc2_w            #2                      // double 1.7e308
34: dstore            9
36: dload             9
38: d2i
39: istore            11
```

In this Java code, we witness both promotions and shortening conventions in action. The bytecode snippets focus specifically on the instructions associated with these conventions, providing a detailed look at how the JVM handles the enlargement and shortening of variable types.

In our exploration of value conversions within the JVM, we've dissected the bytecode instructions orchestrating promotions and considerations for precision loss or overflow. These intricacies underscore the nuanced dance of data types in Java programming. As we conclude this segment, the seamless translation of high-level code to bytecode becomes clearer, revealing the meticulous choreography of the JVM. In the next section, we shift our focus to the captivating realm of object manipulation within bytecode, unraveling the threads that weave the tapestry of Java's object-oriented paradigm. In this forthcoming journey, we'll scrutinize bytecode instructions that mold and maneuver through objects, delving into the heart of dynamic, versatile Java programming.

Object manipulation

In this immersive session, we embark on a comprehensive exploration of object manipulation within the intricate fabric of Java bytecode. Our journey unveils the bytecode instructions instrumental in creating and manipulating instances, forging arrays, and accessing both static and instance attributes of a class. We scrutinize instructions that load values from arrays, save to the stack, inquire about array lengths, and perform crucial checks on instances or arrays. From the foundational new instruction to the dynamic intricacies of multianewarray, each bytecode command propels us deeper into the realm of object-oriented manipulation.

In the bytecode tapestry of Java, the new instruction stands as a gateway to the realm of object creation and manipulation. It not only allocates memory for an object but also invokes its constructor, initiating the birth of a dynamic entity. Join us in this deep dive into the bytecode intricacies, where the seemingly simple new instruction unveils the foundational steps involved in bringing Java objects to life. As we dissect this bytecode command, the underlying symphony of memory allocation and constructor invocation becomes clearer, paving the way for a richer understanding of instance creation within the JVM.

- `new`: This instantiates a new object, allocating memory and invoking the object's constructor. The reference to the newly created object is placed on the stack.

Within the orchestration of Java bytecode, the commands for array creation emerge as a tapestry of versatility. In this segment, we delve into the bytecode instructions that sculpt arrays, offering a dynamic canvas for data storage. From the foundational `newarray` for primitive types to the nuanced `anewarray` for object references and the sophisticated `multianewarray` for multi-dimensional arrays, each bytecode instruction contributes to the vibrant array ecosystem within the JVM. As we dissect these commands, the artistry behind array instantiation within the JVM comes to light, opening the door to a deeper comprehension of data structure dynamics in Java programming.

- `newarray`: Creates a new array of primitive types
- `anewarray`: Creates a new array of object references
- `multianewarray`: Creates a multi-dimensional array

In the intricate dance of Java bytecode, the instructions for accessing static or instance attributes of a class—`getfield`, `putfield`, `getstatic`, and `putstatic`—take center stage. From gracefully retrieving instance field values to dynamically setting static field values, each bytecode instruction contributes to the nuanced choreography of object-oriented programming. Join us in unraveling the elegance of bytecode access, where the delicate balance between instance and class attributes unfolds, revealing the underlying mechanisms that govern data manipulation within the JVM. As we dissect these instructions, the ballet of accessing class attributes comes alive, paving the way for a profound understanding of object-oriented intricacies in Java programming.

- `getfield`: Retrieves the value of an instance field from an object
- `putfield`: Sets the value of an instance field in an object
- `getstatic`: Retrieves the value of a static field from a class
- `putstatic`: Sets the value of a static field in a class

In the bytecode symphony of Java, the loading instructions — `baload`, `caload`, `saload`, `iaload`, `laload`, `faload`, `daload`, and `aaload` — take center stage, defining the choreography for retrieving values from arrays. In this segment, we immerse ourselves in the rhythmic bytecode commands that gracefully bring array elements to the forefront. From extracting bytes and characters to loading integers, longs, floats, doubles, and object references, each instruction plays a crucial role in the harmonious interaction between arrays and the JVM. These loading instructions unveil the orchestrated ballet that unfolds as Java bytecode seamlessly navigates through arrays, showcasing the versatility and precision of array element retrieval. As we explore these loading commands, the intricate dance of loading values from arrays comes alive, providing a deeper insight into the fluid dynamics of Java programming.

In the bytecode masterpiece of Java, the saving instructions — `bastore`, `castore`, `sastore`, `iastore`, `lastore`, `fastore`, `dastore`, and `aastore` — intricately command the canvas of array manipulation. These instructions are pivotal for storing values into arrays of different types. Let's delve into their significance with examples:

- `bastore`: Stores a byte or Boolean value into a byte array

- `castore`: Stores a character value into a char array

- `sastore`: Stores a short value into a short array

- `iastore`: Stores an integer value into an int array

- `lastore`: Stores a long value into a long array

- `dastore`: Stores a double value into a double array

These instructions play a fundamental role in array manipulation, allowing for the precise storage of various data types within arrays.

The `arraylength` instruction serves as a compass in Java bytecode, guiding developers through the metrics of arrays by providing the length of the array:

- `arraylength`: Retrieves the length of an array and pushes it onto the stack.

Within the realm of Java bytecode, the instructions `instanceof` and `checkcast` serve as vigilant guardians, ensuring the integrity of object types and their alignment with specified classes. While our earlier exploration delved into array manipulation, let's now shift our focus to these instructions' essential roles in type checking. `Instanceof` assesses whether an object belongs to a particular class, providing crucial insights into object types. On the other hand, `checkcast` meticulously scrutinizes and casts objects, ensuring their harmonious alignment with designated classes. Together, these bytecode guardians play pivotal roles in maintaining the robustness and coherence of object-oriented paradigms within the JVM:

- `instanceof`: Checks if an object is an instance of a particular class

- `checkcast`: Checks and casts an object to a given class, ensuring type compatibility

These bytecode instructions provide the foundation for manipulating objects in Java, allowing for the creation, access, and modification of instances and arrays. Whether it's instantiating new objects, working with arrays, accessing class attributes, or performing dynamic checks, each instruction contributes to the flexibility and power of object-oriented programming in Java bytecode. Understanding these instructions is key to mastering the intricacies of Java's object manipulation capabilities.

In our previous discussion, we explored essential bytecode instructions, offering a deeper understanding of Java's underlying mechanisms. Now, let's put that knowledge into practice with an illustrative Java code snippet. Here, we introduce a streamlined representation of the `Person` class, focusing on a single attribute: `name`. This class encapsulates fundamental principles of object manipulation, featuring methods for accessing and modifying the attribute. As we navigate this example, we'll delve into the bytecode generated from this code, offering insights into the low-level intricacies of object manipulation within the JVM. These bytecode instructions underpin the dynamic nature of Java programming, and this practical illustration will shed light on their real-world application:

```java
public class Person {
    private String name;

    public Person(String name) {
        this.name = name;
    }

    public String getName() {
        return name;
    }

    public void setName(String newName) {
        this.name = newName;
    }

    public static void main(String[] args) {
        // Creating an instance of Person
        Person person = new Person("John");

        // Accessing and displaying the name attribute
        System.out.println("Original Name: " + person.getName());

        // Changing the name attribute
        person.setName("Alice");

        // Displaying the updated name
        System.out.println("Updated Name: " + person.getName());
    }
}
```

Compile and display bytecode:

```
javac Person.java
javap -c Person.class
```

Let's focus on relevant parts of the bytecode that correspond to object manipulation, including object creation (new), attribute access (getfield, putfield), and method invocation:

```
Compiled from "Person.java"
public class Person {
```

```
private java.lang.String name;

public Person(java.lang.String);
```

Code:

```
0: aload_0
1: invokespecial #1              // Method java/lang/
                                 Object."<init>":()V
4: aload_0
5: aload_1
6: putfield       #2             // Field name:Ljava/lang/
                                 String;
9: return
```

public java.lang.String getName();

Code:

```
0: aload_0
1: getfield       #2             // Field name:Ljava/lang/
                                 String;
4: areturn
```

public void setName(java.lang.String);

Code:

```
0: aload_0
1: aload_1
2: putfield       #2             // Field name:Ljava/lang/
                                 String;
5: return
```

public static void main(java.lang.String[]);

Code:

```
0: new            #3             // class Person
3: dup
4: ldc            #4             // String John
6: invokespecial #5             // Method "<init>":(Ljava/
                                 lang/String;)V
9: astore_1
```

```
10: getstatic      #6          // Field java/lang/System.
                                out:Ljava/io/PrintStream;
13: ldc            #7          // String Original Name:
15: invokevirtual  #8          // Method java/io/
      PrintStream.println:(Ljava/lang/String;)V
18: getstatic      #6          // Field java/lang/System.
                                out:Ljava/io/PrintStream;
21: aload_1
22: invokevirtual  #9          // Method getName:()Ljava/
                                lang/String;
25: invokevirtual  #8          // Method java/io/
      PrintStream.println:(Ljava/lang/String;)V
28: aload_1
29: ldc            #10         // String Alice
31: invokevirtual  #11         // Method setName:(Ljava/
                                lang/String;)V
34: getstatic      #6          // Field java/lang/System.
                                out:Ljava/io/PrintStream;
37: ldc            #12         // String Updated Name:
39: invokevirtual  #8          // Method java/io/
      PrintStream.println:(Ljava/lang/String;)V
42: getstatic      #6          // Field java/lang/System.
                                out:Ljava/io/PrintStream;
45: aload_1
46: invokevirtual  #9          // Method getName:()Ljava/
                                lang/String;
49: invokevirtual  #8          // Method java/io/
      PrintStream.println:(Ljava/lang/String;)V
52: return
}
```

Let's break down the key bytecode instructions:

- Object creation (new):

  - 0: new #3: Creates a new object of type Person

  - 3: dup: Duplicates the object reference on the stack

  - 4: ldc #4: Pushes the constant string "John" onto the stack

  - 6: invokespecial #5: Invokes the constructor (<init>) to initialize the object

- Attribute access (getfield, putfield):

  - 1: getfield #2: Retrieves the value of the name field

  - 2: putfield #2: Sets the value of the name field

- Method invocation:

    - `22: invokevirtual #9`: Invokes the `getName` method

    - `31: invokevirtual #11`: Invokes the `setName` method

These bytecode snippets highlight the fundamental instructions associated with object manipulation, offering insights into the dynamic nature of Java programming at the low-level bytecode level.

In navigating the bytecode tapestry of object manipulation within the simplified `Person` class, we've uncovered the orchestration of instructions governing object creation, attribute access, and method invocation. As the bytecode symphony unfolds, we transition seamlessly to the next segment, where we will delve into the dynamic realm of method calls and returns. Join us in deciphering the bytecode instructions that underpin the essence of method invocation, shedding light on the intricacies that define the flow of program execution within the JVM. As we move forward, the exploration of method calls and returns promises to enrich our understanding of the bytecode symphony, unveiling the next layer of Java programming intricacies.

Method calls and returns

Let us embark on a journey into the intricate dynamics of method calls and the nuanced return of values within the Java programming landscape. We will unveil the subtleties of dynamically invoking methods and agile invocation of interface methods and explore the distinctive chord of calling private or superclass methods and the powerful tone resonating from the invocation of static methods. Amidst this exploration, we will encounter the introduction of dynamic construction, showcasing the adaptability of Java programming. Remember the rhythm of value return is defined by specific instructions.

Exploring the symphony of method invocation in Java bytecode, the following instructions orchestrate various tones in the melody of method calls, each contributing uniquely to the language's dynamic and versatile nature:

- **invokevirtual:** Initiating the melody of method invocation, this instruction calls a method from an instance, providing the backbone for dynamic and polymorphic behavior in Java

- **invokeinterface:** Adding a harmonic note, this instruction calls a method from an interface, contributing to the flexibility and adaptability of Java's object-oriented paradigm

- **invokespecial:** Introducing a distinctive chord, this instruction calls a private or superclass method, encapsulating privileged method invocations

- **invokestatic:** Striking a powerful tone, this instruction calls a static method, emphasizing the invocation of methods that don't rely on instance creation

- **invokedynamic:** Playing a versatile tune, this instruction constructs an object dynamically, showcasing the dynamic capabilities of Java's method invocation

The rhythm of method execution is complemented by return instructions (`ireturn`, `lreturn`, `freturn`, `dreturn`, and `areturn`), defining the cadence of values returned from methods. In the event of unexpected interruptions with exceptions, the `athrow` call takes center stage, managing the orchestration of error handling.

We dive further into the intricacies of synchronous methods, where the monitor, marked by the `ACC_SYNCHRONIZED` flag, orchestrates a controlled dance. With the `monitorenter` instruction, the method enters the monitor, ensuring exclusive execution, and gracefully exits with `monitorexit` upon completion, crafting a synchronous symphony within the bytecode tapestry. Let's now delve into a live demonstration of method calls and returns within Java code. The following is a simple Java program that performs calculations through method calls. We'll then scrutinize the bytecode to decipher the orchestration of these method invocations:

```java
public class MethodCallsExample {

    public static void main(String[] args) {
        int result = performCalculation(5, 3);
        System.out.println("Result of calculation: " + result);
    }

    private static int performCalculation(int a, int b) {
        int sum = add(a, b);
        int product = multiply(a, b);
        return subtract(sum, product);
    }

    private static int add(int a, int b) {
        return a + b;
    }

    private static int multiply(int a, int b) {
        return a * b;
    }

    private static int subtract(int a, int b) {
        return a - b;
    }
}
```

Compile and display bytecode:

```
javac MethodCallsExample.java
javap -c MethodCallsExample.class
```

In the bytecode, we'll focus on the instructions related to method calls (`invokevirtual`, `invokespecial`, `invokestatic`) and the return instructions (`ireturn`).

The following is a simplified excerpt compiled from `MethodCallsExample.java`:

```
public class MethodCallsExample {
  public MethodCallsExample();
    Code:
       0: aload_0
       1: invokespecial #1          // Method java/lang/
                                     Object."<init>":()V

       4: return

  public static void main(java.lang.String[]);
```

Code:

```
       0: iconst_5
       1: iconst_3
       2: invokestatic  #2          // Method
                                     performCalculation:(II)I
       5: istore_1
       6: getstatic     #3          // Field java/lang/System.
                                     out:Ljava/io/PrintStream;
       9: new           #4          // class java/lang/
                                     StringBuilder
      12: dup
      13: ldc           #5          // String Result of
                                     calculation:
      15: invokespecial #6          // Method java/lang/
                  StringBuilder."<init>":(Ljava/lang/String;)V
      18: iload_1
      19: invokevirtual #7          // Method java/lang/
                  StringBuilder.append:(I)Ljava/lang/StringBuilder;
      22: invokevirtual #8          // Method java/lang/
                  StringBuilder.toString:()Ljava/lang/String;
      25: invokevirtual #9          // Method java/io/
                  PrintStream.println:(Ljava/lang/String;)V
      28: return

  private static int performCalculation(int, int);
```

Code:

```
       0: iload_0
       1: iload_1
```

```
     2: invokestatic   #2                // Method
                                         performCalculation:(II)I
     5: iload_0
     6: iload_1
     7: invokestatic   #11               // Method multiply:(II)I
    10: invokestatic   #12               // Method subtract:(II)I
    13: ireturn
```

private static int add(int, int);

Code:

```
    0: iload_0
    1: iload_1
    2: iadd
    3: ireturn
```

private static int multiply(int, int);

Code:

```
    0: iload_0
    1: iload_1
    2: imul
    3: ireturn
```

private static int subtract(int, int);

Code:

```
    0: iload_0
    1: iload_1
    2: isub
    3: ireturn
}
```

This bytecode excerpt showcases the essential instructions related to method calls and returns, providing a glimpse into the bytecode symphony of the provided Java code.

As we draw the curtains on our exploration of method calls and returns within the Java bytecode, we've uncovered the intricate dance of instructions orchestrating the flow of our program. The symphony of invokevirtual, invokeinterface, invokespecial, and invokestatic has echoed through our bytecode tapestry, showcasing the dynamic nature of method invocation and the rhythmic return of values. As we pivot to the next section, the spotlight shifts to conditional instructions, where bytecode decisions shape the course of program execution. Join us in decoding the bytecode intricacies of conditional statements, unraveling the logic that guides the JVM through pathways defined by conditions, and in our continuous journey through the depths of Java programming intricacies.

Conditional instructions

In this section, we delve into the nuanced realm of conditional instructions, unraveling the intricacies of decision-making within the JVM. These instructions form the backbone of conditional statements, guiding the JVM through pathways dictated by Boolean outcomes. Join us as we decipher the bytecode intricacies of conditional instructions, unveiling the logic that dynamically shapes program flow within the JVM. This exploration provides insights into the fundamental principles that govern the execution of conditional statements in Java programming.

Navigating the realm of Java bytecode unveils a set of instructions that intricately control conditional logic within the JVM. These commands stand as the architects of conditional statements, orchestrating precise decision-making and influencing program flow based on Boolean outcomes. This exploration peels back the layers of bytecode intricacies, offering insights into the dynamic pathways shaped by these fundamental instructions within the JVM.

Let's explore a set of bytecode instructions that wield unique powers to control program flow and decision-making in Java. These instructions encompass a range of conditions, switches, and jumps, each playing a distinct role in directing the execution path of a Java program:

- **ifeq:** Branches to the target instruction if the top value on the stack is equal to 0

- **ifne:** Branches to the target instruction if the top value on the stack is not equal to 0

- **iflt:** Branches to the target instruction if the top value on the stack is less than 0

- **ifle:** Branches to the target instruction if the top value on the stack is less than or equal to 0

- **ifgt:** Branches to the target instruction if the top value on the stack is greater than 0

- **ifge:** Branches to the target instruction if the top value on the stack is greater than or equal to 0

- **ifnull:** Branches to the target instruction if the top value on the stack is null

- **ifnonnull:** Branches to the target instruction if the top value on the stack is not null

- **if_icmpeq:** Branches to the target instruction if the two integer values on the stack are equal

- **if_icmpne:** Branches to the target instruction if the two integer values on the stack are not equal

- **if_icmplt:** Branches to the target instruction if the second integer value on the stack is less than the first

- **if_icmple:** Branches to the target instruction if the second integer value on the stack is less than or equal to the first

- **if_icmpgt:** Branches to the target instruction if the second integer value on the stack is greater than the first

- **if_icmpge:** Branches to the target instruction if the second integer value on the stack is greater than or equal to the first

- **if_acmpeq:** Branches to the target instruction if the two object references on the stack are equal

- **if_acmpne:** Branches to the target instruction if the two object references on the stack are not equal

- **tableswitch:** Provides a more efficient way to implement a switch statement with consecutive integer cases

- **lookupswitch:** Similar to `tableswitch`, but supports sparse case values

- **goto:** Unconditionally branches to the target instruction

- **goto_w:** Unconditionally branches to the target instruction (wide index)

- **jsr:** Jumps to a subroutine, saving the return address on the stack

- **jsr_w:** Jumps to a subroutine (wide index), saving the return address on the stack

- **ret:** Returns from a subroutine, using the return address saved by a previous `jsr` instruction

These instructions play a crucial role in constructing conditional statements and controlling the flow of program execution based on various conditions and comparisons. Understanding their behavior is key to deciphering and optimizing Java bytecode.

Let's now explore the realm of conditional logic in Java, where our code becomes a canvas for decision-making. In this illustrative example, we've crafted a simple Java program featuring conditional statements. The code examines the relationship between two integers and two strings, guiding the flow based on equality conditions. As we delve into the bytecode representation of this Java snippet, we'll decipher the underlying instructions, including `if_icmpne` and `if_acmpeq`, responsible for steering the program through divergent paths. Join us in this exploration, unraveling the dynamic interplay of Java code and bytecode that shapes the outcomes of logical decisions within the JVM.

```
public class ConditionalExample {

    public static void main(String[] args) {
        int a = 5;
        int b = 3;

        if (a == b) {
            System.out.println("a is equal to b");
        } else {
            System.out.println("a is not equal to b");
```

```
        }

        String str1 = "Hello";
        String str2 = "Hello";

        if (str1.equals(str2)) {
            System.out.println("Strings are equal");
        } else {
            System.out.println("Strings are not equal");
        }
    }
}
```

Compile and display bytecode:

```
javac ConditionalExample.java
javap -c ConditionalExample.class
```

In the bytecode, we'll focus on conditional instructions, such as `ifeq`, `ifne`, and `if_acmpeq`, which handle the branching based on equality conditions. The following is a simplified excerpt:

Compiled from `ConditionalExample.java`

```
public class ConditionalExample {
  public ConditionalExample();
    Code:
       0: aload_0
       1: invokespecial #1              // Method java/lang/
                                        Object."<init>":()V
       4: return

  public static void main(java.lang.String[]);
```

Code:

```
       0: iconst_5
       1: istore_1
       2: iconst_3
       3: istore_2
       4: iload_1
       5: iload_2
       6: if_icmpne    19
       9: getstatic    #2              // Field java/lang/System.
                                        out:Ljava/io/PrintStream;
```

```
12: ldc             #3         // String a is equal to b
14: invokevirtual   #4         // Method java/io/
                               PrintStream.println:(Ljava/lang/String;)V
17: goto            32
20: getstatic       #2         // Field java/lang/System.
                               out:Ljava/io/PrintStream;
23: ldc             #5         // String a is not equal
                               to b
25: invokevirtual   #4         // Method java/io/
                               PrintStream.println:(Ljava/lang/String;)V
28: goto            32
31: astore_3
32: ldc             #6         // String Hello
34: astore_3
35: ldc             #6         // String Hello
37: astore          4
39: aload_3
40: aload           4
42: if_acmpeq       55
45: getstatic       #2         // Field java/lang/System.
                               out:Ljava/io/PrintStream;
48: ldc             #7         // String Strings are not
                               equal
50: invokevirtual   #4         // Method java/io/
                               PrintStream.println:(Ljava/lang/String;)V
53: goto            68
56: getstatic       #2         // Field java/lang/System.
                               out:Ljava/io/PrintStream;
59: ldc             #8         // String Strings are equal
61: invokevirtual   #4         // Method java/io/
                               PrintStream.println:(Ljava/lang/String;)V
64: goto            68
67: astore          5
69: return
[...]
}
```

This bytecode excerpt showcases the conditional instructions (if_icmpne and if_acmpeq) in action, directing the program flow based on the equality conditions specified in the Java code.

In this exploration of Java bytecode, we've deciphered the intricate dance of conditional instructions that shape the logic within the JVM. From branching based on equality to unconditional jumps, these bytecode commands have guided decision-making processes. As we conclude this section on *Conditional instructions*, the horizon broadens, leading us to the next leg of our journey. The upcoming segment delves into the bytecode representation of entire classes, unraveling the layers of instructions that encapsulate the essence of Java programs. Join us in this transition, where the focus expands from isolated conditions to the holistic view of classes in bytecode, illuminating the inner workings of Java's runtime environment.

Show me the bytecode

As our exploration of Java bytecode continues, we now set our sights on the entire class, a comprehensive dive into the binary representation of Java programs. It's worth noting that the bytecode we examine may vary depending on the JVM version and the specific JVM vendor. In this session, we unravel the intricacies of compiling and examining the bytecode that encapsulates the essence of a complete Java class. From class initialization to method implementations, every facet of the class manifests in bytecode. Together, let us lift the veil on the holistic view of Java programs, exploring the nuances of how our code transforms into a language understood by the JVM.

In our journey through Java bytecode, let's begin by crafting a simple yet versatile Animal class. The following is the Java code snippet that defines the class:

```java
public class Animal {

    private String name;

    public String name() {
        return name;
    }

    public int age() {
        return 10;
    }

    public String bark() {
        return "woof";
    }
}
```

Now, let's navigate through the process of compiling and peering into the bytecode:

```
javac Animal.java
javap -verbose Animal
```

With this, we embark on a fascinating exploration, compiling our Java class and unveiling the intricacies of bytecode that lie beneath the surface. Join us as we decode the language of the JVM and illuminate the bytecode representation of our Animal class.

This section of the bytecode output provides metadata about the compiled class file. Let's break down the key information:

```
Last modified Nov 16, 2023; size 433 bytes
  SHA-256 checksum
  0f087fdc313e02a8307d47242cb9021672ca110932ffe9ba89ae313a4f963da7
  Compiled from "Animal.java"
public class Animal
  minor version: 0
  major version: 65
  flags: (0x0021) ACC_PUBLIC, ACC_SUPER
  this_class: #8                            // Animal
  super_class: #2                           // java/lang/Object
  interfaces: 0, fields: 2, methods: 4, attributes: 1
```

- Last modified: Indicates the date of the last modification to the class file; in this case, it's November 16, 2023.

- Size: Specifies the size of the class file in bytes, which is 433 bytes in this instance.

- SHA-256 checksum: Represents the SHA-256 checksum of the class file. This checksum serves as a unique identifier for the file and ensures its integrity.

- Compiled from "Animal.java": Informs us that this bytecode is compiled from the source file Animal.java.

- Class declaration: Declares the class named Animal.

- Version information:

  - minor version: Set to 0.

  - major version: Set to 65, indicating compatibility with Java 11.

- Flags: Displays hexadecimal flags indicating the access control modifiers applied to the class. In this case, it is a public class (ACC_PUBLIC) with additional properties (ACC_SUPER).

- **Class hierarchy:**

  - this_class: Points to the constant pool index (#8) representing the current class, which is Animal.

  - super_class: Points to the constant pool index (#2) representing the superclass, which is java/lang/Object.

- Interfaces, fields, methods, and attributes: Provides counts for these elements in the class.

This metadata offers a snapshot of the class file's properties, including its version, access modifiers, and structural details.

The `Constant pool` section in the bytecode output provides a glimpse into the constant pool, a table of structures used to store various constants, such as strings, method and field references, class names, and more. Let's decipher the entries in this constant pool:

```
Constant pool:
   #1 = Methodref          #2.#3                 // java/lang/
                                                 Object."<init>":()V
   #2 = Class              #4                    // java/lang/Object
   #3 = NameAndType        #5:#6                 // "<init>":()V
   #4 = UTF-8              java/lang/Object
   #5 = UTF-8              <init>
   #6 = UTF-8              ()V
   #7 = Fieldref           #8.#9                 // Animal.name:Ljava/lang/
                                                 String;
   #8 = Class              #10                   // Animal
   #9 = NameAndType        #11:#12               // name:Ljava/lang/String;
  #10 = UTF-8              Animal
  #11 = UTF-8              name
  #12 = UTF-8              Ljava/lang/String;
  #13 = Fieldref           #8.#14                // Animal.age:I
  #14 = NameAndType        #15:#16               // age:I
  #15 = UTF-8              age
  #16 = UTF-8              I
  #17 = String             #18                   // woof
  #18 = UTF-8              woof
  #19 = UTF-8              Code
  #20 = UTF-8              LineNumberTable
  #21 = UTF-8              ()Ljava/lang/String;
  #22 = UTF-8              ()I
  #23 = UTF-8              bark
  #24 = UTF-8              SourceFile
  #25 = UTF-8              Animal.java
```

This will show field points here:

- Method reference to `Object`'s constructor:

  - `#1 = Methodref #2.#3 // java/lang/Object."<init>":()V`

    - This entry references the constructor of the `java/lang/Object` class, denoted as `<init>`. It indicates the initialization method that every class implicitly inherits from the `Object` class.

- Class reference to `Object` class:
  - `#2 = Class #4 // java/lang/Object`
    - Points to the class reference for `java/lang/Object`, indicating that the `Animal` class extends `Object`.

- Name and type for `Object`'s constructor:
  - `#3 = NameAndType #5:#6 // "<init>":()V`
    - Specifies the name and type of the constructor (`<init>`) with no parameters and returns void.

- UTF-8 entry for `Object` class name:
  - `#4 = UTF-8 java/lang/Object`
    - Represents the name of the `java/lang/Object` class in UTF-8 encoding.

- UTF-8 entries for constructor and parameter type:
  - `#5 = UTF-8 <init>`
  - `#6 = UTF-8 ()V`
    - Denotes the constructor's name (`<init>`) and its type (no parameters and returning void) in UTF-8 encoding.

- Field reference to `Animal`'s name field:
  - `#7 = Fieldref #8.#9 // Animal.name:Ljava/lang/String;`
    - Refers to the name field in the `Animal` class, which is of type `java/lang/String`.

- Class reference to `Animal` class:
  - `#8 = Class #10 // Animal`
    - Points to the class reference for the `Animal` class.

- Name and type for the name field:
  - `#9 = NameAndType #11:#12 // name:Ljava/lang/String;`
    - Specifies the name and type of the name field: its name (`name`) and type (`String`).

- UTF-8 entry for `Animal` class name:
  - `#10 = UTF-8 Animal`
    - Represents the name of the `Animal` class in UTF-8 encoding.

- UTF-8 entries for the name field:

  - #11 = UTF-8 name

  - #12 = UTF-8 Ljava/lang/String;

    - Denote the name of the name field and its type (String) in UTF-8 encoding.

Similar entries exist for the age field and bark method, referencing field and method names, their types, and class names in the constant pool. Overall, the constant pool is a crucial component for resolving symbolic references during the execution of the bytecode.

The bytecode snippets provided represent the methods within the Animal class. Let's break down each method:

- Constructor method (public Animal();):

  - **Descriptor**: ()V (no parameters, returns void)

  - **Flags**: ACC_PUBLIC (public method)

  - **Code**:

    ```
    stack=1, locals=1, args_size=1
       0: aload_0
       1: invokespecial #1 // Method java/lang/Object."<init>":()V
       4: return
    ```

This constructor initializes the Animal object by invoking the constructor of its superclass (Object). The aload_0 instruction loads the object reference (this) onto the stack, and invokespecial invokes the superclass constructor. The LineNumberTable indicates that this code corresponds to line 1 in the source file.

- Method public java.lang.String name();:

  - **Descriptor**: ()Ljava/lang/String; (no parameters, returns String)

  - **Flags**: ACC_PUBLIC (public method)

  - **Code**:

    ```
    stack=1, locals=1, args_size=1
       0: aload_0
       1: getfield #7 // Field name:Ljava/lang/String;
       4: areturn
    ```

The method name() retrieves the value of the name field and returns it. aload_0 loads the object reference (this), and getfield fetches the value of the name field. The LineNumberTable indicates that this code corresponds to line 9 in the source file.

- Method `public int age();`:

  · **Descriptor**: `()I` (no parameters, returns int)

  · **Flags**: `ACC_PUBLIC` (public method)

  · **Code**:

```
stack=1, locals=1, args_size=1
    0: aload_0
    1: getfield #13 // Field age:I
    4: ireturn
```

  Similar to the `name` method, this retrieves the value of the `age` field and returns it. `getfield` fetches the value, and `ireturn` returns it. The `LineNumberTable` indicates that this code corresponds to line `13` in the source file.

- Method `public java.lang.String bark();`:

  · **Descriptor**: `()Ljava/lang/String;` (no parameters, returns `String`)

  · **Flags**: `ACC_PUBLIC` (public method)

  · **Code**:

```
stack=1, locals=1, args_size=1
    0: ldc #17 // String woof
    2: areturn
```

  The `bark()` method directly returns the string `woof` without accessing any fields. `ldc` loads a constant string and `areturn` returns it. The `LineNumberTable` indicates that this code corresponds to line `17` in the source file.

These bytecode snippets encapsulate the logic of each method within the `Animal` class, showcasing the low-level operations performed during method execution.

In Java bytecode, each variable and method parameter is assigned a type descriptor to indicate its data type. These descriptors are compact representations used to convey information about the variable type or parameter. Here's a detailed explanation:

- **B (byte)**: Represents a signed 8-bit integer
- **C (char)**: Denotes a Unicode character
- **D (double)**: Stands for a double-precision floating-point value
- **F (float)**: Represents a single-precision floating point value
- **I (int)**: Denotes a 32-bit integer
- **J (long)**: Represents a 64-bit long integer

- **L Classname (reference)**: Points to an instance of the specified class; the fully qualified class name follows the L and ends with a semicolon

- **S (short)**: Represents a 16-bit short integer

- **Z (Boolean)**: Indicates a Boolean value (true or false)

- **[(array reference)**: Denotes an array. The type of the array elements is determined by additional characters following the [

For array references:

- [L Classname: Represents an array of objects of the specified class

- [[B: Represents a two-dimensional array of bytes

These type descriptors are crucial when examining the bytecode instructions related to method declarations, field definitions, and variable usage within Java classes. They enable a concise representation of data types in the low-level bytecode representation of Java programs.

Summary

As we conclude our exploration of Java bytecode and its intricate conditional instructions, readers have acquired a solid understanding of the nuanced control flow within Java programs. Armed with knowledge about bytecode's decision-making capabilities, readers are well-equipped to optimize their code for efficiency and precision. The journey now propels us into the heart of the JVM with a focus on the execution engine in the upcoming chapter. Readers can anticipate delving into the mechanics of bytecode interpretation and the transformative realm of **just-in-time** (**JIT**) compilation. These skills are invaluable in real-life workplaces, where optimizing Java applications for performance is a critical task. Join us in unraveling the secrets of the JVM's Execution Engine, where the binary dance of bytecode evolves into optimized machine instructions, empowering readers to enhance the runtime magic of Java applications.

Questions

Answer the following questions to test your knowledge of this chapter:

1. Which bytecode instruction is used to compare if two integers are equal and branch accordingly?

    A. `ifeq`

    B. `if_icmpeq`

    C. `if_acmpeq`

    D. `tableswitch`

2. What does the bytecode instruction `ifeq` do?

    A. Branches if the top value on the stack is equal to 0

    B. Branches if two integers on the stack are equal

    C. Jumps to a subroutine

    D. Loads an integer from an array

3. Which bytecode instruction is used for unconditional branching?

    A. `goto`

    B. `ifne`

    C. `jsr_w`

    D. `lookupswitch`

4. In Java bytecode, what does the `jsr` instruction do?

    A. Jumps to a subroutine

    B. Calls a static method

    C. Compares two doubles

    D. Branches if the top value on the stack is null

5. Which bytecode instruction is used to check if two object references are not equal and branches to the target instruction?

    A. `if_acmpeq`

    B. `if_acmpne`

    C. `ifnull`

    D. `goto_w`

Answers

Here are the answers to this chapter's questions:

1. B. `if_icmpeq`
2. A. Branches if the top value on the stack is equal to 0
3. A. `goto`
4. A. Jumps to a subroutine
5. B. `if_acmpne`

Part 2:
Memory Management
and Execution

Continuing our exploration, we dive into the JVM's execution engine, uncovering how bytecode is interpreted and the nuances of just-in-time compilation for optimal performance. Shifting focus, we venture into memory management, unraveling the intricacies of the heap and stack, and the art of memory allocation. Delving deeper, our journey extends into garbage collection algorithms and memory profiling techniques. Together, these chapters offer a concise yet comprehensive guide to the critical aspects of execution and memory within the JVM.

This part has the following chapters:

- *Chapter 4, Execution Engine*
- *Chapter 5, Memory Management*
- *Chapter 6, Garbage Collection and Memory Profiling*

4

Execution Engine

In the intricate landscape of the **Java Virtual Machine (JVM)**, the execution engine takes center stage, playing a pivotal role in interpreting bytecode and executing **just-in-time (JIT) compilation** for performance optimization. Bytecode, the intermediary language between Java source code and the JVM, undergoes interpretation as the execution engine dynamically translates it into native machine code during program execution. The stack-based execution model employed by the JVM manipulates an operand stack, pushing and popping operands as bytecode instructions are interpreted. While bytecode interpretation ensures platform independence, it cannot consistently deliver peak performance due to an additional abstraction layer.

To address performance challenges, the JVM incorporates JIT compilation. This strategic optimization technique identifies frequently executed code segments, or hotspots, and dynamically compiles them into native machine code at runtime. By selectively optimizing hotspots, the JVM balances portability and performance, significantly enhancing the execution speed of Java applications. This chapter delves into the nuances of bytecode interpretation and the intricacies of JIT compilation, unraveling how these processes synergize to make the JVM a robust and adaptive runtime environment for Java programs.

In this chapter, we'll explore the following topics:

- The foundation of execution
- System operation layers
- Decoding JVM execution
- JIT compilation
- Class loading

The foundation of execution

With a solid understanding of the compilation process that transforms Java source code into class files and bytecode, we now focus on the fascinating realm of JVM execution. This crucial phase is where the magic happens, as the JVM takes the reins to bring our Java programs to life.

As the JVM receives the compiled class files containing bytecode, the execution engine kicks into action. Bytecode, the intermediary representation of our Java programs, is interpreted in a stack-based execution model. The execution engine dynamically executes the bytecode instructions, manipulating an operand stack. This stack-based approach allows the JVM to process the instructions efficiently, pushing and popping operands onto and from the stack. While bytecode interpretation ensures platform independence, it may introduce performance considerations, which leads us to the next crucial step in the execution journey.

When a JVM program is executed, several steps unfold to bring the Java application to life:

- **Loading**: The class loader locates and loads the compiled Java class files (bytecode) into the JVM. This includes the core Java libraries and any user-defined classes.

- **Verification**: The loaded bytecode undergoes a verification process to ensure it adheres to Java language specifications, preventing potentially harmful code from being executed.

- **Preparation**: Memory space is allocated for class variables and static fields, initializing them with default values.

- **Resolution**: Symbolic references in the bytecode are resolved to concrete references, ensuring that classes and methods can be linked correctly.

- **Initialization**: The static blocks and variables of the class are executed, initializing the class for use.

- **Execution**: The `main()` method or the designated entry point is invoked, and the program begins its execution.

As a Java class file takes center stage within the JVM, a sophisticated orchestration of processes unfolds, paving the way for the execution of a Java application. The class file, a compiled representation of Java source code, becomes the focal point as the JVM's class loader meticulously locates and loads it into the runtime environment. Once loaded, the JVM undertakes a series of steps, from verifying the bytecode's adherence to language specifications to resolving symbolic references and initializing class variables. The culmination of these steps results in the transformed class file operating within the JVM. With the `main()` method or designated entry point invoked, the application embarks on its runtime journey, with each line of code dynamically interpreted and executed. The synergy between the class file, JVM, and the running application exemplifies the intricate dance that underlies the execution of Java programs within the versatile and adaptive environment of the JVM, as the following diagram shows:

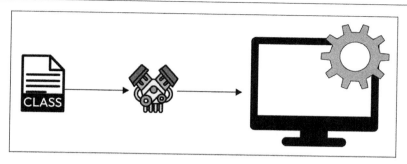

Figure 4.1: The process to execute a class in the JVM

Each time a Java application is executed, the JVM creates a unique runtime environment. However, it's important to note that the JVM optimizes performance within each runtime using various techniques. One notable optimization technique is the JIT compiler. In repeated executions of the same application, the JVM identifies frequently executed code paths, known as hotspots, within that specific runtime and dynamically compiles them into native machine code. This compiled code is stored in memory within the same runtime, reducing the need for repeated interpretation of the same bytecode and significantly improving execution speed within that particular runtime. Additionally, JVM implementations may employ caching mechanisms to store frequently accessed classes and resources, further optimizing the application's performance within the scope of each runtime.

To summarize, the JVM optimizes performance within each runtime, and the benefits of JIT compilation and caching mechanisms apply to a single execution instance, ensuring that the application runs efficiently within its specific runtime environment.

Despite these optimizations, it's important to note that they are lost when the Java application stops. Therefore, with each run of an application on the same or another machine, the entire optimization and compilation of the native code process must happen again. Ongoing projects, such as the Project Leyden (`https://openjdk.org/projects/leyden/`), aim to address this challenge. The primary goal of the Leyden project is to improve startup time, time-to-peak performance, and the overall footprint of Java programs by giving developers more control over which optimizations are applied. However, it's worth noting that the extent of such control may be limited in the project's current state.

Another noteworthy project in this context is **Coordinated Restore at Checkpoint (CRaC)** (`https://docs.azul.com/core/crac/crac-introduction`), which is a JDK project designed to optimize the startup time and resource utilization of Java programs. CRaC allows you to start Java programs with a shorter time to the first transaction and requires fewer resources to achieve complete code speed. It accomplishes this by taking a snapshot of the Java process (checkpoint) when it is fully warmed up. It then uses that snapshot to launch multiple JVMs from this captured state, leveraging native Linux features. It's worth mentioning that alternatives such as **InstantOn from Open Liberty** also exist, and both are proprietary technologies. Additionally, the CRaC API is used by AWS Lambda SnapStart, showcasing real-world applications of this checkpointing approach. Popular frameworks such as Spring, Micronaut, and Quarkus also support CRaC checkpointing, making it a promising approach to optimize Java application performance further.

The bytecode interpreter, a critical component within the JVM, plays a pivotal role in executing Java programs. When a Java application is launched, the JVM loads bytecode generated from previously compiled Java source code, typically packaged into a JAR file. This bytecode is then meticulously interpreted by the bytecode interpreter, following a step-by-step process of fetching, decoding, and executing each instruction.

At its core, the bytecode interpreter adheres to the platform independence principle. Executing the same bytecode on any device equipped with a JVM enables Java applications to run seamlessly across diverse environments without modification. This adaptability is fundamental to Java's renowned *Write Once, Run Anywhere* philosophy, liberating developers from concerns about underlying hardware and operating systems.

Operating on a stack-based model, the interpreter navigates through bytecode instructions, pushing operands onto and popping them off a stack as operations are executed. This stack-oriented approach allows efficient bytecode processing and contributes to Java applications' adaptability and quick startup times. While interpreted code may not match the speed of natively compiled counterparts, the bytecode interpreter strikes a balance by providing the agility of fast startup combined with the portability that defines Java's strength in cross-platform development.

As we transition from the nuanced workings of the JVM to a broader perspective, our journey now unfolds in the layers of system operation. The system's foundation, the hardware layer, provides the raw power, while the **Instruction Set Architecture** (**ISA**) layer is the intermediary language. Operating atop these, the operating system orchestrates the harmony of resources, paving the way for the application layer to shine. As we explore each layer's significance, we uncover how the JVM collaborates with hardware, communicates through the ISA, dances with the operating system, and eventually manifests Java applications at the pinnacle of the computing symphony. Let's embark on this layered expedition to understand the intricate dynamics of system operation.

System operation layers

System operation layers constitute the fundamental architecture that underpins the seamless functionality of modern computing. These layers are hierarchical strata, each serving a distinct purpose in orchestrating the collaboration between hardware and software. Let's unravel the significance of these layers and understand why they are crucial to the operation of a computer system:

- **Hardware layer**: At the lowest level, the hardware layer consists of the physical components of a computer system—processors, memory, storage devices, and input/output devices. It provides the foundation upon which all higher-level operations and software function.

- **ISA layer**: Above the hardware layer lies the ISA layer, defining the interface between software and the hardware. It includes the instruction set and the architecture, which the processor understands. The ISA layer acts as a bridge, allowing software to communicate with and utilize underlying hardware resources.

- **Operating system layer**: Sitting above the ISA layer, the operating system is a crucial intermediary between application software and the hardware. It manages resources, provides a runtime environment for applications, and facilitates communication between software and hardware components.

- **Application layer**: The topmost layer encompasses the application software, which includes programs and tools designed to fulfill specific user needs. This layer interacts with the operating system to efficiently execute tasks and leverage hardware resources.

In this visual snapshot, witness the layered ballet of computing as hardware, the tangible powerhouse, lays the foundation. The ISA layer is a vital bridge, defining the language between software and hardware. Ascending, the operating system is a conductor, orchestrating the dynamic interplay. This diagram encapsulates the essence of computing layers, showcasing the interconnected dance that brings our digital landscape to life:

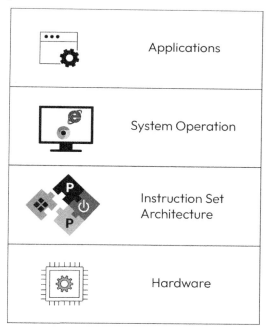

Figure 4.2: The layers of system operation

In the intricate choreography of computing, the JVM emerges as a graceful dancer, seamlessly bridging gaps between system layers. A captivating narrative unfolds as we explore the symbiotic relationship between the JVM and the foundational layers of hardware, ISA, and the operating system:

- **Interaction with ISA and hardware**: The JVM indirectly interacts with the ISA layer and hardware through the operating system. It relies on the ISA layer's instruction set to execute bytecode while the operating system manages hardware resources on behalf of the JVM.

- **Collaboration with the operating system**: The JVM works closely with the operating system layer, utilizing its services for memory management, file operations, and other system-related tasks. The JVM abstracts the underlying hardware and operating system differences, providing a platform-independent execution environment for Java applications.

- **Application execution**: The JVM is a runtime environment for Java applications residing within the application layer. It interprets and executes Java bytecode, ensuring that Java programs can run consistently across various platforms without direct concern for the underlying hardware or operating system specifics.

In essence, the JVM operates as a crucial bridge between the high-level application layer and lower-level system layers, abstracting away hardware and operating system details to provide a standardized and portable execution environment for Java applications.

As we draw the curtains on our exploration of system operation layers and their intricate dance, we find ourselves on the precipice of a more profound revelation—the nuanced execution of the JVM. At this point, we have navigated the significance of abstraction, resource management, interoperability, and security, witnessing how these pillars shape the very essence of computing. Our journey propels us to unravel the layers beneath the JVM's execution. Join us in the next section as we delve into the intricacies of JVM execution, decoding the magic that transpires when Java applications come to life. The continuum of our exploration promises a deeper understanding of the symbiotic relationship between the JVM and the layers we've unraveled.

Decoding JVM execution

In the orchestration of JVM execution, the performance unfolds across distinct stages, each contributing to the seamless functionality of Java applications. The overture commences with the loading of the JVM, where the class loader diligently fetches and loads class files and bytecode into the memory, setting the stage for the ensuing performance.

As the curtains rise, the JVM's execution engine takes the lead, dynamically interpreting bytecode in a stack-based execution model. Simultaneously, the data area is meticulously initialized, allocating memory spaces for the runtime components such as the heap and stack. This orchestrated dance culminates in integration with native elements, seamlessly linking native libraries to augment the application's capabilities. Join us in the upcoming section as we delve deeper into the intricacies of

JVM execution, unraveling the magic that transpires as Java applications come to life in this finely tuned symphony.

When the JVM application executes, it follows these steps:

1. The overture begins with the loading of the JVM itself. This pivotal phase involves the class loader locating and loading the necessary class files and bytecode into the JVM's memory. The class loader acts as a gatekeeper, ensuring that the required classes are accessible for execution.

2. With the stage set, the JVM's execution engine takes the spotlight. Initially, the bytecode is interpreted in a stack-based execution model. As each bytecode instruction is dynamically executed, the application begins to take shape, and the JVM transforms the high-level code into actionable instructions.

3. Simultaneously, the JVM initializes its data area, carving out memory spaces for the program's runtime components. It includes sites for the heap, where objects are allocated, and the stack, which manages method calls and local variables. The meticulous organization of the data area ensures efficient memory management during the application's life cycle.

4. As the application gains momentum, the JVM seamlessly integrates with the native environment. It entails linking native libraries and incorporating them into the execution. The native integration bridges the gap between Java and platform-specific functionality, enhancing the application's capabilities and performance. The following diagram indicates the flow of the process:

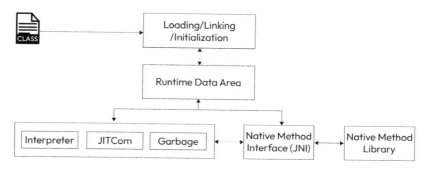

Figure 4.3: JVM in execution

This symphony of stages encapsulates the dynamic execution of a Java application within the JVM. From the initial loading to the interpretation of bytecode, meticulous organization of the data area, and seamless integration with native elements, each stage contributes to the harmonious performance of Java applications. Join us in the next section as we delve deeper into each stage, unraveling the intricacies of JVM execution and demystifying the magic behind Java's adaptability and cross-platform prowess.

In the intricate symphony of JVM execution, we've navigated through the stages of loading, bytecode interpretation, data area initialization, and native integration, witnessing the seamless orchestration that brings Java applications to life. As this chapter concludes, it serves as a prelude to the forthcoming exploration into the transformative realm of JIT compilation. In the next section, we will unravel the dynamic optimization orchestrated by JIT compilation, where bytecode is translated into native machine code during runtime, unlocking new dimensions of performance for Java applications. Join us as we delve deeper into the evolving symphony of JVM execution, exploring the art of on-the-fly optimization and the unparalleled adaptability that JIT compilation brings to the world of Java programming.

JIT compilation

JIT compilation stands as a pivotal component in the JVM, revolutionizing the execution of Java applications. Unlike traditional **ahead-of-time** (**AOT**) compilation, where the entire code is translated into machine code before execution, JIT compilation occurs dynamically during runtime. This on-the-fly translation transforms Java bytecode into native machine code just before execution, optimizing performance and adaptability for the machine it runs on, considering which parts of the code are used the most and need to be optimized. This dynamic optimization process ensures that the JVM focuses on the most frequently executed portions of the code, effectively enhancing performance and adaptability to the specific runtime conditions.

The adoption of JIT compilation within the JVM is rooted in the pursuit of striking a balance between portability and performance. By interpreting bytecode initially and then selectively compiling frequently executed code paths into native machine code, the JVM harnesses the advantages of both interpreted and compiled approaches. This approach allows Java applications to maintain platform independence while achieving performance comparable to natively compiled languages.

Within the intricate tapestry of JVM execution, the tiers of JIT compilation play a pivotal role in balancing adaptability with performance. Let's delve into these levels, understanding why they exist and how they collectively enhance the execution of Java applications.

The presence of multiple JIT compilation levels allows the JVM to strike a delicate balance between the advantages of interpretation and the performance benefits of native machine code. The interpreter provides agility and platform independence, while the JIT compilers optimize hotspots, ensuring that Java applications adapt dynamically to their execution environment. This adaptive compilation approach is pivotal in achieving high-performance results without sacrificing the cross-platform nature of Java. Join us in the upcoming section as we dissect the inner workings of JIT compilation, unveiling how these levels collaborate to empower the Java runtime environment:

- **Interpreter level**: At the interpreter level, the JVM utilizes an interpreter to execute Java bytecode dynamically. This interpreter is the initial bridge between the platform-independent bytecode and the underlying hardware. When a Java program is executed, the interpreter reads the bytecode instructions individually and translates them into machine code on the fly. While this approach offers advantages such as quick startup and platform independence, it introduces inherent overhead due to the interpretation process, which can impact execution speed.

The interpreter essentially acts as a swift executor, enabling Java applications to run on any platform without the need for precompiled native code. However, because of the real-time translation of bytecode to machine code during execution, the overall performance might not be as optimized as it could be. It is where the subsequent JIT compilation levels come into play, aiming to enhance performance by selectively translating and optimizing frequently executed code paths, known as hotspots, into native machine code. The interpreter level, therefore, provides a balance between agility and adaptability, laying the groundwork for the more advanced JIT compilation stages.

- **Baseline JIT compilation**: Baseline JIT compilation represents the next tier in the dynamic compilation process within the JVM. After the initial interpretation of bytecode, the JVM identifies specific sections of code frequently executed, known as hotspots. These hotspots are candidates for further optimization to enhance overall performance. It is where the baseline JIT compiler steps in.

In the baseline JIT compilation stage, the compiler employs selective compilation, targeting identified hotspots rather than the entire program. Focusing on frequently executed portions of the code translates them into native machine code just before execution. Emphasizing quick compilation for immediate performance enhancement, the baseline JIT compiler utilizes simple and rapid translation techniques, significantly improving over repeated interpretation. Dynamic adaptation is key, as the compiler continuously monitors the application's execution, identifying and selectively compiling hotspots. This agile response ensures optimization efforts are concentrated on the most impactful areas, aligning with the evolving runtime behavior and optimizing for immediate performance gains.

- **Dynamic adaptation**: Dynamic adaptation within baseline JIT compilation refers to the compiler's agile response to the evolving runtime behavior of a Java application. Continuously monitoring the execution, the compiler identifies frequently executed code sections or hotspots and selectively compiles them into native machine code. This adaptive strategy ensures that the baseline JIT compiler focuses its optimization efforts on the most impactful areas, optimizing for immediate performance gains.

The significance of dynamic adaptation lies in its ability to balance quick compilation and effective performance improvement. By tailoring its approach based on the runtime behavior, the compiler remains responsive to changes in the workload, refining its strategies to match the evolving execution patterns of the Java program. It ensures that the baseline JIT compilation, also known as the C1 compiler, remains a dynamic and effective component, optimizing Java applications in real time as they navigate diverse and dynamic workloads.

Notably, this dynamic adaptation is the main difference from AOT compiled code. Such code always works the same way and is not capable of adapting to the *use case of the day*, something the JIT compiler handles perfectly. The JIT compiler's ability to adjust its optimization strategies based on runtime behavior makes it a powerful tool for maximizing Java application performance in a wide range of scenarios.

In the culmination of our exploration into JIT compilation, we've witnessed the transformative power it wields in dynamically optimizing Java bytecode for enhanced performance. From the swift adaptability of the interpreter to the selective compilation prowess of the baseline JIT compiler, the intricate dance of JIT has unfolded. As we draw the curtain on this chapter, the stage is set for a more profound revelation—the role of class loading in Java's runtime dynamics. Join us in the next section, where we will unravel the nuances of class loading, exploring how dynamically loading classes into the JVM forms the cornerstone of Java's extensibility and dynamic nature. The continuum of our journey promises a seamless transition from the dynamic compilation orchestration of JIT to the backstage marvels of class loading.

Class loading

In this enlightening section, we dive deep into the intricate world of class loading, a cornerstone of Java's dynamic and extensible nature. Join us as we unravel the mechanisms behind dynamic class loading, which allows Java applications to adapt and extend their functionality during runtime. We'll explore `ClassLoader`, the unsung hero responsible for dynamically loading Java classes into the JVM. Gain insights into the nuances of the class loader hierarchy, understanding how different class loaders collaborate to assemble the rich tapestry of Java applications. From system class loaders to custom class loaders, we'll traverse the layers underpinning Java's ability to incorporate new classes and extend its functionality dynamically. Prepare for a journey into the heart of Java's runtime dynamics, where the magic of class loading unfolds.

The realm of class loading in Java is delineated by two distinct entities: the bootstrap class loader, an integral part of the JVM, and user-defined class loaders. Each user-defined class loader, an instantiation of a subclass of the `ClassLoader` abstract class, empowers applications to customize how the JVM dynamically generates classes. These user-defined class loaders serve as conduits for extending the traditional means by which the JVM creates classes, allowing for the incorporation of classes from sources beyond the typical classpath.

When the JVM delegates the task of locating a binary representation for a class or interface named N to a class loader, denoted as L, it sets in motion a dynamic process. Class loader L, upon receiving this request, loads the specified class or interface C associated with N. This loading can occur directly, with L acquiring the binary representation and instructing the JVM to instantiate C from it. Alternatively, L may opt for an indirect loading approach by deferring the task to another class loader. This indirect loading may involve the delegated class loader loading C directly or employing further layers of delegation until C is eventually loaded. Such flexibility allows Java applications to seamlessly integrate classes from diverse sources, including those fetched over a network, generated on the fly, or extracted from encrypted files. The dynamics of user-defined class loaders thus play a pivotal role in shaping the extensibility and adaptability of Java applications.

Comprehending class loading and creation is essential for Java's adaptability, facilitating the dynamic addition of classes during runtime. With the bootstrap class loader, the JVM checks if it has previously recorded this loader as the initiator for a given class or interface. The process concludes if recorded, and the identified class or interface is present. If not, the bootstrap class loader finds a representation, instructs the JVM to derive the class from it, and then creates it.

User-defined class loaders introduce a dynamic layer to this process. The JVM checks if a user-defined class loader has been recorded as the initiator for the identified class or interface. No further action is taken if recorded and the class or interface is present. Otherwise, the JVM invokes the class loader's `loadClass` method, instructing it to either directly load and create the class or interface from the obtained bytes or delegate the loading process to another class loader.

The dynamic nature of class loading and creation, whether through the bootstrap class loader or user-defined class loaders, empowers Java applications with unparalleled flexibility. This adaptability allows for integrating classes from various sources, contributing to the extensibility and dynamism that define the Java programming language. Our exploration into class loading forms the foundation for understanding how Java seamlessly adapts and evolves at runtime, setting the stage for further revelations in the intricate symphony of Java's runtime environment.

Summary

As we conclude our exploration into the intricate realms of bytecode interpretation and execution within the JVM, we find ourselves standing at the gateway to a profound symphony—the orchestration of memory. The bytecode interpreter, a conductor in its own right, sets the tempo for the next chapter, where we will unravel the nuances of memory management within the JVM.

In the preceding chapters, we deciphered bytecode's journey, its interpretation, and the dynamic adaptations that breathe life into Java applications. Now, our journey propels us to the heart of the JVM's inner workings—memory orchestration. Join us in the upcoming chapter as we navigate how the JVM allocates, utilizes, and deallocates memory, unveiling the artistry that ensures optimal performance and resource efficiency. The continuum of our exploration promises a deeper understanding of the symbiotic relationship between bytecode's execution and the meticulous ballet of memory within the JVM.

Questions

Answer the following questions to test your knowledge of this chapter:

1. What is the purpose of the bytecode interpreter in the JVM?

   A. Static code analysis

   B. Dynamic code execution

   C. Memory allocation

   D. Platform-specific compilation

2.   What does the term "hotspot" refer to in the context of baseline JIT compilation?

A.   Code segments rarely executed

B.   Frequently executed code sections

C.   Compilation errors

D.   Interpreted bytecode

3.   How does the bytecode interpreter contribute to platform independence in Java?

A.   It performs static analysis

B.   It interprets bytecode on the fly

C.   It relies on platform-specific compilation

D.   It only works on certain operating systems

4.   What is the primary role of the baseline JIT compiler in JVM optimization?

A.   Quick compilation for all code segments

B.   In-depth analysis of code behavior

C.   Static translation of bytecode

D.   Selective compilation of frequently executed code

5.   How does dynamic adaptation contribute to baseline JIT compilation's effectiveness?

A.   By ignoring runtime behavior

B.   By compiling the entire program at once

C.   By adapting to changes in workload

D.   By prioritizing seldom-executed code

Answers

Here are the answers to this chapter's questions:

1.   B. Dynamic code execution

2.   B. Frequently executed code sections

3.   B. It interprets bytecode on the fly

4.   D. Selective compilation of frequently executed code

5.   C. By adapting to changes in workload

5
Memory Management

This chapter explores the intricate realm of memory management within the JVM. Understanding the inner workings of memory allocation and utilization is paramount for Java developers seeking to optimize their applications for performance and scalability. As the heartbeat of any Java program, the JVM's memory management system juggles various components, including the heap, stack, and garbage collection mechanisms, each playing a crucial role in the efficient execution of Java applications.

Throughout this chapter, we'll delve into the intricacies of these components, unraveling the mysteries of how the JVM dynamically allocates and manages memory resources. We'll explore the foundational concepts behind the heap, where objects reside and are managed by the garbage collector, and the stack, which handles method calls and local variables. This journey through memory management demystifies the complexities of garbage collection algorithms, shedding light on best practices for efficient object memory allocation. By the end of this chapter, you will have not only grasped the fundamental principles governing memory management in the JVM but also acquired practical insights to fine-tune your Java applications for optimal memory utilization. Whether you're a seasoned Java developer or a newcomer to the language, this exploration promises to be a gateway to mastering the art of memory management in the Java ecosystem.

In this chapter, we'll explore the topics:

- Memory management in the JVM
- Program counter
- Java stack
- Native method stacks
- Method area
- Heap
- Code Cache and JIT

Technical requirements

For this chapter, you will require the following:

- Java 21
- This chapter's GitHub repository, found at - `https://github.com/PacktPublishing/Mastering-the-Java-Virtual-Machine/tree/main/chapter-05`

Memory management in the JVM

In this enlightening exploration of memory management within the JVM, we'll delve into the intricacies of memory allocation and utilization, recognizing the pivotal role memory plays in the life cycle of a Java application. Once your Java code has been compiled into bytecode, the journey into memory management begins. As the bytecode executes, it invokes the JVM, the cornerstone of Java's platform independence, which steps forward to claim the necessary memory from the underlying system. We'll explore the mechanisms by which the JVM interacts with the system, acquiring the memory needed for efficient program execution.

Within the rich memory landscape of the JVM, crucial components such as the heap and the stack come into play. The heap, a dynamic area where objects are stored, undergoes garbage collection to reclaim memory occupied by objects no longer in use. The stack manages method calls and local variables, providing a structured and efficient way to handle memory during program execution.

A distinctive feature of the JVM is its ability to dynamically adapt to changing memory needs. The garbage collector, which is integral to the JVM, identifies and reclaims memory occupied by unreferenced objects. This dynamic memory management ensures optimal resource utilization, enhancing the overall performance of your Java programs. One of the most significant differences between Java and languages such as C/C++ is that in Java, memory assignment and cleanup are managed automatically by the JVM. It alleviates developers from the burden of explicit memory management tasks. However, while you don't need to concern yourself with memory management, understanding the underlying memory structures and their management by the JVM, as explained in this chapter, is crucial for effective Java development.

Understanding how the JVM interfaces with the system is vital to obtaining the required memory. We'll delve into the communication protocols and mechanisms that enable the JVM to allocate and release memory seamlessly, ensuring a harmonious integration with the underlying operating system. Armed with this knowledge, you'll be better equipped to optimize your code for memory efficiency, contributing to your Java applications' enhanced performance and scalability. So, let's embark on this journey into the heart of the JVM's memory management, where every byte matters!

In this exploration, our focus is on unraveling the intricate memory architecture of the JVM, with a specific emphasis on its key components: the method area, the heap, Java stacks, the **program counter** (**PC**) register, and native method stacks. Collectively, these elements orchestrate the dynamic execution of Java programs, each playing a unique role in managing class-level information, object allocation, method execution, program flow control, and the integration of native code. As we delve into the nuances of these memory areas, we aim to provide a comprehensive understanding of how the JVM handles memory, enabling developers to optimize their code for enhanced performance and scalability. So, let's embark on this journey through the JVM's memory landscape, where each memory area has its role in shaping the runtime behavior of Java applications.

The method area is a critical segment of the JVM's memory architecture. It is a repository for class-level data that houses method code, static variables, and the constant pool. Each loaded class has its dedicated space in the method area, making it a shared resource among all threads in the JVM. This area is indispensable for the efficient management of class-related information.

On the other hand, the heap is a dynamic and shared memory space where the JVM allocates memory for objects during runtime. All objects, irrespective of their scope, reside in the heap. It plays a pivotal role in garbage collection, ensuring that unreferenced objects are identified and their memory is reclaimed to prevent resource exhaustion.

Java stacks are employed for the execution of Java methods. Each thread in a Java application possesses its stack, containing the method call stack and local variables. The stack is fundamental for managing method calls, providing a clean and isolated environment for executing each thread.

The PC register is a small yet significant area within a thread's memory. It stores the address of the currently executing instruction, maintaining the program's flow by indicating the next instruction to be executed. The PC register is crucial for upholding the sequential order of program execution within a thread.

Additionally, native method stacks are dedicated memory areas for native methods written in languages such as C or C++. These stacks operate separately from the Java stacks and handle the execution of native code, facilitating seamless integration between Java and native languages.

Within the intricate architecture of the JVM, the allocation and management of memory are orchestrated by several distinct areas. This visual representation captures the dynamic interplay of key memory components, showcasing the **method area**, **heap**, **Java stacks**, **PC registers**, and **native method stacks**:

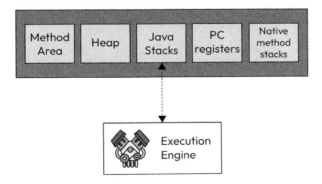

Figure 5.1: The JVM running and its memory

In the forthcoming sections, we will delve into the intricacies of these memory areas within the JVM. Our exploration will encompass understanding how the method area manages class-level information, the dynamic nature of the heap and its role in object allocation, the significance of Java stacks in method execution, the function of the PC register in controlling program flow, and how native methods are handled through native method stacks. By the chapter's conclusion, you will comprehensively understand the JVM's memory architecture and how these components collaboratively facilitate the execution of Java programs.

As we conclude our exploration into the diverse memory areas within the JVM, we've gained valuable insights into the dynamic interplay of components such as the method area, heap, Java stacks, PC register, and native method stacks. Understanding these elements is pivotal for developers seeking to optimize memory usage and enhance the performance of their Java applications.

In the next section, we will focus on a crucial aspect of the JVM's inner workings – the PC. It plays a central role in guiding the flow of program execution, storing the address of the currently executing instruction. Join us in the upcoming section as we unravel the significance of the PC register, delving into its function and impact on the seamless execution of Java programs. This journey through the intricate layers of the JVM promises to deepen our understanding of its core mechanisms, empowering us to write more efficient and robust Java code.

Program counter

Our focus sharpens on the PC within the JVM, a crucial component intricately tied to the execution flow. Unique for each thread, the PC serves as a guidepost, carrying essential information about the ongoing instruction execution. Join us as we delve into the nuances of the PC, unraveling its role in managing program flow, and understanding its significance in both native and non-native method executions.

The PC is a specialized register that's created for every thread within the JVM. It carries crucial data, primarily as a pointer and a return address. This dynamic duo holds the key to understanding the ongoing execution state of the thread. The pointer directs the thread to the next instruction to be executed, while the return address ensures a seamless return to the previous execution point after method completion.

Distinguishing native and non-native methods is crucial in understanding the PC's behavior. The PC's value is clearly defined in non-native methods, representing the instruction address. However, in the context of native methods, the PC transforms into a pointer, showcasing its adaptability in accommodating the diverse nature of method executions within the JVM.

The following visual representation offers a glimpse into the intricate dance of thread execution within the JVM, with a particular focus on the PC. The figure vividly illustrates how the PC, which is unique to each thread, carries critical information such as a return address and a pointer to guide the thread through its execution path. In the realm of native methods, the PC takes on a mysterious quality, represented by an unknown value, symbolizing the dynamic nature of its role in navigating between Java code and native executions:

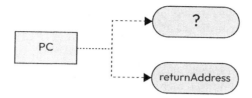

Figure 5.2: A PC that might have returnAddress or an unknown value

The PC's role in managing the thread's execution is paramount. It acts as a sentinel, constantly updating to reflect the current instruction in progress. As threads navigate method calls, the PC ensures a smooth transition between instructions, orchestrating the program flow precisely.

Beyond its role in execution control, the PC has implications for code optimization. While the JVM implementation controls the PC, developers can still influence code optimization by understanding how the PC operates. This understanding allows developers to optimize their code strategically, aligning with the JVM's execution model to enhance performance and efficiency. While direct control over the PC might be limited, insights into its behavior empower developers to write code better suited for the JVM's execution, ultimately leading to improved application performance.

As we conclude our exploration of the PC and its pivotal role in guiding thread execution within the JVM, we find ourselves on the brink of unraveling yet another layer of the JVM's intricacies. Join us in the upcoming session as we delve into the dynamic world of the Java stack. This essential component is central in managing method calls, providing dedicated spaces for call stacks and local variables within each thread. Understanding the Java stack is paramount for developers seeking to optimize their code for efficient execution. So, let's seamlessly transition from exploring the PC to a deep dive into the Java stack, where each method call leaves its mark, shaping the robust architecture of Java applications.

Java stack

In this section, we'll delve into the intricacies of the Java stack – a fundamental component within the JVM. Like the PC, the Java stack is a private register exclusive to each thread, functioning as a repository for method execution information. This section delves into the Java stack's operation, drawing parallels with classical languages such as C and shedding light on its role in storing local variables, partial results, method invocations, and results.

Like classical languages such as C, the Java stack operates by storing frames, each encapsulating crucial information related to method execution. These frames hold parameters, local variables, and other essential data. The Java stack's functionality extends beyond direct variable modifications; instead, it gracefully inserts and removes frames to accommodate the evolving state of thread execution.

When a thread calls a method, the Java stack undergoes a dynamic transformation by inserting a new frame. This frame encapsulates details such as parameters and local variables, orchestrating a dedicated space for the method's execution. As the method concludes, whether in a normal fashion or due to an exception, the frame is discarded. This life cycle ensures a well-organized and efficient execution environment within the Java stack.

The Java stack's flexibility is underscored by its ability to be fixed or dynamically determined in size. This feature allows for tailored resource allocation based on the specific needs of the executing Java application, contributing to optimized memory utilization.

The fundamental building block of the Java stack is the frame. This unit comes into existence upon creating a method and ceases to exist when the method concludes, whether by normal completion or due to an exception. Each frame encapsulates key components, including a list of local variables, a stack of operations, and references to the current class and method. This tripartite structure divides the frame into three essential parts:

- **Local variables**: The stack variables section within the frame is a storage space for local variables. These variables are specific to the method currently in execution and are crucial for storing intermediate results and parameters relevant to the method's functionality.

- **Operand stack**: Operating in tandem with the stack variables, the stack operand section houses the stack of operations. This stack is instrumental in managing the flow of operations within the method, facilitating the execution of instructions, and ensuring a structured approach to method execution.

- **Frame data**: This section encapsulates critical information about the method's execution context. It includes references to the current class and method, providing the necessary contextual information for the JVM to navigate the program's structure effectively.

This tripartite division of the frame into local variables, stack operand, and frame data is pivotal for maintaining the integrity and functionality of the Java stack. It ensures systematic information organization, allowing for efficient method execution and seamless handling of variables and operations within the JVM's memory architecture.

Each frame within the Java stack incorporates a crucial reference to the runtime constant pool corresponding to the type of the current method. This inclusion supports the dynamic linking of method code, a process essential for translating symbolic references in class file code. Symbolic references, denoting methods to be invoked and variables to be accessed, undergo dynamic linking to transform into concrete references during runtime. This dynamic linking process involves resolving undefined symbols and potentially loading classes as needed. The outcome is a translation of variable accesses into precise offsets within storage structures linked to the runtime location of these variables. This late binding mechanism enhances adaptability and reduces the likelihood of code breakage when modifications are made to other classes that a method may use.

The following visual representation briefly overviews the Java stack's core unit: the frame. This fundamental building block, created with the inception of a method and dismantled upon method termination, encapsulates three key components:

- **Stack variables**: Stores method-specific local variables

- **Stack operand**: Manages a stack of operations for method execution
- **Frame data**: Contains crucial references to the current class and method

Together, these elements define the structure of the frame and play a pivotal role in orchestrating efficient and organized method execution within the JVM, as shown here:

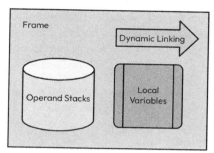

Figure 5.3: A Java stack representation

A frame within the JVM serves as a fundamental unit for storing data, handling partial results, dynamic linking, returning values for methods, and managing exceptions. Its life cycle is tightly bound to method invocations, with a new frame created each time a method is invoked and subsequently destroyed upon the completion of that invocation, whether it concludes normally or abruptly due to an uncaught exception. These frames are allocated from the thread's JVM stack and possess distinct arrays of local variables, operand stacks, and references to the runtime constant pool of the class associated with the current method. Implementation-specific details, such as debugging information, can be appended to a frame, offering extended functionality.

The sizes of the local variable array and operand stack are predetermined at compile-time and accompany the method's code. Consequently, the frame's size relies solely on the JVM's implementation, allowing for concurrent memory allocation during method invocation. In the realm of a given thread's control, only one frame – the active frame for the executing method – is designated as the current frame, with operations on local variables and the operand stack predominantly referencing this frame. As a method invokes another or concludes its execution, the current frame evolves, passing results back to the previous frame. Importantly, frames are thread-local, ensuring they remain inaccessible to other threads.

A StackOverflow error is an exception when the call stack, a region of memory used to manage method calls in a program, exceeds its maximum limit. A method calls itself in recursive programming, creating a new stack frame for each invocation. Each stack frame contains information about the method's state, including local variables and return addresses.

As the method calls itself repeatedly, new stack frames are created and pushed onto the call stack. If this recursion goes too deep without returning, it can consume all the available memory for the call stack, leading to a StackOverflow error. This error serves as a safeguard to prevent a program from running indefinitely and potentially crashing the system.

The StackOverflow error practically demonstrates how the call stack works in programming. Each method call pushes a new frame onto the stack, and when the stack becomes too deep, it results in an error. To avoid this error, programmers can optimize their recursive algorithms to use less stack space or switch to iterative solutions.

The StackWalker API (`https://openjdk.org/jeps/259`) API that was introduced in Java provides a standardized and efficient way to walk through the execution stack. It allows developers to access information about the stack frames, including class instances, without capturing the entire stack trace. This API offers more flexibility and performance than methods such as `Throwable::getStackTrace` or `Thread::getStackTrace`.

StackWalker is particularly useful for scenarios where you must traverse selected frames on the execution stack efficiently and access class instances of each frame. It helps address the limitations of existing APIs by allowing lazy access to stack frame information and filtering of frames, making it a valuable tool for tasks such as the following:

- Determining the immediate caller's class for caller-sensitive APIs
- Filtering out specific implementation classes in the stack
- Finding protection domains and privileged frames
- Generating stack traces for throwable objects and implementing debugging features

StackOverflow errors are a practical outcome of recursive programming when the call stack becomes too deep. The StackWalker API, introduced in Java, provides an efficient and flexible way to traverse and access information from the execution stack, addressing limitations in existing stack-tracing methods.

In the intricate tapestry of the JVM, each frame harbors an array of variables known as its local variables. The length of this array is predetermined at compile time and embedded in the binary representation of the associated class or interface, accompanying the method code within the frame. A single local variable can accommodate Boolean, byte, char, short, int, float, reference, or returnAddress values, while pairs of local variables can collectively hold values of long or double types.

Local variables

Local variables are accessed through indexing, with the index of the first local variable being zero. The JVM's addressing mechanism allows integers to serve as indices in the local variable array and are only valid if the integer falls between zero and one less than the array's size. Importantly, values of the long or double type span two consecutive local variables, which necessitates using the lesser index for addressing. While storing in the second variable is permissible, it invalidates the contents of the first.

The JVM showcases its remarkable flexibility through its capacity to accommodate non-even indices (n) when handling long and double values, which deviates from the traditional concept of 64-bit alignment in the local variables array. This adaptability empowers implementors to decide how to represent these values, leveraging the allocation of the two reserved local variables. This unique feature of the JVM enables it to seamlessly adapt to various system architectures, including 32-bit and 64-bit systems, optimizing memory utilization and performance based on the specific hardware configurations.

Practically, local variables play a vital role in method invocation. For class method invocation, parameters find their place in consecutive local variables, commencing from local variable 0. In the case of instance method invocation, local variable 0 acts as the conduit for passing a reference to the invoking object (akin to this in Java), with subsequent parameters residing in consecutive local variables starting from index 1. This systematic use of local variables ensures the effective passing of parameters during method execution within the JVM.

The following visual representation shows the dynamic choreography of local variables within the JVM. This figure encapsulates the local variables within each frame, portraying the organized spaces for Boolean, byte, char, short, int, float, reference, returnAddress, long, and double types. Notably, pairs of local variables seamlessly accommodate long or double values, challenging traditional alignment norms with non-even indexing flexibility. Here, we can see how the JVM efficiently employs local variables during method invocation, systematically arranging parameters in consecutive local variables. This concise visual offers a clear roadmap for understanding the nuanced interplay of values within the JVM's memory architecture:

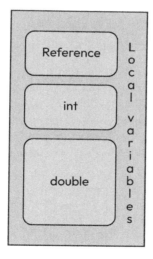

Figure 5.4: Local variables representation

In concluding our exploration of local variables within bytecode, we've peeled back the layers of method execution, witnessing how these variables serve as dynamic containers for values, parameters, and references. This understanding sets the groundwork for our next section: *Operand stacks*. As we transition, anticipate an in-depth examination of how the operand stack interfaces with local variables, directing the flow of operations and ensuring the seamless execution of methods within the intricate dance of the JVM. Join us as we unravel the pivotal role of operand stacks in the symphony of bytecode execution.

Operand stacks

Within the intricate structure of the JVM, each frame boasts a **last-in-first-out** (**LIFO**) stack known as the operand stack. This session peels back the layers of bytecode execution to unveil the role of operand stacks in managing data during method execution.

The maximum depth of the operand stack is a compile-time decision that's intricately intertwined with the method's code. This depth parameter shapes the operand stack's behavior within each frame.

While often referred to simply as the operand stack, it's essential to recognize its dynamic nature. Starting empty upon frame creation, the operand stack becomes a dynamic repository for constants, local variables, field values, and method results.

The JVM supplies instructions to load, manipulate, and store values on the operand stack. Operations range from loading constants to intricate computations. For instance, the `iadd` instruction adds two int values, necessitating their presence as the top two values on the operand stack.

The operand stack enforces strict type constraints to maintain integrity. Each entry can hold any JVM type, including long or double values. Type-appropriate operations are essential, preventing, for example, the treatment of two int values as a long.

The depth of an operand stack at any given moment reflects the cumulative contributions of its values. Type-specific units, such as two units for long or double, shape the associated depth.

The following visual representation unveils the operand stack dynamics in the realm of integers within the JVM. Picture an operand stack initiated with two values, 10 and 20, poised for addition. As the bytecode execution unfolds, the `iadd` instruction orchestrates the addition operation, summing up these integers. Witness the seamless flow of values on the operand stack, capturing the transformation of 10 and 20 into the final result of **30**. This illustrative snapshot encapsulates the essence of operand stack manipulation, showcasing the fluid exchange and computation of values within the intricate dance of bytecode execution:

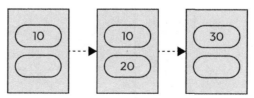

Figure 5.5: The operand stack of int a + int b

This figure shows operand stacks handling double values within the JVM. Picture an operand stack initialized with two double values, 10.10 and 20.20, poised for addition. However, unlike integers, doubles occupy a larger size in the operand stack due to their inherent nature. As the bytecode's execution unfolds, the relevant instructions orchestrate the addition operation, seamlessly handling the larger size of double values. Witness the transformation of 10.10 and 20.20 into the final result of 30.30, reflecting the arithmetic operation and the nuanced accommodation of double values within the operand stack. The following figure captures the intricacies of operand stack dynamics, emphasizing the size considerations essential for handling diverse data types in the JVM:

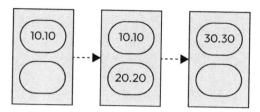

Figure 5.6: The operand stack of double a + double b

As we conclude our exploration of operand stacks, we've unraveled the intricate dance of values within the JVM, witnessing their dynamic exchange and computation. From integers to doubles, the operand stack is a versatile stage for bytecode execution. Now, our journey leads us to the heart of method execution – the Java stack. In the next session, we will dissect the Java stack at the bytecode level, delving into how it orchestrates the flow of method calls, manages frames, and navigates the intricacies of the call stack. Join us as we embark on a deeper dive into the stack-based architecture of the JVM, unlocking the layers that define the journey of method invocation and execution.

Java stack at the bytecode

When we explored Java's internal mechanics, we shifted our focus to a pivotal aspect – the Java stack at the bytecode level. We've already delved into the intricate world of bytecode execution, unraveling how Java instructions translate into low-level operations within the JVM. If you're keen on delving deeper into bytecode specifics, we encourage you to revisit *Chapter 3*.

Now, our journey takes us to scrutinizing the Java stack, a fundamental component in the JVM's stack-based architecture. This section is designed to dissect the Java stack's role in managing method calls, handling frames, and navigating the call stack. It's a journey into the core of method execution, shedding light on how the JVM organizes and executes Java code.

So, join us as we navigate the Java stack in bytecode, revealing the layers that shape the intricacies of method invocation and execution. For those eager to deepen their understanding of Java's internal workings, this section explores the stack-based foundations of Java's runtime environment.

Let's create a Java class named `Math` that encapsulates various arithmetic operations, showcasing static and instance methods. Our class will feature fundamental operations such as addition, multiplication, subtraction, and division while employing integer and double data types:

```java
public class Math {

    int sum(int a, int b) {
        return a + b;
    }

    static int multiply(int a, int b) {
        return a * b;
    }

    double subtract(double a, int b) {
        return a - b;
    }

    static double divide(double a, long b) {
        return a + b;
    }
}
```

Once the class definition is complete, we can compile it using the `javac` command. Subsequently, we can inspect the bytecode representation of the `Math` class using the `javap` command with the `-verbose` flag. This insightful exploration into the generated bytecode allows us to delve into the low-level instructions the JVM interprets to execute arithmetic operations. Join us in this hands-on journey to uncover the bytecode intricacies of both static and instance methods, providing a deeper understanding of their implementation within the JVM.

We'll meticulously analyze the bytecode that's generated for each method within our `Math` class. Bytecode, the intermediate representation of Java code that the JVM comprehends, unfolds with insights into each method's low-level operations. Let's meticulously dissect the bytecode for our arithmetic operations, delving into the stack, local variables, and argument size for two methods.

First, we will explore the sum using an integer; as you can see, the arg size is three because, beyond the parameter, there is also the instance, once it is not a static method:

```java
int sum(int, int);
```

- **Descriptor**: `(II)I`
- **Flags**: `(0x0000)`

- **Code explanation**:

```
stack=2, locals=3, args_size=3
   0: iload_1
   1: iload_2
   2: iadd
   3: ireturn
```

- **Analysis**:

  - `locals=3` indicates that the method has three local variables. In this case, it includes the instance and the two parameters.

  - `stack=2` signifies that the maximum stack size during method execution is 2, accommodating the values pushed onto the stack.

  - `args_size=3` denotes that three arguments are passed to the method.

This method is a multiply operation that's declared as static. In Java, when a method is static, it belongs to the class itself, not to instances of the class. Therefore, static methods don't have a reference to an instance of the class, unlike instance methods.

In method descriptors, `args_size` specifies the total number of arguments the method expects when it's invoked. For instance methods, one of those arguments is reserved for the instance itself, commonly referred to as `this` in Java. However, in static methods, this instance argument is not present because static methods are not associated with any particular instance of the class. Consequently, static methods have "one less `args_size`" because they don't require the instance argument that instance methods do.

```
static int multiply(int, int);
```

- **Descriptor**: `(II)I`
- **Flags**: `(0x0008) ACC_STATIC`
- **Code explanation**:

```
stack=2, locals=2, args_size=2
   0: iload_0
   1: iload_1
   2: imul
   3: ireturn
```

- **Analysis**:

  - `locals=2` indicates that the method has two local variables, corresponding to the two parameters

- `stack=2` signifies that the maximum stack size during method execution is 2

- `args_size=2` denotes that two arguments are passed to the method

By observing the bytecode characteristics of the provided methods, we can see that operations involving `double` and `long` data types result in a doubling of both stack size and local variables. This is because these data types occupy two spaces, necessitating increased allocation in memory. As we further explore bytecode intricacies, we lay the groundwork for optimizing and refining Java applications within the confines of the JVM's interpretation.

By unraveling the bytecode's size characteristics, including the stack, local variables, and argument size for each method, we understand the memory management and execution intricacies embedded within these operations. This exploration lays the groundwork for optimizing and refining Java applications as we navigate the JVM's bytecode interpretation depths.

In delving into the Java stack, we've unraveled the intricacies of method execution within the JVM. Understanding the stack's role as a private register for each thread, accommodating frames, and facilitating the storage of local variables and partial results is pivotal in navigating the landscape of Java memory management. We explored various methods and observed how the stack dynamically adjusts to method invocations, managing parameters, local variables, and method results.

This comprehension sets the stage for what we'll cover next: native method stacks. Native methods, which bridge the gap between Java and platform-specific functionality, introduce a layer of complexity to the JVM's memory model. Join us in the upcoming session as we dissect the mechanics of native method invocation, exploring how native method stacks contribute to the seamless integration of Java applications with underlying platform capabilities.

Native method stacks

In the JVM realm, the execution of native methods, those penned in languages beyond Java's domain, introduces a distinctive memory management facet: native method stacks. These stacks, often synonymous with "C stacks," serve as the scaffolding for the execution of native methods and may even be leveraged by JVM interpreters implemented in languages such as C.

A JVM implementation employing native method stacks may allocate these stacks per thread, aligning with the thread's creation. The flexibility of these stacks can manifest in either fixed sizes or dynamic resizing to accommodate the demands of the computation. When fixed, each native method stack's size can be independently determined upon creation.

For fine-tuning and optimization, JVM implementations might offer control over the initial, maximum, and minimum sizes of native method stacks, empowering programmers or users to tailor the runtime environment to specific requirements.

However, treading into the domain of native method stacks isn't without its caveats. The JVM sets forth exceptional conditions associated with these stacks. `StackOverflowError` looms if a thread's computation demands a more giant native method stack than what's allowed. This error can also affect the Java stack, not just the native memory stack, and occurs when the call stack becomes too deep due to excessive method invocations. Additionally, attempts at dynamic expansion may encounter `OutOfMemoryError` if the system fails to furnish the required memory, either during expansion or the creation of an initial native method stack for a new thread. These exceptional conditions highlight the importance of efficient memory management within the JVM, affecting both native and Java stacks.

In unraveling the intricacies of native method stacks, we've navigated a crucial layer of the JVM's memory management, which is essential for executing native methods and bridging the gap between Java and other languages. As we conclude our exploration of these specialized stacks, our journey seamlessly transitions to the heart of the JVM's internal workings – the method area. This pivotal region is the repository for class and method information and a dynamic space where method invocations and their corresponding frames come to life. Join us in the next section as we delve into the method area, unveiling the repository that shapes the foundation for executing Java applications within the JVM.

Method area

Within the complex architecture of the JVM, the method area serves as a shared space accessible to all JVM threads, much like the storage for compiled code in traditional languages or the "text" segment in an operating system process. This essential region contains structures unique to each class, including the runtime constant pool, data for fields and methods, and the code for methods and constructors. It also accommodates unique class, interface, and instance initialization methods.

Created at the inception of the virtual machine, the method area, while logically part of the heap, may differ in garbage collection and compaction policies. This specification does not dictate its implementation specifics, such as location and management policies, offering flexibility to JVM implementations. The method area's size, whether fixed or dynamic, can be controlled by the programmer or user, providing flexibility in tuning the runtime environment. However, the potential exceptional condition of `OutOfMemoryError` looms if memory allocation within the method area cannot satisfy a request. Join us as we embark on a detailed exploration of the method area, unraveling its role as the repository for class and method information, and setting the stage for the seamless execution of Java applications within the JVM.

Nestled within the JVM's intricate architecture, the method area emerges as a shared realm among all JVM threads, akin to the compiled code storage in conventional languages or the "text" segment in an operating system process. This vital space is the repository for per-class structures, housing the runtime constant pool, field and method data, and the code for methods and constructors. Special methods intricately linked to class, interface initialization, and instance initialization find their abode within this domain.

Initiated at the birth of the virtual machine, the method area, though logically part of the heap, may diverge in garbage collection and compaction policies. Its implementation specifics, including location and management policies, grant flexibility to JVM implementations. The method area's size, whether fixed or dynamic, can be fine-tuned by the programmer or user, offering control over the runtime environment. However, an imminent `OutOfMemoryError` looms as a potential exceptional condition if memory allocation within the method area falls short.

As we unravel the layers of the method area, delving into its role as the repository for class and method information, we pave the way for the seamless execution of Java applications within the JVM. Join us on this exploration that not only demystifies the intricacies of the method area but also sets the stage for our next journey into the expansive terrain of the heap – a critical component in the dynamic memory management orchestration of the JVM.

Heap

At the heart of the JVM lies the heap, a shared space among all JVM threads, and the dynamic runtime data area responsible for allocating memory to all class instances and arrays. As a foundational component created during virtual machine startup, the heap plays a pivotal role in executing Java applications.

An automatic storage management system, commonly known as a garbage collector, orchestrates memory management within the heap. Notably, objects in the heap are never explicitly deallocated, relying on the automatic system to reclaim storage. The JVM remains agnostic to a specific storage management technique, allowing flexibility in its implementation to cater to varied system requirements. The heap's size can be fixed or dynamically adjusted based on computational needs, expanding or contracting as necessary. This adaptability, combined with non-contiguous memory allocation, ensures efficient utilization.

By empowering JVM implementations with flexibility, programmers and users can control the heap's initial, maximum, and minimum sizes. However, the looming exceptional condition is `OutOfMemoryError`, which is triggered when a computation demands more heap space than the automatic storage management system can provide. Join us on this exploration of the heap, where we'll uncover its critical role in dynamically managing memory and understanding the nuances of its configuration for optimized Java application execution.

The following figure shows the birth of an object, its inception marking the creation of a reference – a pointer to the essence encapsulated within:

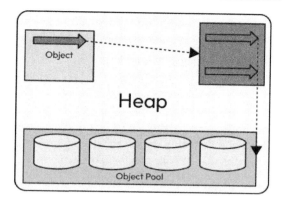

Figure 5.7: Heap overview

As the reference extends its influence, two subtle pointers come into play, delineating the path to essential domains:

- **Object pool**: A reservoir of detailed information, the object pool harbors the intricacies that breathe life into the object

- **Method area**: Nestled within, the constant pool within the method area stands as a repository of class details – attributes, methods, encapsulations – offering a comprehensive view of the object's origins

This figure captures the symbiosis between instances, references, and the heap's intricate web of memory allocation. Join us in deciphering this symphony of memory, where objects find their abode, and the threads converge in a collective memory space, painting a vivid tableau of Java's dynamic runtime environment.

With the birth of an instance, its essence finds a dwelling within the heap – a shared memory space threading through the very fabric of JVM. This dynamic realm, collectively accessed by threads, not only stores object information but also boasts a sophisticated memory reclamation mechanism, skillfully maneuvering objects to sidestep the perils of space fragmentation.

The representation of reference type variables within the heap diverges from primitive types, akin to the pointer mechanisms in C/C++. These reference objects, devoid of detailed information, act as pointers, directing toward the reservoir of object information. In essence, a reference object comprises two succinct pointers:

- One aligns with the object pool, housing the coveted details

- The other extends toward the constant pool, a treasure trove of class insights encompassing attributes, methods, encapsulations, and more, gracefully nestled within the method area

Venturing into the representation of vectors within this dynamic expanse, they echo the behavior of reference variables. However, vectors adorn themselves with two additional fields:

- **Size**: An indicator defining the vector's dimensions
- **Reference list**: A curated compilation of pointers, weaving connections to the objects nestled within this vector

As we traverse this intricate landscape, envisioning the symbiotic relationship between instances, references, and pools, an illustrative depiction unveils the dance of memory within the heap – where objects find residence, and threads share a collective memory space.

As we delve into the intricacies of the heap, understanding its dynamic nature and the vital role it plays in memory allocation, our journey converges on the seamless interplay between the method area and the heap. Collectively, these integral components form the backbone of the JVM's memory management, shaping the runtime environment for Java applications. Join us in the next section as we navigate this symbiotic relationship, exploring the interaction and synergy between the heap and the method area in the realm of the JVM's internal workings.

As we conclude our exploration of the heap, the heartbeat of shared memory among threads, we prepare to delve into the dynamic realms of the Code Cache and **just-in-time** (**JIT**) compilation. In the next section, we'll unravel the intricacies of code execution optimization, where the Code Cache plays a pivotal role in storing compiled code snippets. Join us as we journey into the world of adaptive and efficient runtime performance, unlocking the mechanisms that enhance the execution speed of Java applications. Welcome to the realm of Code Cache and JIT, where the magic of optimized code unfolds.

Code Cache and JIT

In this section, we'll unravel the dynamic duo of Code Cache and JIT compilation, pivotal components that elevate the runtime performance of Java applications to new heights. The Code Cache serves as a sanctuary for brilliance – housing compiled code snippets ready to be executed optimally. As Java applications run, the JIT compilation engine translates Java bytecode into native machine code, dynamically generating optimized versions of frequently executed methods. These gems of compiled code find their haven in the Code Cache, ensuring swift access for subsequent invocations.

Code Cache, the powerhouse behind runtime optimization, plays a pivotal role in enhancing the execution speed of Java applications. Let's explore its intricacies to understand the magic it brings to Java programming.

In the dynamic landscape of Java runtime optimization, the Code Cache emerges as a central protagonist, orchestrating a symphony of compiled brilliance to enhance the execution speed of applications. Let's embark on a journey to unravel the intricacies of Code Cache dynamics, delving into the mechanisms that make it a powerhouse within the JVM:

- **Compilation sanctuary**: As Java applications execute, the JIT compilation engine dynamically translates Java bytecode into native machine code. The compiled code, representing optimized versions of frequently executed methods, aka hotspots, finds its haven in the Code Cache.

- **Optimized code storage**: The Code Cache serves as a repository for compiled brilliance, storing these optimized code snippets for swift access during subsequent invocations. It acts as a dynamic storage space, adapting to the evolving needs of the application as it runs.

- **Management of hotspots**: The Code Cache is particularly adept at managing hotspots – code sections that are frequently executed during the application's runtime. By focusing on these hotspots, the Code Cache ensures that the most crucial pathways undergo efficient and tailored optimization.

- **Space utilization**: The Code Cache dynamically adjusts its size based on the demands of the executing application. This adaptive resizing mechanism ensures that the most relevant and frequently used code segments find their place within the cache.

- **Swift access and execution**: The optimized code snippets stored in the Code Cache enable swift access during subsequent method invocations, contributing to the overall performance boost of the Java application.

Understanding the dynamics of the Code Cache unveils its crucial role in the JIT compilation process, contributing significantly to the efficiency and adaptability of Java applications. As we delve into the intricacies of runtime optimization, the Code Cache emerges as a cornerstone, ensuring that the compiled brilliance is readily available for the application's accelerated execution.

Summary

In this chapter, we delved into the intricate mechanisms that govern the execution of Java applications within the JVM. From understanding the intricacies of memory management, exploring the Java stack, and unraveling the mysteries of native method stacks, to witnessing the dynamic compilation prowess of the JIT compiler and the crucial role played by the Code Cache, our journey has been one of decoding the inner workings of a Java application in action.

As we bid farewell to the realm of code execution dynamics, our next destination awaits, where we'll explore a fundamental aspect of runtime management: the garbage collector. Join us in the upcoming chapter as we unravel the intricacies of memory cleanup and resource management, which is essential for maintaining the health and efficiency of Java applications. The garbage collector beckons, promising insights into how the JVM gracefully handles memory de-allocation and ensures the longevity of Java applications. Let's embark on the next chapter to uncover the secrets of garbage collection in the dynamic landscape of the JVM.

Questions

Answer the following questions to test your knowledge of this chapter:

1. What is the primary role of the Code Cache in the JVM?

    A. Storage for object instances

    B. A repository for compiled code

    C. Memory cleanup and resource management

    D. Dynamic adjustment of heap size

2. What does the Java stack store for each thread in the JVM?

    A. Compiled code snippets

    B. Garbage collector information

    C. Frames, local variables, and the operand stack

    D. Native method stacks

3. Which memory area is shared among all JVM threads and stores the runtime constant pool, field and method data, and method code?

    A. Heap

    B. Method area

    C. Code Cache

    D. Native method stack

4. Which memory area in the JVM is responsible for storing class instances and arrays, with memory reclaimed by a garbage collector?

    A. Code Cache

    B. Native method stack

    C. Java stack

    D. Heap

5. What is the primary purpose of the Java stack in the JVM?

    A. Storage for compiled code snippets

    B. A repository for object instances

    C. Dynamic adjustment of heap size

    D. To store frames, local variables, and the operand stack for each thread

Answers

Here are the answers to this chapter's questions:

1. B. A repository for compiled code
2. C. Frames, local variables, and the operand stack
3. B. Method area
4. D. Heap
5. D. To store frames, local variables, and the operand stack for each thread

6

Garbage Collection and Memory Profiling

In the intricate dance of **Java Virtual Machine** (**JVM**) internals, where bytecode is compiled and programs are executed within the confines of register memory, an indispensable aspect emerges the artful orchestration of memory resources. After traversing the realms of bytecode compilation and program execution, it is paramount to delve into the nuanced domain of memory management within the JVM. This chapter embarks on a comprehensive exploration of **garbage collectors** (**GCs**), unraveling the intricate tapestry governing Java programs' sustenance.

Our journey through the inner workings of the JVM reaches a crucial juncture as we unravel the mysteries of memory allocation, heap structures, and the ever-pivotal garbage collection mechanisms. By comprehending the nuances of memory management, including distinctions between heap and stack, and mastering the intricacies of garbage collection, you will enhance your understanding of JVM internals and acquire the skills to wield precise control over memory usage. Join us as we navigate the intricate terrain of GCs, unlocking the keys to optimizing memory efficiency in Java applications.

In this chapter, we'll explore the following topics:

- GC overview
- JVM tuning and ergonomics

GC overview

In the intricate landscape of JVM internals, the GC role stands as a critical component, influencing the efficiency and reliability of Java applications. Our exploration delves into the fundamental concept of garbage collection and its pivotal role in managing memory within the JVM.

At its core, the purpose of the GC is to automatically reclaim memory occupied by objects no longer in use by the program. In languages such as Java, which employ automatic memory management, developers are spared the burden of explicitly deallocating memory, enhancing productivity and reducing the likelihood of memory-related errors.

Imagine a scenario where each dynamically allocated object had to be manually deallocated by the programmer. Not only does this introduce a considerable cognitive load, but it also opens the door to memory leaks and inefficiencies. In the absence of a GC, the responsibility of memory management falls entirely on the developer's shoulders, increasing the likelihood of bugs and hindering the development process.

Java, with its *Write Once, Run Anywhere* philosophy, utilizes garbage collection to provide a seamless and robust memory management system. The JVM's GC identifies and reclaims unreachable objects, preventing memory leaks and ensuring optimal resource utilization. The Java approach allows developers to focus on application logic rather than micromanaging memory, contributing to the language's popularity in enterprise-level applications.

While Java champions automatic memory management through its GC, other programming languages have embraced various memory management strategies. For instance, languages such as C and C++ frequently depend on manual memory management, granting developers explicit control but also leaving them susceptible to potential pitfalls. Conversely, languages such as Python and C# implement their own garbage collection mechanisms, each meticulously crafted to address the unique requirements of their respective languages.

Even among languages with garbage collection, the implementations can differ significantly. Java's GC is known for its generational approach, dividing the heap into different generations (young and old) and applying different collection algorithms to each. Within the JVM itself, multiple GCs exist, each with its strategies and trade-offs. This contrasts with, for instance, Python's reference counting mechanism or the GCs used in languages such as Go or C#.

Memory leaks often result from programming errors, such as failing to release dynamically allocated memory or inadvertently maintaining references to objects beyond their useful lifespan. Common scenarios include neglecting to free memory in languages that require manual memory management, such as C or C++, or unintentionally creating circular references in languages with automatic memory management, such as Java.

The GC plays a pivotal role in mitigating the risk of memory leaks in languages that employ automatic memory management. Its primary function is to identify and reclaim memory occupied by objects no longer reachable or in use by the program. By automating the memory deallocation process, the GC significantly reduces the likelihood of memory leaks.

In automatic memory management, the GC acts as a vigilant defender, crucially mitigating the risk of memory leaks. Automating the identification and reclamation of unused memory in languages such as Java streamlines the development process and enhances system stability. With a generational approach that swiftly handles short-lived objects and smart memory management adapting to dynamic applications, the GC stands as a pivotal chapter in fortifying software integrity against the subtle menace of memory leaks:

- **Automated memory management**: In languages such as Java, where automatic memory management is integral, the GC regularly scans the heap to identify objects with no reachable references. Once identified, these unreferenced objects are marked for collection and deallocated, freeing up memory for new allocations.

- **Generational approach**: Java's GC often employs a generational approach, categorizing objects into different generations based on their age. Younger objects, which are more likely to become unreachable quickly, are collected more frequently, while older objects undergo less frequent, more comprehensive garbage collection. It helps quickly identify and collect short-lived objects, reducing the chances of memory leaks.

- **Smart memory management**: Modern GCs are designed to be intelligent and adaptive. They utilize algorithms and heuristics to optimize memory management based on the application's behavior. This adaptability ensures efficient garbage collection and minimizes the risk of memory leaks, even in complex and dynamic applications.

Within the intricate tapestry of JVM internals, the *Mark and Sweep* GC algorithm emerges as a cornerstone in managing memory efficiently. This fundamental process operates in two key phases: the mark phase, where the GC discerns the utilization status of memory, marking objects as either reachable or unreachable, and the subsequent sweep phase, where the collector liberates the heap by reclaiming memory occupied by objects marked as unreachable. The advantages of this approach are profound, offering automatic memory management, mitigating dangling pointer issues, and significantly contributing to memory leak management, as the following diagram shows:

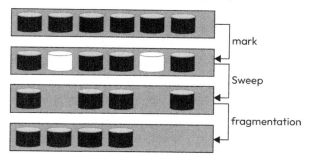

Figure 6.1: Mark and Sweep steps of the GC

As we delve into the nuances of Mark and Sweep, we navigate the benefits and challenges inherent in this automatic memory management paradigm. While it liberates developers from the intricacies of manual memory handling, it introduces considerations such as increased CPU power consumption and relinquishing control over object cleanup scheduling. Join us on this exploration into the heart of JVM internals, where the Mark and Sweep algorithm plays a pivotal role in shaping the reliability and efficiency of Java applications.

In our exploration, we've uncovered the automatic process of Mark and Sweep: its ability to effortlessly handle memory allocation and deallocation, its role in mitigating dangling pointers, and its significant contribution to managing memory leaks.

However, no architectural marvel comes without its trade-offs. In the case of Mark and Sweep, a prominent consideration emerges in the form of memory fragmentation. As we unravel this aspect, we delve into the intricacies of how the algorithm, while adept at reclaiming memory, can leave behind fragmented pockets in the memory space. These fragments, akin to scattered puzzle pieces, introduce challenges to the efficient allocation of contiguous memory blocks, impacting the overall efficiency of the application.

Our narrative thus far has illuminated the delicate balancing act between the advantages of automatic memory management and the potential drawbacks, emphasizing the need for a nuanced approach. The trade-off between seamless automation and the specter of fragmentation prompts developers to weigh the benefits against the efficiency requirements of their applications.

Within the intricate realm of JVM internals, the choice of GC can profoundly impact the performance of Java applications. **Serial GC**, a simple and single-threaded collector, suits applications with modest memory requirements, offering a straightforward approach to garbage collection. Conversely, **Parallel GC** steps up for throughput-centric scenarios, leveraging multiple threads to expedite garbage collection tasks and enhance overall system efficiency. Java's default collector since version 9, **Garbage-First (G1) GC**, strikes a balance between low latency and high throughput, making it a versatile choice for various applications. Introducing a new paradigm, the **Z GC (ZGC)** in Java 11 promises minimal pause times and enhanced scalability, catering to the demands of modern, resource-intensive applications. As we embark on a journey through the intricacies of each collector, a nuanced understanding will empower developers to make informed decisions, optimizing garbage collection strategies to align with the specific needs of their Java projects.

Serial GC

Within the tapestry of JVM internals, Serial GC is a fundamental player in garbage collection strategies. We will dissect the essence of Serial GC, a collector distinguished by its simplicity and singular-threaded approach to memory management. As we delve into the intricacies of its operation, we explore why such a straightforward design is essential and the scenarios in which Serial GC shines. Unveiling its advantages and limitations, we navigate the landscape to understand the optimal scenarios where this minimalist collector becomes a strategic choice for Java developers. We will explore Serial GC, where the pursuit of simplicity intertwines with efficiency in the orchestration of memory within the JVM.

Serial GC is characterized by its sequential, **stop-the-world** approach to garbage collection. It halts the application's execution during the collection process, ensuring that no parallel threads interfere with identifying and reclaiming unreachable objects. This simplicity allows Serial GC to streamline memory management without the complexity of concurrent operations.

The elegance of Serial GC comes with trade-offs, notably in the realm of throughput and responsiveness. Given its single-threaded nature, there may be more efficient choices for applications with large heaps or those requiring low pause times. Stop-the-world pauses, while brief, can impact the user experience, making Serial GC better suited for scenarios where these pauses are acceptable.

Serial GC seamlessly integrates with the Mark and Sweep algorithm. It identifies reachable and unreachable objects during the mark phase, marking them accordingly. In the subsequent sweep phase, it clears memory occupied by unreachable objects. The sequential nature of Serial GC ensures a straightforward execution of these phases, simplifying the coordination between marking and sweeping, as the following diagram shows:

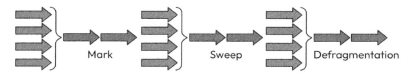

Figure 6.2: Serial GC working

The simplicity of Serial GC shines in scenarios where the memory footprint is modest and the application's performance is not overly sensitive to brief pauses. It is well suited for client applications or environments with limited resources, where the straightforward, stop-the-world approach aligns seamlessly with the system's demands.

As we immerse ourselves in the orchestration of memory within the JVM, a crucial aspect unfolds through the configuration options tailored for Serial GC. The following table presents a harmonious ensemble of commands, each holding the power to influence and optimize the behavior of Serial GC. From enabling or disabling the use of Serial GC to fine-tuning ratios, sizes, and thresholds, these commands offer a conductor's wand to shape the memory management symphony. Join us in deciphering the significance of each command, providing developers and administrators with the means to sculpt an optimal performance for their Java applications by adjusting the parameters that govern the workings of Serial GC:

Command	Description
`-XX:+UseSerialGC`	Enables the use of Serial GC.
`-XX:-UseSerialGC`	Disables Serial GC (default for server-class machines).
`-XX:NewRatio=<value>`	Sets the ratio of the young generation to the old generation.

Command	Description
`-XX:NewSize=<size>`	Sets the initial size of the young generation.
`-XX:MaxNewSize=<size>`	Sets the maximum size of the young generation.
`-XX:SurvivorRatio=<value>`	Sets the ratio of Eden space to survivor space.
`-XX:MaxTenuringThreshold=<value>`	Sets the maximum tenuring threshold for objects in the young generation.
`-XX:TargetSurvivorRatio=<value>`	Sets the desired survivor space size as a percentage of the young generation size.
`-XX:PretenureSizeThreshold=<size>`	Sets the threshold for object allocation in the old generation. Objects larger than this size go directly to the old generation.
`-XX:MaxHeapSize=<size>`	Sets the maximum heap size.

Table 6.1: Serial GC commands

These options allow developers and administrators to configure aspects of Serial GC, such as the size of the young generation, the ratio of survivor spaces, and overall heap size. Adjusting these parameters enables fine-tuning of memory management for specific application requirements and hardware characteristics.

The harmonious coordination of memory management orchestrated by Serial GC has illuminated its advantages, trade-offs, and strategic scenarios in which its singular approach excels. As we transition to our next section, the stage is set for a parallel performance as we delve into Parallel GC. The evolution from singular to parallel threads promises an exploration of efficiency at scale and enhanced throughput.

Parallel GC

As we embark on the next movement in our exploration of JVM internals, the spotlight now shifts to Parallel GC. In this section, we dive into the world of parallelism, where the efficiency of memory management takes center stage. Parallel GC, with its multithreaded prowess, orchestrates a symphony of garbage collection, promising enhanced throughput and optimized performance for Java applications. Through a nuanced lens, we unravel the complexities of Parallel GC—its characteristics, advantages, and scenarios where its parallel threads harmonize seamlessly with the demands of large-scale, data-intensive environments. Join us in this section as we traverse the parallel rhythms of JVM internals, uncovering parallel threads that propel memory management to new heights.

Parallel GC's hallmark lies in its multithreaded approach, making it particularly adept at handling more enormous heaps and achieving higher throughput compared to its single-threaded counterparts. It divides the heap into sections, employing parallel threads to perform garbage collection tasks concurrently, resulting in faster execution and reduced pause times.

Parallel GC orchestrates a synchronized dance of efficiency within the JVM, seamlessly integrating with the Mark and Sweep algorithm. In the intricate garbage collection process, Parallel GC leverages the power of multiple threads to execute the crucial steps of marking and sweeping concurrently. During the mark phase, each thread traverses a designated heap section, identifying and marking objects as reachable or unreachable. This simultaneous marking across threads ensures a swift and parallel assessment of the memory space. As the mark phase concludes, the collective effort of threads harmonizes in the sweep phase, where Parallel GC efficiently reclaims memory by discarding unreachable objects identified during marking. The parallelism embedded in the Mark and Sweep process under Parallel GC optimizes throughput. It showcases the synchronized brilliance of multiple threads working in unison to choreograph a performance that elegantly balances responsiveness and efficiency in memory management, as the following diagram shows:

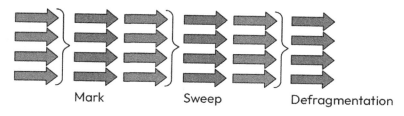

Mark   Sweep   Defragmentation

Figure 6.3: Parallel GC working

While Parallel GC excels in throughput, its reliance on parallelism introduces trade-offs, notably in responsiveness. Stop-the-world pauses, while minimized, can still impact the application's responsiveness, making it less suitable for scenarios where low latency is paramount. Additionally, the increased CPU usage due to parallelism might be a consideration for resource-constrained environments.

Parallel GC shines brightest in scenarios where large heaps and data-intensive applications are the norm. It is well suited for batch processing, scientific computing, and scenarios where maximizing throughput is crucial. However, its trade-offs make it a strategic choice for applications that can tolerate brief pauses in exchange for optimized overall performance.

As we unravel the intricacies of Parallel GC, we explore how its parallel threads choreograph a performance that balances the demands of large-scale memory management. Join us in this section as we navigate the landscape of parallel garbage collection, understanding when its parallel prowess becomes a strategic choice for optimizing memory orchestration within the JVM.

In our exploration of Parallel GC within the intricacies of JVM internals, the ability to finely tune its behavior becomes paramount. The following table offers a comprehensive ensemble of commands, each a key to unlocking the potential of Parallel GC's efficiency and throughput. From turning its use on or off to configuring the number of threads, setting pause-time goals, and employing adaptive sizing policies, these options empower developers and administrators to shape the orchestration of memory management within the JVM. As we delve into the nuances of each command, this ensemble becomes a conductor's guide, enabling the crafting of a performance optimized to meet the unique demands of Java applications. Join us in deciphering the significance of these commands, providing a symphony of possibilities for molding Parallel GC to harmonize seamlessly with the diverse landscapes of JVM environments:

Command	Description
`-XX:+UseParallelGC`	Enables the use of Parallel GC.
`-XX:-UseParallelGC`	Disables Parallel GC.
`-XX:ParallelGCThreads=<value>`	Sets the number of threads for garbage collection.
`-XX:MaxGCPauseMillis=<value>`	Sets the maximum desired pause-time goal for garbage collection.
`-XX:GCTimeRatio=<value>`	Sets the target ratio of garbage collection time to application time.
`-XX:UseAdaptiveSizePolicy`	Enables adaptive sizing policies for heap and survivor spaces.
`-XX:AdaptiveSizeThroughPutPolicy`	Configures the adaptive sizing policy for throughput-oriented garbage collection.
`-XX:AdaptiveSizePolicyOutputInterval=<n>`	Sets the interval, in the number of collections, for adaptive sizing policy output.
`-XX:ParallelGCVerbose`	Enables verbose output from Parallel GC.

Table 6.2: Parallel GC commands

These options provide a means to configure and fine-tune the behavior of Parallel GC, allowing developers and administrators to optimize garbage collection for specific application requirements and hardware characteristics.

As we conclude our exploration into the Parallel GC world, we find ourselves enriched with insights into the parallel threads that orchestrate a harmonious performance within the JVM. The multithreaded efficiency of Parallel GC, showcased through its configuration options, provides a powerful toolkit for developers and administrators seeking to optimize memory management in diverse JVM environments. Our journey through the parallel rhythms has set the stage for the next act—G1 GC. Join us in the upcoming section as we delve into the nuances of G1, unraveling its characteristics, advantages, and intricacies that position it as a pivotal player in the symphony of garbage collection strategies within the JVM.

G1

As we continue our exploration of JVM internals, our spotlight now turns to G1 GC. Positioned as a modern successor to its predecessors, G1 introduces a paradigm shift in garbage collection strategies. In this section, we delve into the intricacies of G1, unraveling its characteristics, operational nuances, and the innovative approaches it brings to the forefront of memory management. G1's meticulous focus on achieving low latency, predictable pause times, and efficient heap utilization marks it as a key player in the symphony of garbage collection within the JVM. Join us in this section as we explore the evolution of garbage collection strategies, dissect the principles that underpin G1, and unveil the symphonic efficiency it brings to the dynamic landscape of JVM internals.

G1 GC is designed to address the challenges posed by traditional garbage collection strategies. It introduces a region-based approach, dividing the Java heap into smaller, uniformly sized regions. This departure from the monolithic heap structure allows G1 to manage memory more flexibly and precisely.

G1 divides the heap into regions and categorizes them into three main types: Eden, survivor, and old. The size and configuration of these regions are dynamic, allowing G1 to adapt to the memory needs of the application.

The concept of the liveness space is central to G1's efficiency. The liveness space comprises regions with live objects—objects still actively referenced by the application. G1 identifies and prioritizes regions with the least live data for garbage collection. This strategic approach optimizes the collection process by targeting areas where reclaimable memory is most concentrated, reducing both the frequency and duration of garbage collection pauses, as the following diagram shows:

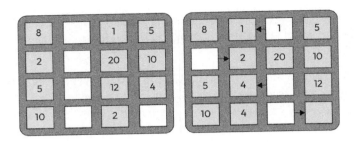

Figure 6.4: G1 process and liveness space working

G1's primary goal is to achieve low latency and predictable pause times. By prioritizing regions with the least live data, G1 minimizes the impact on application responsiveness. It makes G1 particularly well suited for scenarios where maintaining consistent and low pause times is critical, such as in interactive and real-time applications.

G1 employs adaptive collection strategies to adjust its approach based on the application's dynamic behavior. It can dynamically resize regions, alter the garbage collection frequency, and adapt its overall strategy to align with the evolving demands of the application.

In essence, G1 GC's utilization of liveness spaces, along with its region-based approach, positions it as a sophisticated and efficient solution for memory management in modern Java applications. The focus on predictability and adaptability makes G1 valuable in the landscape of garbage collection strategies within the JVM.

In our journey through the orchestration of memory within the JVM, the following table unfolds as a conductor's guide to G1. Each command within this ensemble provides a key to unlocking the precision and efficiency that G1 brings to garbage collection. From turning G1 on or off to fine-tuning parameters such as heap region size, pause-time goals, and adaptive strategies, these options empower developers and administrators to sculpt the symphony of memory management within the JVM. As we delve into the significance of each command, we navigate the intricacies that define G1's performance, crafting a balance between predictability and adaptability. Join us in deciphering this symphony of configurations, where each note resonates with the nuanced precision that G1 introduces to the dynamic landscape of JVM internals:

Command	Description
`-XX:+UseG1GC`	Enables the use of G1 GC.
`-XX:-UseG1GC`	Disables G1 GC.
`-XX:G1HeapRegionSize=<value>`	Sets the size of G1 garbage collection regions.

Command	Description
`-XX:MaxGCPauseMillis=<value>`	Sets the maximum desired pause-time goal for G1 garbage collection.
`-XX:InitiatingHeapOccupancyPercent=<value>`	Sets the percentage of heap occupancy to start a G1 garbage collection cycle.
`-XX:G1NewSizePercent=<value>`	Sets the percentage of heap size to use as the minimum for the young generation in G1.
`-XX:G1MaxNewSizePercent=<value>`	Sets the maximum percentage of heap size to use as the maximum for the young generation in G1.
`-XX:ParallelGCThreads=<value>`	Sets the number of parallel garbage collection threads for G1.
`-XX:ConcGCThreads=<value>`	Sets the number of parallel garbage collection threads for the concurrent phase in G1.
`-XX:G1ReservePercent=<value>`	Sets the target percentage of heap to reserve as space for future garbage collection cycles.
`-XX:G1TargetSurvivorOccupancy=<value>`	Sets the target occupancy of survivor space within each G1 region.
`-XX:G1HeapWastePercent=<value>`	Sets the target percentage of wasted space within a G1 region before a region is considered for reclamation.

Table 6.3: G1 commands

These options provide a means to configure and fine-tune the behavior of G1 GC, allowing developers and administrators to optimize garbage collection for specific application requirements and hardware characteristics.

On our exploration into the intricacies of G1 GC, we stand enriched with insights into the precision and adaptability that define its symphony of memory management within the JVM. The meticulous configuration options presented in our ensemble guide offer a conductor's wand, shaping G1's performance to align seamlessly with the diverse demands of Java applications. As we set our sights on the next section, the stage is set for a crescendo as we unravel the innovative nuances of ZGC.

ZGC

In our continued exploration of JVM internals, our focus shifts to the forefront of innovation by introducing ZGC. Positioned as a game-changer in garbage collection strategies, ZGC emerges as a beacon of efficiency and low-latency performance. This section serves as our gateway into the world of ZGC, unraveling its cutting-edge features, adaptive techniques, and commitment to minimizing pause times. With the pursuit of responsiveness at its core, ZGC redefines the dynamics of garbage collection, offering a solution tailored for modern, dynamic applications. Join us in this section as we delve into the revolutionary advancements that ZGC brings to the JVM, marking a pivotal milestone in the evolution of garbage collection strategies.

ZGC stands at the forefront of modern garbage collection strategies, introducing groundbreaking features that redefine the dynamics of memory management within the JVM. At its core, ZGC prioritizes low latency and responsiveness, aiming to minimize pause times for applications with stringent performance requirements. One of ZGC's key innovations is its concurrent approach to garbage collection. Unlike traditional collectors that halt the application during certain phases, ZGC performs major garbage collection tasks concurrently with the application threads, ensuring that pause times are kept to a minimum. This concurrent model is particularly advantageous for applications where responsiveness is critical, such as in real-time systems, interactive applications, or services where downtime must be minimized.

In computer memory, multi-mapping refers to a technique in which specific addresses in the virtual memory space point to the same ones in physical memory. It means that multiple virtual addresses correspond to the same physical location. Applications interact with data through virtual memory, and they remain oblivious to the underlying multi-mapping mechanism. This abstraction is crucial for the applications, allowing them to access data without being aware of the complexities involved in mapping virtual to physical memory, as the following diagram shows:

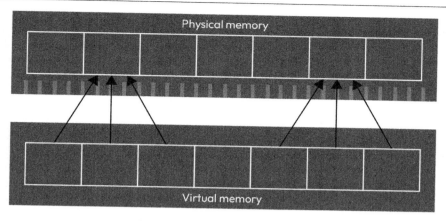

Figure 6.5: ZGC process mapping

Dynamic memory allocation, a common practice in programming, contributes to memory fragmentation over time. When objects are allocated and deallocated, free space gaps can emerge in the memory layout. Over time, these gaps accumulate, leading to **fragmentation**, wherein the memory resembles a chessboard with alternating areas of free and used space. To address this, there are two main strategies.

One approach involves scanning the memory for free space large enough to accommodate the desired object. This method, while feasible, is resource-intensive, especially if performed frequently. Additionally, it does not entirely eliminate fragmentation, as finding an exact match for the required space size can be challenging, leaving gaps between objects.

The alternative strategy is to periodically relocate objects from fragmented memory areas to free spacein a more compact format. It involves dividing the memory space into blocks and relocating entire blocks of objects simultaneously. By doing so, the allocation of memory becomes faster, as known empty blocks are available. This strategy helps manage memory fragmentation more efficiently, balancing the need for dynamic allocation and the desire for a more contiguous and organized memory layout.

Trade-offs are inherent in any garbage collection strategy, and ZGC is no exception. While it excels in reducing pause times, it may not achieve the same throughput as collectors optimized for throughput at the expense of latency. Additionally, ZGC might not be optimal for applications with extremely large heaps, as its concurrent approach may introduce some overhead. However, for scenarios where low latency is paramount, and the application's responsiveness takes precedence over maximum throughput, ZGC emerges as a powerful solution.

Another notable feature of ZGC is its ability to resize the heap dynamically. ZGC adapts the heap size to the application's demand, allowing it to manage memory in response to changing workloads efficiently. This adaptability is particularly beneficial in environments where workloads vary, providing an agile and responsive memory management solution.

In essence, ZGC represents a paradigm shift in garbage collection, offering a sophisticated solution for applications demanding low latency and responsiveness without compromising memory management efficiency. Its innovative features and concurrent design make it a compelling choice for modern Java applications operating in dynamic and resource-intensive scenarios.

In the dynamic realm of JVM internals, ZGC takes center stage as a cutting-edge solution, prioritizing low-latency performance and responsiveness. This table serves as a compass in navigating the configuration landscape of ZGC, providing developers and administrators with a curated set of commands to sculpt its behavior. From turning ZGC on or off to fine-tuning parameters such as pause times, thread counts, and memory uncommit policies, these options empower users to tailor ZGC to the specific demands of their Java applications. As we delve into the significance of each command, this guide becomes an essential resource for optimizing ZGC performance, ensuring a harmonious balance between efficiency and adaptability. Join us in unlocking the potential of ZGC, where each command becomes a note in the symphony of precision that defines the future of garbage collection strategies within the JVM:

Command	Description
`-XX:+UseZGC`	Enables the use of ZGC.
`-XX:-UseZGC`	Disables ZGC.
`-XX:MaxGCPauseMillis=<value>`	Sets the maximum desired pause time goal for ZGC garbage collection.
`-XX:GCPauseIntervalMillis=<value>`	Sets the maximum interval between ZGC pauses.
`-XX:ConcGCThreads=<value>`	Sets the number of parallel garbage collection threads for ZGC.
`-XX:ParallelGCThreads=<value>`	Sets the number of parallel garbage collection threads for the parallel phase of ZGC.
`-XX:ConcGCThreads=<value>`	Sets the number of parallel garbage collection threads for the concurrent phase of ZGC.
`-XX:ZUncommitDelay=<value>`	Sets the delay for uncommitting memory after a region is no longer needed.

Command	Description
`-XX:ZUncommitDelayMax=<value>`	Sets the maximum delay for uncommitting memory after a region is no longer needed.
`-XX:ZUncommitDelayPolicy=<adaptive|fixed>`	Sets the uncommit delay policy for ZGC. Options include adaptive and fixed.
`-XX:SoftMaxHeap=<value>`	Sets the soft maximum heap size for ZGC.
`-XX:ZHeapSize=<value>`	Sets the ZGC heap size.

Table 6.4: ZGC commands

These options provide a means to configure and fine-tune the behavior of ZGC, allowing developers and administrators to optimize garbage collection for specific application requirements and hardware characteristics.

As we wrap up our exploration into the intricacies of ZGC, we find ourselves immersed in the world of precision performance and low-latency responsiveness. The table of ZGC commands presented here serves as a guide, unlocking the potential for users to fine-tune and optimize ZGC for their Java applications. This section has laid the foundation for understanding how ZGC reshapes the landscape of garbage collection strategies.

Our journey doesn't end here but gracefully transitions into the next act—ergonomics and tuning. In the forthcoming chapters, we will delve into the art of optimizing Java applications, exploring strategies to fine-tune the performance of the JVM to meet the nuanced demands of diverse workloads. Join us as we navigate the realm of JVM tuning, where each adjustment becomes a brushstroke in the canvas of crafting optimal Java application performance.

JVM tuning and ergonomics

In the dynamic landscape of Java application development, the twin pillars of ergonomics and profiling emerge as crucial elements in achieving optimal performance. This section marks our journey into fine-tuning Java applications, exploring the principles of ergonomics to adapt the JVM automatically to varying workloads. Simultaneously, we delve into profiling, a powerful tool for gaining insights into the runtime behavior of applications. As we navigate the nuances of optimizing Java performance, ergonomics and profiling become our guiding lights, offering strategies to sculpt applications for responsiveness and efficiency. Join us in this section as we uncover the synergy between adaptive tuning and insightful profiling, unlocking the potential to elevate Java applications to new levels of performance and responsiveness.

Ergonomics in the context of Java refers to the adaptive tuning capabilities embedded within the JVM to adjust its configuration automatically based on the characteristics of the underlying hardware and the application's behavior. The primary goal of ergonomics is to enhance the performance and responsiveness of Java applications without requiring manual intervention from developers. By dynamically adjusting parameters such as garbage collection algorithms, heap sizes, and thread counts, ergonomics aims to strike an optimal balance for a given runtime environment.

However, the default configuration set by ergonomics is often considered a form of premature optimization. It is because the default settings are determined at JVM startup, relying on heuristics and assumptions about the environment. While these defaults may work reasonably well for a broad range of applications and hardware, they might not be the most efficient configuration for specific use cases. Premature optimization occurs when the JVM makes assumptions about application behavior without sufficient runtime information, potentially leading to suboptimal performance.

Ergonomics can choose between Serial GC and G1 based on the system's capabilities. Serial GC is typically chosen as the default, especially for single-processor systems or when memory is limited. On the other hand, G1 may be selected when there are more than two processors and a sufficient amount of memory (1792 MB or more) available.

Furthermore, ergonomics adjusts the default maximum heap size based on the available memory. The default maximum heap size can be set to 50%, 25%, or 1/64 of the available memory, providing flexibility to accommodate different application requirements and system constraints. In essence, ergonomics acts as an intelligent conductor, dynamically tailoring the JVM's configuration to orchestrate a performance symphony that aligns with the unique characteristics of each runtime environment.

The recommendation to *always set the configuration of GC and avoid the ergonomic* stems from the idea that manually configuring GC parameters gives developers more control and predictability over the JVM's behavior. While ergonomic settings are designed to adjust the JVM configuration based on heuristics and runtime characteristics, this automated approach may not always produce the most optimized performance for specific use cases.

When developers manually configure the GC, they can tailor the JVM settings according to the application's unique requirements, workload characteristics, and the underlying infrastructure. This manual tuning allows more fine-grained control over parameters such as heap size, thread counts, and garbage collection algorithms.

Avoiding ergonomic settings becomes especially relevant when applications have specific performance goals, stringent latency requirements, or when the default configurations generated by the ergonomic tuning may not align with the application's optimal needs. Manual tuning allows developers to experiment with, analyze, and adjust JVM parameters to achieve the desired performance outcomes.

However, it's crucial to note that while manual tuning provides greater control, it also requires a deep understanding of the application's behavior, garbage collection algorithms, and JVM internals. Developers must carefully assess the impact of their configurations and regularly monitor the application's performance to ensure that the chosen settings align with evolving application demands.

In summary, the recommendation to manually set the configuration of the GC and avoid relying solely on ergonomic settings reflects a desire for more precise control over JVM behavior, particularly in scenarios where tailored performance optimization is crucial for the application's success.

In Bruno Borges' insightful *Secrets of Performance Tuning Java on Kubernetes* presentation, he shared invaluable recommendations for optimizing Java applications running on Kubernetes. Borges discussed the performance implications associated with different garbage collection algorithms, namely Serial, Parallel, G1, and Z, considering key factors such as the number of cores, multithreaded environments, Java heap size, pause times, overhead, and tail-latency effects. Each garbage collection strategy was dissected in the context of its suitability for specific scenarios. Whether an application benefits from the simplicity of Serial, the parallel processing of Parallel, the adaptability of G1, or the low-latency focus of Z, Borges provided nuanced insights into choosing the most effective garbage collection approach. The recommendations presented by Borges offer a comprehensive guide for Java developers navigating the complexities of performance tuning in Kubernetes environments, shedding light on the intricate dance between application demands and garbage collection strategies:

	Serial	**Parallel**	**G1**	**Z**
Number of cores	1	+2	+2	+2
Multithreaded	No	Yes	Yes	Yes
Java heap size	> 4 GB	< 4 GB	> 4 GB	> 4 GB
Pause	Yes	Yes	Yes	Yes (> 1 ms)
Overhead	Minimal	Minimal	Moderate	Moderate
Tail-latency effect	High	High	High	Low
Best for	Single-core small heaps	Multi-core small heaps. Batch jobs, with any heap size.	Responsive in medium-to-large heaps (request-response/DB interactions)	Responsive in medium-to-large heaps (request-response

Table 6.5: Comparing all GCs' aspects

In our exploration of JVM tuning, we've delved into the realms of ergonomics, profiling, and the delicate balance between automated adaptation and manual precision. Ergonomics dynamically tunes the JVM configuration for varying workloads, yet the recommendation emerges to configure the GC for greater control manually. A distilled summary awaits as we approach the conclusion, crystallizing the wisdom gained in navigating JVM tuning intricacies.

Summary

As we draw the curtain on our exploration into the intricate GC world, we've navigated diverse strategies, nuances, and configurations that shape the memory management landscape within the JVM. From the adaptive finesse of ergonomics to the precision of Serial, Parallel, G1, and ZGC GCs, our journey has been a symphony of choices, each tuned to orchestrate optimal performance based on distinct application needs.

However, our expedition through JVM internals doesn't pause here. The next chapter awaits, inviting us into the avant-garde realm of GraalVM. Beyond the confines of traditional Java, GraalVM emerges as a revolutionary platform, blurring the boundaries between languages and unleashing new possibilities for performance, polyglot capabilities, and efficient execution. Join us in the forthcoming chapters as we delve into the paradigm-shifting landscape of GraalVM, where the symphony of languages converges in harmony, marking a dynamic evolution in the ever-evolving tapestry of JVM technologies.

Questions

Answer the following questions to test your knowledge of this chapter:

1. What is the primary goal of ergonomics in JVM tuning?

    A. Minimizing code compilation time

    B. Automatically adjusting JVM configuration based on runtime characteristics

    C. Maximizing heap size for all applications

    D. Disabling garbage collection for enhanced performance

2. Which GC is often chosen by ergonomics as the default for single-processor systems or when memory is limited?

    A. Serial GC

    B. Parallel GC

    C. G1 GC

    D. ZGC

3. In the context of garbage collection, what does "multi-mapping" refer to?

    A. Multiple mapping of virtual memory addresses to physical memory

    B. The use of multiple garbage collection algorithms simultaneously

    C. Multithreading during garbage collection

    D. Allocating memory in multiple regions simultaneously

4. Why might developers prefer manual GC configuration over ergonomics?

   A. Manual tuning is more cost-effective

   B. Ergonomics is not compatible with modern JVM versions

   C. Developers have better control over performance parameters

   D. Manual configuration reduces the need for garbage collection

5. Which GC is known for its focus on low latency and responsiveness, making it suitable for real-time systems?

   A. Serial GC

   B. Parallel GC

   C. G1 GC

   D. ZGC

Answers

Here are the answers to this chapter's questions:

1. B. Automatically adjusting JVM configuration based on runtime characteristics

2. A. Serial GC

3. A. Multiple mapping of virtual memory addresses to physical memory

4. C. Developers have better control over performance parameters

5. D. ZGC

Part 3: Alternative JVMs

Advancing in our exploration, we introduce GraalVM—a versatile alternative JVM supporting multiple languages with ahead-of-time compilation. Broadening our perspective further, we delve into the broader JVM ecosystem in *Chapter 8*, exploring alternative JVMs such as OpenJ9 and Correto. These chapters collectively expand our understanding of diverse JVM implementations, providing insights into their features and use cases.

This part has the following chapters:

- *Chapter 7, GraalVM*
- *Chapter 8, JVM Ecosystem and Alternative JVMs*

7
GraalVM

In the ever-evolving landscape of JVMs, GraalVM stands out as a revolutionary and versatile alternative. This chapter delves into the intricacies of GraalVM, unraveling its unique features and shedding light on its role as a game-changer in the realm of JVM internals. GraalVM, developed by Oracle Labs, transcends the traditional boundaries of a conventional JVM by providing a polyglot runtime that supports multiple languages, including Java, JavaScript, Python, Ruby, and more. This flexibility opens up new avenues for developers, allowing them to integrate different languages within a single application seamlessly. As we navigate the pages of this chapter, you'll gain a comprehensive understanding of GraalVM's architecture, its distinctive components, and its pivotal role in reshaping the landscape of Java development.

GraalVM's architecture is a testament not only to its engineering prowess but also to its commitment to performance and efficiency. The chapter not only explores the underlying architecture and components of GraalVM but also highlights its innovative JIT compiler, which is at the heart of its efficiency. Understanding the nuts and bolts of GraalVM's architecture is essential for developers looking to harness its power to optimize and enhance the performance of their applications. Additionally, we'll delve into real-world use cases, showcasing scenarios where GraalVM excels and the unique problems it addresses. Whether you're aiming to boost the execution speed of your Java applications or seeking a seamless integration of multiple languages, GraalVM emerges as a compelling solution, and this chapter will guide you through its capabilities and potential applications. Get ready to explore the cutting-edge features of GraalVM and unlock a new dimension of possibilities in the ever-evolving landscape of JVM internals.

In this chapter, we'll explore the topics:

- GraalVM overview
- Native Image
- Creating a Native Image

Technical requirements

For this chapter, you will require the following:

- GraalVM 21
- Git
- Maven
- Any preferred IDE
- This chapter's GitHub repository, found at - `https://github.com/PacktPublishing/Mastering-the-Java-Virtual-Machine/tree/main/chapter-07`

GraalVM overview

In this enlightening section, we'll embark on a journey through the groundbreaking landscape of GraalVM, an innovation that has redefined the expectations of a JVM. GraalVM's rise to prominence can be attributed to its sensational features, with a special emphasis on its high-performance compiler, **ahead-of-time** (**AOT**) compilation, and prowess in managing diverse language runtimes.

At the heart of GraalVM's exceptional performance lies its state-of-the-art JIT compiler. This compiler is meticulously engineered to optimize the execution of Java applications, pushing the boundaries of speed and efficiency. Unlike traditional JVMs, GraalVM's JIT compiler boasts advanced techniques and optimizations, resulting in faster startup times and reduced memory footprint. Therefore, developers experience a significant boost in the overall performance of their applications, making GraalVM an invaluable tool for those striving for excellence in execution speed.

GraalVM introduces a paradigm shift with its AOT compilation, enabling developers to pre-compile their programs into native machine code. This approach eliminates the need for JIT compilation during runtime, resulting in faster startup times and lower memory consumption. AOT compilation opens up new horizons for GraalVM, making it an ideal choice for scenarios where rapid startup and reduced latency are critical. This section will explore the intricacies of AOT compilation and guide you on harnessing its power to optimize your applications.

GraalVM transcends the confines of a traditional JVM by offering a multilingual runtime environment. This means developers can seamlessly integrate and execute programs written in multiple languages within the same application. From Java and JavaScript to Python, Ruby, and more, GraalVM supports various languages, fostering a polyglot ecosystem. This section will delve into the implications of polyglot capabilities, demonstrating how developers can leverage this feature to build versatile and efficient applications that transcend language barriers.

While GraalVM brings many innovative features, like any technology, it comes with trade-offs. This section aims to shed light on these considerations, helping developers make informed decisions on when and where to harness the power of GraalVM.

While balancing benefits such as enhanced runtime and polyglot capabilities, developers must also consider factors like increased memory usage, longer compilation times, and compatibility nuances. Exploring these trade-offs will empower developers to make informed decisions tailored to their project requirements. Understanding these intricacies enables a strategic application of GraalVM's strengths while mitigating potential challenges in specific use cases:

- **Memory overhead**: A slight increase in memory usage often accompanies GraalVM's impressive performance gains. The advanced optimizations and versatile language support contribute to a more substantial memory footprint than some traditional JVMs. Developers must weigh the performance benefits against the potential impact on memory resources, particularly in environments with stringent memory constraints.

- **Compilation time**: While GraalVM's JIT compiler is a powerhouse for runtime performance, it's worth noting that the initial compilation time may be longer compared to other JVMs. Developers working on short-lived applications or scenarios where quick startup is critical should carefully assess whether the benefits of runtime performance outweigh the longer compilation times during application initialization.

- **Compatibility**: While GraalVM supports a wide array of languages, certain language features or libraries might not be fully compatible. Developers need to consider their projects' specific language requirements and ensure that GraalVM provides adequate support. Compatibility issues may require additional effort in adapting or optimizing code to work seamlessly with GraalVM.

Identifying the optimal scenarios for leveraging GraalVM's strengths requires a targeted assessment of best use cases. In microservices and serverless architectures, GraalVM's superior performance and reduced memory footprint align seamlessly with the agility demands of these environments. Its polyglot capabilities make it ideal for projects involving multiple languages, fostering a cohesive runtime environment. High-performance computing applications benefit from GraalVM's advanced JIT compilation, accelerating computation-intensive tasks. Additionally, resource-intensive applications in cloud environments can capitalize on GraalVM's efficiency in resource utilization without compromising performance. Developers can strategically employ GraalVM to maximize its advantages in diverse application scenarios by pinpointing these use cases:

- **Microservices and serverless architectures**: GraalVM's impressive performance gains and reduced memory footprint make it well-suited for microservices and serverless architectures. The faster startup times and efficient resource utilization align with the demands of these environments where agility and responsiveness are paramount.

- **Polyglot applications**: The polyglot capabilities of GraalVM shine in scenarios where applications are built using multiple programming languages. If your project involves components written in Java, JavaScript, Python, Ruby, and more, GraalVM's ability to seamlessly integrate these languages within a single runtime environment becomes a decisive advantage.

- **High-performance computing**: Applications with a focus on high-performance computing, such as scientific simulations or data processing, can benefit from GraalVM's advanced JIT compilation. The enhanced runtime performance can significantly accelerate computation-intensive tasks.

- **Resource-intensive applications**: GraalVM's efficiency in resource utilization makes it an excellent choice for resource-intensive applications, particularly in cloud-based environments. Developers can leverage GraalVM to optimize resource consumption without compromising on performance.

In conclusion, GraalVM presents a compelling option for various scenarios, especially where the trade-offs align with the project's priorities and constraints. By carefully evaluating the application's specific needs, developers can harness the full potential of GraalVM in scenarios where its strengths shine the brightest.

As we conclude our exploration of GraalVM and its nuanced considerations, it becomes evident that this innovative JVM alternative is a force to be reckoned with in the ever-evolving landscape of Java development. From its high-performance JIT compiler to polyglot language runtimes, GraalVM offers a compelling set of features that can elevate application development to new heights. While we've discussed the trade-offs involved, it's crucial to recognize that these considerations are integral to making informed decisions in line with specific project requirements.

Moreover, our journey through GraalVM's best use cases has unveiled scenarios where its strengths shine brightest, from microservices architectures to resource-intensive cloud applications. However, the story doesn't end here. GraalVM's Native Image functionality takes the narrative further by allowing developers to compile applications ahead of time into standalone executables, completely sidestepping the need for a JVM during deployment. It sets the stage for a deeper dive into Native Image, where GraalVM's capabilities are extended to provide an even more streamlined, efficient, and resource-friendly approach to application deployment. As we unravel the possibilities unlocked by GraalVM's Native Image, reshaping the landscape of Java development with unparalleled efficiency and innovation.

Native Image

Welcome to an illuminating session dedicated to GraalVM, a game-changing technology that transcends the conventional boundaries of JVMs. Developed by Oracle Labs, GraalVM emerges as a multifaceted solution, introducing revolutionary features that redefine the application development landscape. This section serves as your gateway to understanding the key facets of GraalVM, from its high-performance JIT compiler to its polyglot language runtimes and innovative AOT compilation. As we delve into GraalVM's architecture and capabilities, you'll gain insights into how it addresses the evolving needs of modern applications. Join us on this exploration of GraalVM, where innovation meets versatility, and discover how it empowers developers to create efficient, polyglot applications that push the boundaries of what's possible in the Java ecosystem.

One of the most distinctive features of GraalVM is its Native Image functionality, a transformative capability that propels application deployment into a new era. Unlike traditional Java applications running on a JVM, GraalVM's Native Image empowers developers to compile their applications ahead of time into standalone executables. Instead of relying on a JVM during deployment, the application is packaged as a self-contained binary directly interacting with the operating system, bypassing the need for an intermediary virtual machine.

The key advantage of the Native Image approach lies in its efficiency gains during both startup time and runtime performance. By eliminating the need for a JVM to interpret and execute the code, Native Image significantly reduces the application's startup time, making it ideal for scenarios where rapid responsiveness is crucial. Moreover, the absence of a JVM reduces the application's memory footprint, enhancing resource utilization and making it more suitable for resource-constrained environments.

However, it should also be highlighted that AOT compilation removes the exact benefits of JIT compilation as the bytecode is no longer available at runtime to optimize the code concerning changing code behavior. In many cases where applications run for a longer time, the gain of a quick startup, while notable, may be partially offset because the overall performance is lower due to the absence of dynamic runtime optimizations. For a detailed exploration of this trade-off between AOT and JIT, you can refer to this insightful presentation: `https://www.azul.com/blog/jit-performance-ahead-of-time-versus-just-in-time/`.

While GraalVM's Native Image feature brings notable advantages in terms of startup time, memory efficiency, and resource utilization, it also comes with trade-offs that developers should carefully consider:

- **Build time and complexity**: Creating a Native Image involves AOT compilation, which occurs during the build phase. This compilation process is more time-consuming compared to traditional JIT compilation used in JVM-based applications. Additionally, configuring the Native Image build can be more intricate, requiring developers to manage native libraries, reflective access, and other considerations to achieve optimal results.

- **Dynamic class loading and reflection**: Native Image requires a static analysis of the application's code during compilation, which can pose challenges for applications that heavily rely on dynamic class loading or reflection. Since the Native Image compiler needs to know the complete set of classes and methods at build time, dynamically loaded or generated code may need special handling, potentially requiring adjustments to the application code.

- **Limited runtime profile**: AOT compilation necessitates a comprehensive understanding of the application's behavior during the build phase. It can be challenging for applications with complex runtime behaviors or those dynamically adapting to various scenarios. In such cases, the Native Image may not capture the complete runtime profile, leading to potential performance trade-offs.

- **Platform dependencies**: Native Image produces platform-specific binaries, potentially introducing challenges for cross-platform compatibility. While GraalVM provides some level of cross-compilation support, developers must be mindful of potential platform dependencies and thoroughly test their applications on target platforms.

- **The footprint of included libraries**: Including certain libraries in a Native Image can increase size, potentially offsetting some of the gains in memory efficiency. Developers must carefully choose and optimize the dependencies included in the native image to strike the right balance between footprint and functionality.

Navigating the landscape of application deployment, it becomes essential to comprehend the fundamental distinctions between Native Image applications and those running on a JVM. The divergence lies in their approach to execution and resource utilization. Native Image applications, crafted through GraalVM's innovative AOT compilation, stand out for their streamlined startup times and reduced memory footprints. They eschew the need for a JVM during deployment, directly interacting with the operating system as standalone executables. In contrast, JVM-based applications boast portability across platforms and can run on any environment equipped with a compatible JVM. Next, we'll delve into the nuances of these differences, shedding light on considerations such as startup time, memory efficiency, and the impact on application portability. By unraveling these distinctions, developers can make informed choices tailored to the specific demands of their projects, unlocking the optimal balance between performance, portability, and resource utilization:

- **Startup time**: Native Image applications excel in terms of startup time as they eliminate the overhead associated with initializing a JVM. This is particularly advantageous for short-lived applications or microservices where rapid responsiveness is paramount. In contrast, JVM-based applications typically have a longer startup time as the JVM needs to interpret and compile the code at runtime.

- **Memory footprint**: Native Image applications generally have a smaller memory footprint compared to their JVM counterparts. Without the need for a JVM, the overhead associated with running the virtual machine is eliminated, resulting in more efficient resource utilization. This makes Native Image applications well-suited for environments with stringent memory constraints.

- **Portability**: JVM applications are known for their portability – the ability to run on any platform with a compatible JVM. On the other hand, Native Image applications, being compiled to platform-specific binaries, may have platform dependencies. While GraalVM provides some level of cross-compilation support, it's essential to consider platform-specific implications when using Native Image.

Diving into the intricate decision-making process of application deployment, the following comparison table illuminates the distinctive characteristics between Native Image applications and those operating on a JVM. Each column encapsulates crucial aspects that influence performance, resource utilization, and adaptability. Native Image applications, sculpted through GraalVM's innovative AOT compilation, boast expedited startup times and diminished memory footprints, making them particularly adept for scenarios prioritizing efficiency. In contrast, JVM-based applications offer the advantage of cross-platform compatibility and dynamic adaptability, leveraging JIT compilation. This table serves as a compass for developers, providing a concise yet comprehensive guide to navigate the trade-offs and make informed decisions based on the specific needs of their projects:

Feature	Native Image Applications	JVM-Based Applications
Startup Time	Generally faster	May be slower, depending on the JIT compilation
Memory Footprint	Smaller	Larger
Build Time	Longer due to AOT compilation	Shorter due to the JIT compilation
Dynamic Class Loading	Limited; requires careful handling	More flexible
Reflection	Limited; requires careful handling	More flexible
Platform Portability	Platform-specific binaries	Cross-platform with a compatible JVM
Resource Utilization	Efficient; lower overheads	May have higher overheads depending on the JVM
Dependency Inclusion	Need to optimize to manage size	Easier management with dependency managers
Adaptability to Runtime Changes	Less dynamic; needs careful handling	More adaptive with JIT compilation
Build Complexity	Higher; requires configuration	Lower; generally handled by the JVM

Table 7.1: Native Image versus JVM

This table provides a high-level overview of the key differences between Native Image and JVM-based applications. It's important to note that the choice between the two depends on specific project requirements, considering factors such as startup time, memory efficiency, platform portability, and flexibility needed in dynamic features.

On exploring the differences between Native Image applications and their counterparts, it becomes clear that the path to optimal application deployment is nuanced and multifaceted. This comparative journey has uncovered both approaches' unique strengths and considerations, guiding developers toward informed decisions that align with project priorities. Now, with a richer understanding of the trade-offs and benefits, we stand at the threshold of hands-on mastery.

In the upcoming session, we'll delve into the practical realm of creating a Native Image using GraalVM. We'll unravel the intricacies of the AOT compilation process, demystifying the steps to transform a Java application into a standalone executable. From optimizing dependencies to navigating platform specific considerations, this hands-on exploration will empower you to harness the efficiency gains of Native Image deployment. Join us in the next section as we embark on a practical journey toward unlocking the potential of Native Image, reshaping the landscape of application deployment with GraalVM's groundbreaking capabilities.

Creating a Native Image

In this immersive and hands-on section, we delve into mastering the creation of Native Images using GraalVM. Building upon the insights gained in our comparative exploration of Native Image applications and JVM counterparts, this section is your gateway to the practical realm of application deployment efficiency. As we shift from theory to practice, our focus now centers on empowering you to wield the transformative capabilities of Native Image compilation. Prepare to embark on a journey where we demystify the AOT compilation process, offering step-by-step guidance on transforming a Java application into a standalone executable.

Throughout this section, we will delve into the intricacies of optimizing dependencies, navigating platform-specific considerations, and unleashing the full potential of Native Image deployment. Whether you're a seasoned developer seeking to enhance application performance or an enthusiast eager to explore the cutting-edge of GraalVM technology, this hands-on experience will equip you with the practical skills to integrate Native Image compilation seamlessly into your development toolkit. Let's dive in and turn theory into practice as we navigate the creation of Native Images, reshaping the landscape of application deployment with GraalVM's revolutionary capabilities.

In this hands-on practice section, we'll dive into the exciting world of Native Image compilation by working on a whimsically simple yet illustrative Java application. The App class is designed to print a greeting to the world and, in a super silly twist, reverse a given string. As we explore the code, you'll notice it's not your typical "Hello, World!" example. Instead, it introduces a method called reverseString that recursively reverses a given string. The application starts by printing a greeting and then reverses the string "Native Image is awesome" using the reverseString method.

This playful sample serves as the canvas for our Native Image experiment. Through this exercise, we'll not only witness the creation of a Native Image but also gain insights into the optimization process and the resulting efficiency gains. So, buckle up as we traverse the creation of a Native Image for this super silly yet instructive Java application. Let's make the whimsical tangible and explore the magic of Native Image with GraalVM:

```java
public class App {
    public static void main(String[] args) {
        System.out.println("Hello, World! with Native image");
        String str = "Native Image is awesome";
        String reversed = reverseString(str);
        System.out.println("The reversed string is: " + reversed);
    }


    public static String reverseString(String str) {
        if (str.isEmpty())
            return str;
        return reverseString(str.substring(1)) + str.charAt(0);
    }
}
```

Setting up GraalVM is a crucial step in our journey toward mastering Native Image compilation. To streamline this process and manage different Java versions effortlessly, we'll leverage the SDKMan project. SDKMan simplifies the installation and switching between different Java versions, providing a seamless experience for developers.

For manual installation, you can refer to the official GraalVM documentation. However, to make our lives easier, let's use SDKMan to install GraalVM. At the time of writing, we're opting for version 21.0.1 with GraalVM support. Execute the following command in your terminal:

```
sdk install java 21.0.1-graal
```

This command fetches and installs GraalVM version 21.0.1 through SDKMan. Once established, you can either set it as the default Java version for your system or use it selectively in the current terminal session. If you wish to set it as the default, employ the following command:

```
sdk use java 21.0.1-graal
```

Now, with GraalVM seamlessly integrated into your development environment, we're well-prepared to explore Native Image creation. Let's embark on the next steps of this hands-on journey, where we'll combine the power of GraalVM with the simplicity of SDKMan.

Creating a Native Image is the pivotal next step in our exploration, and the process involves a series of commands to compile, package, and, finally, generate the native image. Let's break it down:

1. **Compile the App class:**

   ```
   javac -d build src/main/java/expert/os/App.java
   ```

   This command compiles the App class and stores the compiled files in the `build` directory.

2. **Create a JAR file:**

   ```
   jar --create --file App.jar --main-class expert.os.App -C
   build .
   ```

   Here, we package the compiled files into a JAR file named `App.jar` and specify the main class as `expert.os.App`.

3. **Create the Native Image:**

   ```
   native-image -jar App.jar
   ```

   Utilizing GraalVM's `native-image` tool, we generate the native image from the JAR file. This step involves AOD compilation, resulting in a standalone executable.

4. **Execute the Native Image:**

   ```
   ./App
   ```

With the native image created, we can run the executable. Upon execution, the console will display the following output:

```
Hello, World! with Native image
The reversed string is: emosewa si egamI evitaN
```

Congratulations! You've successfully navigated the process of creating a Native Image using GraalVM, turning our whimsically simple Java application into a streamlined, standalone executable. This hands-on experience sets the stage for further exploration of the efficiency gains and optimization possibilities offered by Native Image compilation. Let's revel in the results and continue our journey into the dynamic realm of GraalVM.

As we conclude this section on Native Image creation with GraalVM, it's evident that we've embarked on a transformative journey in application deployment. By seamlessly integrating the power of GraalVM, we've transformed a playful Java application into a standalone executable, unlocking efficiency gains in startup time and resource utilization.

Through meticulous compilation steps and the magic of AOT processing, we've witnessed the birth of a native image. The output of our executable not only echoes the familiar "Hello, World!" greeting but also showcases the whimsical reversal of a string – a testament to the versatility of GraalVM.

This hands-on experience lays a solid foundation for further exploration. Armed with a Native Image, developers can delve into real-world applications, optimizing performance and navigating the intricacies of efficient resource utilization. The journey doesn't end here, though; it extends into the dynamic landscapes of GraalVM's capabilities.

As we celebrate the successful execution of our native image, let this be a catalyst for your continued exploration into the possibilities and efficiencies unlocked by GraalVM. The adventure continues, and the next chapters await, promising deeper insights and mastery in the fascinating world of Java application development.

Summary

In this chapter, we delved into the transformative capabilities of GraalVM, from its high-performance compiler to the creation of a Native Image. Witnessing the efficiency gains achievable through AOT compilation marked a significant milestone, showcasing GraalVM's versatility in reshaping the Java development landscape.

As we conclude, this chapter served as a stepping stone to the broader exploration of the JVM ecosystem and alternative JVMs in the next chapter. The diverse options beyond conventional JVMs, such as OpenJ9 and Azul Zing, will be unraveled, providing insights into their unique features and contributions to the ever-evolving Java ecosystem. Join us in the next chapter as we navigate the diverse paths within the JVM landscape, informed by the knowledge we've gained from our exploration of GraalVM.

Questions

Answer the following questions to test your knowledge of this chapter:

1. What is the primary benefit of GraalVM's Native Image compilation?

    A. Increased memory footprint

    B. Slower startup time

    C. Platform portability

    D. Limited language support

2. Which command is used to compile the App class in the GraalVM Native Image creation process?

    A. `compile -class App`

    B. `javac -d build src/main/java/expert/os/App.java`

    C. `native-image --compile App`

    D. `graalvm-compile App.java`

3. What is the purpose of the `reverseString` method in the provided Java application?

    A. Concatenates strings

    B. Reverses a given string

    C. Checks for a palindrome

    D. Removes whitespace from a string

4. How does GraalVM's Native Image differ from JVM-based applications in terms of startup time?

    A. Native Image has a slower startup time

    B. Both have similar startup times

    C. Native Image has a faster startup time

    D. JVM-based applications have a faster startup time

5. What is SDKMan used for in the context of GraalVM installation?

    A. Managing Java versions and installations

    B. Creating native images

    C. Debugging Java applications

    D. Managing Docker images

6. What does the `native-image` command do in the GraalVM Native Image creation process?

    A. Compiles Java source code

    B. Generates a standalone executable

    C. Downloads Java dependencies

    D. Executes the Java application

Answers

Here are the answers to this chapter's questions:

1. C. Platform portability

2. B. `javac -d build src/main/java/expert/os/App.java`

3. B. Reverses a given string

4. C. Native Image has a faster startup time

5. A. Managing Java versions and installations

6. B. Generates a standalone executable

8

The JVM Ecosystem and Alternative JVMs

The JVM is the cornerstone of Java's *write once, run anywhere* philosophy, enabling the execution of Java bytecode on diverse platforms. While the HotSpot JVM has long been the stalwart choice, the expansive JVM ecosystem extends far beyond, offering alternative implementations that cater to specific needs and performance considerations. In this chapter, we'll explore the JVM landscape comprehensively, delving into alternative JVMs such as OpenJ9 and Correto. As we unravel their nuances, you will gain valuable insights into the diverse options available, each with unique features, optimizations, and trade-offs.

Our journey commences with an in-depth overview of these alternative JVMs, shedding light on their architectures and critical differentiators. Subsequent sections delve into the performance characteristics and benchmarks that distinguish these implementations, providing a nuanced understanding of how alternative JVMs stack up against the conventional HotSpot. Through real-world performance metrics, we aim to empower you with the knowledge to make informed decisions tailored to your specific use cases. Additionally, we'll explore practical scenarios and use points where alternative JVMs shine, showcasing their strengths in various application domains. This chapter will also discuss the seamless integration of these JVMs with Java applications, offering insights into compatibility, tooling support, and interoperability. Finally, we'll wrap up with essential considerations that guide the judicious selection of a JVM, ensuring that you are equipped to navigate the complexities of the JVM ecosystem with confidence and precision.

In this chapter, we'll explore the topics:

- The diversity of the JVM
- Eclipse J9
- Amazon Corretto
- Azul Zulu
- IBM Semeru

- Eclipse Temurin
- Even more JVM vendors and SDKMan

The diversity of the JVM

A captivating exploration of the JVM and its remarkable tapestry is interwoven within the programming world. While Java often takes center stage, the JVM's true prowess lies in its versatility, extending far beyond a mere executor of Java bytecode. Contrary to popular belief, the JVM is not a monolithic entity but a testament to diversity, accommodating a rich ecosystem of alternative implementations and vendors. Let's embark on a journey to uncover the manifold facets of the JVM that make it an unparalleled force in software development.

Despite being the bedrock of Java, the JVM is not confined to a single language. Its extensibility has paved the way for many programming languages to flourish under its aegis. From Kotlin and Scala to Groovy and Clojure, the JVM acts as a unifying platform that fosters an environment where developers can seamlessly harness the power of different languages. Moreover, the landscape of JVM distributors is a testament to the ecosystem's robustness. Beyond Oracle's HotSpot JVM, there's a tapestry of alternatives, each bringing its unique blend of optimizations, features, and licensing models. In fact, over the JVM's storied history, more than 20 implementations have emerged, catering to diverse needs and preferences.

One of the most remarkable aspects of the JVM is its ability to transcend the boundaries of languages and vendors. Thanks to meticulously crafted specifications, developers can write code in one JVM implementation and confidently execute it in another, regardless of vendor disparities. This interoperability fosters code reuse and promotes an ecosystem where innovation can thrive. As we navigate this section, we'll explore how the JVM's universal bridge enables developers to compile code on one JVM and seamlessly run it on another, underscoring the platform's adaptability and resilience.

The question of why there are multiple JVM implementations when code can seamlessly run across them is a multifaceted exploration of software development's diverse needs and specialized contexts. While the ability to run code across different JVMs promotes interoperability, multiple implementations stem from the desire to cater to specific use cases, optimize performance, and adapt to varying hardware and software environments. It's important to note that most distributions are not different JVM implementations but builds of the OpenJDK project, sometimes with slight modifications. Additionally, all distributions must succeed in the Java **Technology Compatibility Kit (TCK)** (`https://foojay.io/pedia/tck/`), ensuring they adhere to Java standards and maintain compatibility across the Java ecosystem. The sources of OpenJDK are available at `https://github.com/openjdk/jdk/`, and you can even build the runtime yourself by following the instructions in the "building" file. This stringent requirement ensures developers can rely on consistent behavior and functionality, regardless of the distribution chosen when running their Java applications.

Each JVM possesses unique strengths that can be harnessed in specific contexts, making them powerful tools for developers. Consider, for instance, the OpenJ9 JVM. Its emphasis on resource efficiency and swift startup times makes it a compelling choice for cloud-based applications, where responsiveness and resource utilization are critical factors. On the other hand, Amazon Corretto, with its focus on **long-term support** (**LTS**) and seamless integration with **Amazon Web Services** (**AWS**), is well-suited for enterprises deeply entrenched in the AWS ecosystem.

Moreover, the JVM's adaptability extends to the hardware level. The ability to run the same code on diverse platforms, whether on Lego Mindstorms or specific hardware such as OpenSolaris, exemplifies the JVM's portability. It simplifies the development process and empowers developers to create applications seamlessly transitioning between different environments without compromising functionality.

The power of each JVM lies in its ability to execute code and in the optimizations and features it brings to the table. For instance, GraalVM, known for its **just-in-time** (**JIT**) compiler and polyglot capabilities, opens the door to language interoperability, allowing developers to seamlessly integrate languages such as JavaScript, Python, and Ruby into their Java applications. This versatility is invaluable in scenarios where diverse languages must coexist within a single code base.

In essence, the existence of multiple JVMs is a testament to the adaptability and diversity of the Java ecosystem. Developers can leverage these implementations to tailor their choices based on performance requirements, integration needs, and the specific characteristics of the target environment. This variety fosters innovation and ensures that the JVM remains a robust and dynamic platform that can evolve alongside the ever-changing software development landscape.

As we conclude this section on the diverse and influential landscape of the JVM, we've unveiled the intricacies that make it a unifying force across programming languages and hardware platforms. The ability to seamlessly run code across multiple JVMs while maintaining compatibility underscores the flexibility and robustness of this foundational technology. Yet, the question lingers: with such compatibility, why do we have a multitude of JVM implementations?

The answer lies in the nuanced strengths and optimizations each JVM brings to the table, catering to specific use cases, performance demands, and integration scenarios. In the next section, we will embark on a hands-on exploration of selected JVM implementations that exemplify this diversity. Join us as we delve into Eclipse J9, Amazon Corretto, Azul, and Eclipse Temurin and dissect their unique features, performance characteristics, and real-world applications. Through this deep dive, we aim to equip you with the knowledge to navigate the rich tapestry of JVM choices, ensuring you can make informed decisions aligned with your development goals.

Eclipse J9

In this dedicated section, we'll delve into the capabilities of Eclipse J9, a JVM implementation that stands out for its emphasis on efficiency, scalability, and resource optimization. As we navigate the intricacies of Eclipse J9, we'll uncover the unique features that set it apart in the vast landscape of JVM implementations and explore why developers should consider this powerhouse for their Java applications.

Eclipse J9, developed by the Eclipse Foundation, represents a cutting-edge JVM implementation that's designed to maximize efficiency and minimize resource footprint. Known for its compact size and swift startup times, Eclipse J9 excels in critical resource utilization scenarios, making it a prime candidate for cloud-based applications, microservices, and other environments where responsiveness is paramount. Its architecture incorporates advanced JIT compilation techniques and aggressive memory management, contributing to a nimble and responsive runtime.

Eclipse J9, as a distinguished JVM implementation, unfolds many advantages that position it as a compelling choice for discerning developers. At the forefront is its commendable commitment to resource efficiency. Eclipse J9's compact footprint optimizes system resources, making it an optimal solution for applications where minimizing overhead is pivotal. This efficiency extends to memory utilization and processor engagement, a crucial feature for applications operating in resource-constrained environments. Swift startup times further amplify its appeal, enhancing user experience and responsiveness, especially in scenarios where time-to-operation is of the essence. Eclipse J9's scalability is another noteworthy benefit, accommodating the dynamic demands of diverse environments, from small-scale applications to expansive enterprise systems. As we explore the landscape of Eclipse J9, these benefits emerge as critical pillars, underlining its capacity to empower developers to create applications that seamlessly balance performance and resource consumption:

- **Resource efficiency**: Eclipse J9's compact footprint ensures efficient utilization of system resources, making it an ideal choice for applications where minimizing overhead is crucial. This efficiency extends to both memory usage and processor utilization, allowing for optimal performance in resource-constrained environments.

- **Swift startup times**: The JVM's startup time is pivotal in particular application domains, and Eclipse J9 shines in this regard. Its rapid startup ensures that applications become operational swiftly, enhancing user experience and responsiveness.

- **Scalability**: Eclipse J9 is designed to scale seamlessly across various environments, adapting to the demands of both small-scale applications and large-scale enterprise systems. Its scalability makes it well-suited for dynamic workloads and applications that may experience fluctuating markets.

Considering Eclipse J9 for your Java applications becomes imperative when efficiency, rapid responsiveness, and optimal resource utilization are paramount. Whether you're developing cloud-native applications or microservices or deploying in resource-constrained environments, Eclipse J9 provides a compelling solution. The benefits of Eclipse J9 translate into tangible advantages, offering developers the flexibility to balance performance and resource consumption according to their application's unique requirements.

As we conclude our exploration into the efficiency and scalability offered by Eclipse J9, we've witnessed how this JVM implementation can be a strategic choice for developers seeking optimal resource utilization and rapid responsiveness in their Java applications. The benefits of Eclipse J9, from its compact footprint to swift startup times and scalable architecture, underscore its versatility across various application landscapes. In the next section, we will seamlessly transition into an in-depth examination of another notable JVM implementation: Amazon Corretto. We'll uncover the distinctive features and advantages that Amazon Corretto brings to the table, further expanding our understanding of the diverse and dynamic world of JVM. The journey continues, and the exploration of JVM implementations remains the key to unlocking the full potential of Java development.

Amazon Corretto

In this section, we'll embark on an insightful journey into Amazon Corretto, a JVM implementation crafted by Amazon that combines reliability, performance, and LTS. As we navigate the nuances of Amazon Corretto, we'll explore its unique features, performance optimizations, and compelling reasons developers should consider integrating this JVM implementation into their Java applications.

Amazon Corretto represents Amazon's commitment to delivering a high-quality, open source JVM that meets the demands of modern Java development. Built on the solid foundation of OpenJDK (Java Development Kit), Corretto is designed to provide a reliable and secure Java runtime environment. Amazon Corretto is free to use and comes with LTS, making it an attractive choice for enterprises looking for a stable and dependable JVM.

In navigating the intricacies of JVM implementations, Amazon Corretto emerges as a beacon of reliability, performance, and sustained support. This segment delves into the distinct advantages that make Amazon Corretto a compelling choice for Java developers across diverse landscapes. From its commitment to LTS to performance optimizations and a steadfast focus on security, Amazon Corretto offers a comprehensive suite of benefits that elevate the development experience and ensure the longevity and stability of Java applications. Join us as we unravel the layers of Amazon Corretto's advantages, providing a nuanced understanding of why this JVM implementation deserves a prominent place in your toolkit:

- **LTS**: One of the standout features of Amazon Corretto is its LTS. Enterprises can benefit from extended support and updates, ensuring the stability and security of their Java applications over an extended period.

- **Performance optimizations**: Amazon Corretto is equipped with performance enhancements that optimize the execution of Java applications. These optimizations improve responsiveness and throughput, making it well-suited for a wide range of use cases.

- **Security and stability**: Built with a focus on security and stability, Amazon Corretto undergoes rigorous testing and quality assurance processes. It ensures developers can rely on a robust, secure runtime environment for their Java applications.

- **Compatibility with OpenJDK**: Amazon Corretto maintains compatibility with OpenJDK, allowing developers to transition from other OpenJDK-based JVMs seamlessly. This compatibility simplifies the migration process while providing the benefits of Amazon's additional optimizations and support.

Considering Amazon Corretto for your Java applications is a strategic decision, especially when LTS, performance optimizations, and a commitment to security are paramount. Whether you are developing cloud-native applications, serverless functions, or traditional enterprise systems, Amazon Corretto offers a compelling JVM solution backed by the reliability and scale of AWS.

As we conclude our exploration of the robust world of Amazon Corretto, we've witnessed the confluence of reliability, performance, and LTS that defines this JVM implementation. The benefits of Amazon Corretto, from its unwavering commitment to security to the optimization of Java applications, resonate as compelling reasons for developers to consider integrating it into their projects. Our journey into the diverse landscape of JVM implementations continues, and in the next section, we will unravel the intricacies of another noteworthy player: Azul. Join us as we explore Azul's distinctive features and advantages to Java development, expanding our understanding of the myriad possibilities that JVM implementations offer. The path to Java excellence unfolds, and the exploration of Azul awaits in the next section.

Azul Zulu and Zing

In this section, we'll delve into the dynamic realm of **Azul Zulu Builds of OpenJDK** (**Azul Zulu**), a JVM implementation that is a pivotal part of Azul's comprehensive offerings in the Java runtime space. Azul, renowned for its commitment to providing JVM runtimes and additional tools to enhance Java performance while reducing costs, brings Azul Zulu to the forefront. As a TCK-certified build of OpenJDK, Azul Zulu aligns with the performance standards of most distributors as they all base their builds on the OpenJDK project. Azul's active participation in monitoring and resolving CVE security issues sets it apart, allowing it to adhere to a 3-month release cycle. It enables Azul to provide free and commercial builds of all supported versions with timely security fixes, ensuring the safe operation of Java applications in production environments.

Furthermore, Azul Zulu's distinction lies in its groundbreaking contributions to the OpenJDK ecosystem. Azul initiated the OpenJDK project known as **Coordinated Restore at Checkpoint** (**CraC**) (`https://openjdk.org/projects/crac/`), making Zulu the first JVM runtime to incorporate this feature, enabling ultrafast startup of Java applications. Zulu's versatility extends to JavaFX integrations, catering to various use cases.

Azul Zing Builds of OpenJDK (**Azul Zing**) emerges as a stalwart in the JVM landscape, offering a tapestry of benefits that elevate Java development to new heights. Azul Zing introduces the innovative **Continuously Concurrent Compacting Collector** (**C4**) Garbage Collector at its core, setting a benchmark for low-latency and pauseless garbage collection. This key feature ensures that Java applications remain responsive, even in the face of intensive workloads. Beyond its cutting-edge garbage collection, Azul Zing is distinguished by its unwavering commitment to enhanced runtime performance. It is a formidable choice for applications demanding high throughput and minimal latency. Its scalability and elasticity further position Azul Zing as a versatile solution, seamlessly adapting to the dynamic requirements of both small-scale applications and large enterprise systems. With a foundation rooted in LTS and stability, Azul Zing becomes a strategic choice for projects with extended life cycles, promising developers a robust platform for crafting Java applications that excel in performance, responsiveness, and reliability. Join us in exploring the manifold benefits of Azul Zing as we uncover how this JVM implementation stands as a beacon of innovation and efficiency in the ever-evolving landscape of Java development:

- **C4 Garbage Collector**: Azul Zing incorporates the innovative C4 Garbage Collector. This collector distinguishes itself by providing low-latency and pauseless garbage collection, ensuring that Java applications maintain consistent responsiveness even under heavy workloads.

- **Enhanced runtime performance**: Azul Zing is engineered to deliver enhanced runtime performance, making it well-suited for high-throughput and low-latency applications. Its optimizations contribute to improved application responsiveness and reduced execution times.

- **Scalability and elasticity**: Azul Zing is designed to scale seamlessly across diverse workloads, adapting to the demands of both small-scale applications and large, enterprise-level systems. Its elasticity ensures optimal performance in dynamic and fluctuating environments.

- **LTS and stability**: Azul Zing offers LTS and stability, providing enterprises with a reliable foundation for their Java applications. This commitment to stability is crucial for projects with extended life cycles and stringent reliability requirements.

Azul Zing for Java development is a strategic choice when performance, scalability, and low latency are non-negotiable. The advanced features, including the C4 Garbage Collector, position Azul Zing as an ideal solution for applications where consistent responsiveness and optimal resource utilization are paramount. Let's unravel the capabilities of Azul Zing and discover how this JVM implementation can be a catalyst for achieving unprecedented levels of performance in your Java applications. This section aims to equip you with insights to make informed decisions and leverage the advantages of Azul Zing across a diverse range of use cases.

In navigating the intricacies of Azul Zulu and Zing, we've unraveled a tapestry of benefits that positions these JVM implementations as a beacon of innovation and efficiency. Azul Zulu is a build of OpenJDK with additional integrations such as CRaC and JavaFX. Azul Zing is a powerful catalyst for achieving peak Java application performance, from the groundbreaking C4 Garbage Collector to its commitment to enhanced runtime performance and scalability. As our journey through diverse JVM implementations continues, our next destination beckons us toward IBM Semeru. In the upcoming section, we'll delve into the distinctive features and advantages that IBM Semeru brings to the forefront, further expanding our understanding of the multifaceted landscape of Java development. Our exploration of IBM Semeru awaits, promising new insights and perspectives in our quest for Java excellence.

IBM Semeru

In this section, we'll explore IBM Semeru, a JVM implementation that encapsulates the expertise and innovation of IBM in the realm of Java development. As we navigate the intricacies of IBM Semeru, we will unravel its distinctive features, optimizations, and compelling reasons developers should consider integrating this JVM implementation into their Java applications.

IBM Semeru, based on the OpenJ9 JVM, represents IBM's commitment to delivering a high-performance, scalable, and efficient Java runtime environment. With a focus on resource efficiency, rapid startup times, and advanced optimizations, IBM Semeru is designed to cater to various application scenarios.

IBM Semeru emerges as a beacon of innovation in Java development, encapsulating a spectrum of benefits that redefine the possibilities of efficient and scalable runtime environments. Anchored by the robust OpenJ9 virtual machine, Semeru introduces a harmonious blend of resource efficiency and rapid startup times, making it an ideal choice for contemporary cloud-native applications and microservices. Integrating **ahead-of-time** (**AOT**) compilation further distinguishes IBM Semeru, translating Java bytecode into machine code before runtime to enhance startup performance and reduce the memory footprint. With a container-friendly architecture optimized for cloud deployments, IBM Semeru caters to the evolving needs of modern application deployment, ensuring adaptability, scalability, and efficiency. For developers seeking a comprehensive solution that aligns with the demands of dynamic cloud environments, IBM Semeru is a compelling choice, promising a sophisticated and optimized Java runtime experience. Join us in exploring the benefits that IBM Semeru brings to the forefront as we delve into a new era of Java development excellence:

- **OpenJ9 virtual machine**: IBM Semeru leverages the OpenJ9 virtual machine, known for its efficient memory usage and fast startup times. This optimization is particularly beneficial for cloud-native applications and microservices where resource efficiency is paramount.

- **AOT compilation**: IBM Semeru incorporates AOT compilation, a feature that translates Java bytecode into machine code before runtime. This approach enhances startup performance, reduces the memory footprint, and contributes to consistent and predictable application behavior.

- **Container-friendly architecture**: With a container-friendly architecture, IBM Semeru is well-suited for deployment in containerized environments. Its efficient resource utilization and compatibility with container orchestration platforms make it ideal for modern, scalable infrastructures.

- **Optimized for cloud deployments**: IBM Semeru is optimized for cloud deployments, aligning with the demands of cloud-native applications. Its adaptability to dynamic and scalable cloud environments positions it as a strategic choice for developers building applications in cloud ecosystems.

Consideration of IBM Semeru becomes imperative when resource efficiency, rapid startup times, and compatibility with modern deployment paradigms are critical for your Java applications. Whether you are developing cloud-native applications microservices or deploying in containerized environments, IBM Semeru offers a robust JVM implementation with the backing of IBM's expertise and commitment to innovation. Join us as we uncover the capabilities of IBM Semeru, providing you with insights to make informed decisions and harness the advantages of this feature-rich JVM implementation for your Java development endeavors.

Our exploration into the world of JVM implementations reaches a crescendo with the comprehensive insights gained from IBM Semeru. The distinctive benefits, from resource efficiency to cloud optimization, underscore its significance in the ever-evolving landscape of Java development. As our journey continues, the spotlight now shifts toward Eclipse Temurin. In the forthcoming section, we will unravel the unique features and advantages that Eclipse Temurin brings to the table, enriching our understanding of JVM implementations. This exploration of Eclipse Temurin promises new perspectives and innovations as we strive toward Java excellence. Join us in continuing our journey through the diverse tapestry of JVM implementations as we uncover Eclipse Temurin's capabilities in the dynamic world of Java development.

Eclipse Temurin

In this section, we'll explore Eclipse Temurin, a robust and versatile JVM implementation that stands as a testament to the collaborative efforts within the Eclipse community. As we navigate the intricacies of Eclipse Temurin, we will uncover its distinctive features, optimizations, and compelling reasons why developers should consider embracing this JVM implementation for their Java applications.

Eclipse Temurin, formerly AdoptOpenJDK, is a community-driven, open source project that provides free, high-quality, and production-ready builds of the OpenJDK. Fueled by a commitment to transparency and collaboration, Eclipse Temurin ensures that developers can access a reliable and well-supported Java runtime environment.

Eclipse Temurin emerges as a beacon of reliability and versatility in the Java development landscape, offering a rich tapestry of benefits that resonate with the needs of modern developers. With a commitment to timely updates and security patches for OpenJDK, Eclipse Temurin ensures developers have access to the latest enhancements, contributing to the security and stability of Java applications. Its platform independence provides the flexibility to deploy Java applications seamlessly across diverse operating systems and architectures, catering to the demands of projects targeting multiple environments. What sets Eclipse Temurin apart is its transparent and open community collaboration within the Eclipse ecosystem. Developers can actively contribute, fostering a sense of community-driven development and ensuring the JVM evolves in sync with the diverse needs of its users. The ease of adoption, coupled with a commitment to providing hassle-free builds of OpenJDK, positions Eclipse Temurin as an essential component in the toolkit of developers seeking a reliable, well-supported, and community-driven Java runtime environment. Join us as we unravel the benefits Eclipse Temurin brings to Java development, fostering a new era of collaboration and innovation within the Eclipse community:

- **Timely updates and security patches**: Eclipse Temurin offers timely updates and security patches for OpenJDK, ensuring developers can access the latest enhancements and fixes. This commitment to regular updates contributes to the security and stability of Java applications.

- **Platform independence**: Eclipse Temurin supports various platforms, allowing developers to deploy Java applications seamlessly across diverse operating systems and architectures. This platform independence is crucial for projects targeting multiple environments.

- **Transparent and open community collaboration**: Being part of the Eclipse community, Eclipse Temurin benefits from transparent and open collaboration. Developers can actively contribute to the project, fostering a sense of community-driven development and ensuring that the JVM evolves in tandem with the diverse needs of its users.

- **Ease of adoption**: Eclipse Temurin's commitment to providing easy-to-adopt OpenJDK builds simplifies incorporating the latest Java features into projects. This ease of adoption is precious for developers seeking a hassle-free integration of new Java capabilities.

Considering Eclipse, Temurin becomes imperative for developers prioritizing access to up-to-date OpenJDK builds, a collaborative community-driven approach, and seamless platform independence. Whether you are developing applications for deployment across various operating systems or contributing to an open source ecosystem, Eclipse Temurin provides a reliable and well-supported foundation.

Our journey through the diverse landscape of JVM implementations has been a rich tapestry of innovation and optimization, from Eclipse Temurin's community-driven excellence to the unique strengths of IBM Semeru, Azul Zulu's performance prowess, Amazon Corretto's reliability, and the efficiency of Eclipse J9. As we conclude these individual explorations, the next section promises a holistic view, showcasing the remarkable diversity that defines the world of JVM implementations. Join us in the upcoming section, where we will navigate multiple JVM implementations in a single section, highlighting the dynamic choices available to developers. From Eclipse Temurin to other notable players, witness how the JVM ecosystem thrives on versatility, offering developers many options to tailor their choices based on specific needs and preferences. The exploration continues, unveiling the depth and breadth of the JVM implementation world.

Even more JVM vendors and SDKMan

In this section, we'll embark on a fascinating exploration of the expansive diversity within the JVM ecosystem. Our focus will extend beyond individual JVM implementations, encompassing a spectrum of specialized builds tailored for distinct use cases and environments. Join us as we delve into the nuances of Dragonwell, Tencent Kona, Liberica, Mandrel, the Microsoft Build of OpenJDK, and SapMachine – each representing a unique facet of JVM diversity, optimized to cater to specific demands and scenarios.

We'll be embarking on a captivating journey into the multifaceted world of JVM diversity, where a kaleidoscope of specialized builds awaits exploration. Each JVM implementation represents a distinctive approach to addressing unique challenges in application development. From extreme scaling demands to cloud computing, big data, and SAP-supported ecosystems, each JVM is meticulously crafted to meet specific use cases. Join us as we unravel the intricacies of these implementations, gaining insights into how they cater to diverse scenarios, thus offering developers a rich palette of options to align with the unique requirements of their projects. This exploration promises a deeper understanding of the adaptability and versatility ingrained in the diverse world of JVMs:

- **Dragonwell (Alibaba)**: Engineered as the in-house OpenJDK implementation at Alibaba, Dragonwell is optimized for the extreme scaling demands of online eCommerce and financial and logistics applications. Dive into how Dragonwell powers the intricate web of Java applications across Alibaba's massive server infrastructure.

- **Tencent Kona**: Serving as Tencent's default JDK for cloud computing, big data, and various Java applications, Kona is a production-ready distribution of OpenJDK with LTS. Uncover the features that make Tencent Kona a robust choice for diverse computing needs within Tencent's ecosystem.

- **Liberica (BellSoft)**: As a 100% open source Java implementation built from OpenJDK, Liberica is thoroughly tested, including passing the **Java Compatibility Kit** (**JCK**). Explore how Liberica's commitment to openness ensures JavaFX support across all its versions.

- **Mandrel (Red Hat)**: Focused on GraalVM's native-image component, Mandrel facilitates the generation of native images for Quarkus applications. Delve into how Mandrel simplifies the journey from Java source code to efficient, native applications, a crucial capability for cloud-native application development.

- **Microsoft Build of OpenJDK**: Microsoft's contribution to JVM diversity comes from a no-cost distribution of OpenJDK. With LTS binaries for Java 11 and Java 16 across multiple operating systems and architectures, understand how Microsoft's build provides a versatile option for developers.

- **SapMachine (SAP)**: As a downstream version of the OpenJDK project, SapMachine is meticulously crafted to support SAP customers and partners. Discover how SAP's commitment ensures the success of Java applications within the SAP ecosystem.

Exploring this rich tapestry of JVM implementations is paramount for developers seeking solutions tailored to specific use cases, from extreme scaling in eCommerce to cloud computing, big data, and beyond.

As we explore the plethora of JVM implementations discussed earlier SDKMAN (`https://sdkman.io/`) emerges as a versatile companion, simplifying the management of various vendors and versions. The need for different JVM versions is common in real-world production scenarios, whether for stability, optimization, or during migration phases. Join us as we delve into how SDKMAN streamlines the process of managing JVM implementations, providing developers with a seamless experience in experimenting with, switching between, and maintaining diverse JVM versions.

In this pivotal segment, we'll embark on a journey to unravel the potent capabilities of SDKMAN. This tool is a linchpin in simplifying the intricate landscape of JVM diversity. As we explore the vast array of JVM implementations and versions, SDKMAN emerges as a versatile ally, streamlining the management process with finesse. It extends the gift of vendor agnosticism, allowing developers to seamlessly navigate between JVM vendors such as Alibaba, Tencent, BellSoft, Red Hat, Microsoft, and SAP. Let's dive into the intricacies of version management, where SDKMAN empowers developers to effortlessly install, switch, and utilize diverse JVM versions, addressing the nuanced needs of projects in real-world production scenarios. With seamless integration into popular build tools and a commitment to community-driven updates, SDKMAN becomes the linchpin in ensuring a smooth and agile development experience, freeing developers to focus on their code in the dynamic and diverse landscape of Java development. Join us as we unlock the power of SDKMAN, demystifying the complexities and enhancing the agility of JVM management for developers worldwide:

- **Vendor agnosticism**: SDKMAN embraces vendor agnosticism, allowing developers to switch between JVM vendors such as Alibaba, Tencent, BellSoft, Red Hat, Microsoft, and SAP. Experience the freedom to choose the most suitable JVM for your specific use case without the hassle of manual installations.

- **Version management**: Managing multiple JVM versions is essential in the dynamic landscape of Java development. SDKMAN simplifies version management, enabling developers to quickly install, switch, and use different versions based on project requirements or migration needs.

- **Seamless integration of and integration with build tools**: SDKMAN integrates with popular build tools such as Maven and Gradle, facilitating a smooth transition between different JVM versions within your build and deployment processes. It ensures that your projects stay aligned with the chosen JVM without disruptions.

- **Community-driven updates**: SDKMAN is a community-driven initiative that ensures continuous updates and support for the latest JVM releases. Stay in sync with the vibrant Java ecosystem (`https://foojay.io/today/disco-api-helping-you-to-find-any-openjdk-distribution`) and access the latest features and optimizations as soon as they become available.

In the ever-evolving landscape of Java development, SDKMAN emerges as a valuable ally for developers seeking agility and flexibility in managing JVM implementations. Whether you are exploring diverse JVM vendors, experimenting with versions, or navigating migration phases, SDKMAN streamlines the process, empowering developers to stay focused on their code.

Summary

As we conclude our exploration of the intricate world of JVM diversity and the instrumental role of SDKMAN, you have gained a profound understanding of alternative JVMs, including Alibaba's Dragonwell, Tencent Kona, Liberica, Mandrel, the Microsoft Build of OpenJDK, and SapMachine. This chapter not only shed light on the unique characteristics of these implementations, catering to diverse use cases, but also emphasized the pivotal role of SDKMAN in simplifying JVM management. The insights garnered set the stage for the upcoming chapter, where you will delve into the fundamental principles shaping Java frameworks. From design patterns to modularity, these principles are essential for creating robust, scalable, and maintainable applications. The practical utility of the information provided in this chapter will become evident, equipping you with the knowledge needed to navigate the dynamic Java development landscape. As we transition into Java framework principles, the comprehensive understanding you've gained here promises to be invaluable, guiding you on a seamless journey toward excellence in your coding endeavors.

Questions

Answer the following questions to test your knowledge of this chapter:

1. What is the primary focus of Alibaba's Dragonwell JVM implementation?

    A. Cloud computing

    B. Online eCommerce and financial and logistics applications

    C. Big data

    D. Microservices

2. Which JVM implementation is Tencent's default JDK for cloud computing and big data?

    A. Amazon Corretto

    B. Tencent Kona

    C. Eclipse Temurin

    D. Azul Zulu

3. What is the primary focus of the Mandrel JVM implementation?

    A. High-performance computing

    B. Running applications on containers

    C. Native image generation for Quarkus applications

    D. Cloud-native application development

4. What is one of the key benefits of Eclipse Temurin (formerly AdoptOpenJDK)?

    A. Closed source development

    B. Timely updates and security patches

    C. Limited platform support

    D. Exclusive focus on cloud environments

5. How does SDKMAN simplify JVM management for developers?

    A. By limiting the number of JVM vendors available

    B. By restricting the use of different JVM versions

    C. By seamlessly integrating with build tools

    D. By supporting only proprietary JVM implementations

6.   What differentiates Azul Zulu from Azul Zing?

   A.   Azul Zulu is not TCK-certified

   B.   Azul Zing is based on OpenJDK

   C.   Azul Zulu incorporates the G1 Garbage Collector

   D.   Azul Zing focuses on small-scale applications

7.   What key feature of Azul Zulu ensures that Java applications remain responsive even under heavy workloads?

   A.   C4 Garbage Collector

   B.   Falcon compiler

   C.   Elasticity

   D.   JavaFX integration

Answers

Here are the answers to this chapter's questions:

1.   B. Online eCommerce and financial and logistics applications

2.   B. Tencent Kona

3.   C. Native image generation for Quarkus applications

4.   B. Timely updates and security patches

5.   C. By seamlessly integrating with build tools

6.   B. Azul Zing is based on OpenJDK

7.   A. C4 Garbage Collector

Part 4: Advanced Java Topics

In the subsequent chapters, our exploration extends to Java framework principles, shedding light on the intricacies of designing and utilizing frameworks, trade-offs, and the role of metadata and annotations. The focus then shifts to the dynamic realm of Java, where reflection unveils aspects such as field access, method invocation, and proxy usage. Another facet of our journey delves into Java annotation processors, revealing their role in reading metadata at build time. Concluding our exploration, we offer final considerations and tips for further exploration, providing a comprehensive overview of our journey through the JVM's intricacies.

This part has the following chapters:

- *Chapter 9, Java Framework Principles*
- *Chapter 10, Reflection*
- *Chapter 11, Java Annotation Processor*
- *Chapter 12, Final Considerations*

9
Java Framework Principles

In the intricate landscape of **Java Virtual Machine** (**JVM**) internals, the development and utilization of Java frameworks stand out as a cornerstone for building robust and scalable applications. This chapter delves into fundamental principles that underpin the art of crafting Java frameworks, offering a comprehensive exploration of the intricacies involved. As architects and developers navigate the dynamic realm of software design, understanding trade-offs inherent in framework development becomes paramount. This chapter illuminates critical considerations in framework design and sheds light on the delicate balance between flexibility and performance. Through insightful analysis and practical examples, readers will gain a profound understanding of decisions that shape the architecture of Java frameworks, empowering them to make informed choices in their software endeavors.

In software development, a framework is a foundational structure that provides pre-defined components, tools, and design patterns to streamline application development. Examples in Java include the Spring Framework, Hibernate for database interaction, Struts for web applications, **JavaServer Faces** (**JSF**) for user interfaces, and Apache Wicket for web apps. Frameworks simplify development, encourage code reuse, and maintain best practices.

A pivotal aspect of this exploration lies in examining metadata and annotations within the Java framework ecosystem. These elements enhance code expressiveness, enabling developers to encapsulate and convey crucial information about classes, methods, and other components. By unraveling the intricacies of metadata and annotations, this chapter equips readers with the knowledge needed to harness the full potential of these tools in crafting flexible and extensible frameworks. Whether unraveling the mysteries of reflection or leveraging annotations for configuration and extension points, this chapter guides navigating the nuanced landscape of Java framework principles. Through a blend of theoretical insights and practical examples, readers will embark on a journey that demystifies the complexities of framework development, empowering them to architect sophisticated solutions on the robust foundation of JVM internals.

In this chapter, we'll explore the following topics:

- Why do we have frameworks?
- Java metadata
- Trade-offs in framework adoption
- Java framework principles

Why do we have frameworks?

We'll explore the underlying reasons for the prevalence and evolution of Java frameworks in software development. Adopting frameworks aligns seamlessly with established software development practices, arising organically as a response to the perpetual quest for efficiency, reliability, and scalability. Developers, faced with the challenges of crafting intricate and feature-rich applications, find in frameworks a strategic ally that provides a structured and standardized foundation, facilitating the reuse of components and streamlining development processes.

A key motivation behind the widespread use of frameworks is their capacity to address challenges related to redundant code and duplicated bugs. By encapsulating best practices, design patterns, and common functionalities, frameworks empower developers to concentrate on distinctive aspects of their applications, fostering code efficiency and reducing the likelihood of errors. It expedites development cycles and enhances the overall quality of software products. As projects mature, the cumulative impact of leveraging frameworks becomes increasingly evident, expediting the journey from conceptualization to deployment.

Moreover, the evolution of these reusable components has given rise to a thriving market of framework-based businesses. By recognizing the intrinsic value of streamlined development practices, companies actively invest in and adopt Java frameworks to catalyze their software development processes. These frameworks boost productivity and contribute to creating robust, maintainable, and scalable applications.

In business-oriented software development, the concept of reusable components takes on a dual significance, manifesting both within the confines of an organization and across diverse companies. Internally, organizations harness inner-source power, fostering an environment where reusable components are cultivated and shared among different teams. This collaborative approach enhances code reusability, accelerates development cycles, and nurtures a culture of knowledge exchange within the organization.

Simultaneously, the broader landscape of Java frameworks extends beyond organizational boundaries, providing functionalities that transcend company-specific needs. Java is a linchpin for integration, seamlessly weaving disparate components and technologies together. Whether it's database integration, handling HTTP requests, implementing caching mechanisms, or facilitating distributed observability, Java frameworks have become indispensable in ensuring interoperability and efficiency across many systems.

What distinguishes Java in this ecosystem is its versatility and the robust open-source community surrounding it. Countless open-source products and proprietary solutions contribute to a rich tapestry of tools that aid software engineers on their development journey. For instance, widely adopted databases such as MySQL and PostgreSQL seamlessly integrate with Java applications, ensuring efficient data management. Advanced caching solutions such as Ehcache enhance application performance by optimizing data retrieval. Distributed observability platforms such as Prometheus and Jaeger also empower developers to monitor and troubleshoot applications effectively. These tools collectively form the backbone of Java's strength in enterprise-level integration, enabling developers to build scalable and efficient solutions quickly.

The multitude of frameworks available for Java, spanning database integration, HTTP requests, caching, and distributed observability, underscores its adaptability and resilience in addressing diverse business challenges. This amalgamation of open source and proprietary tools serves as a testament to the collaborative nature of the software development landscape, where shared resources and frameworks accelerate innovation and empower software engineers to navigate the complexities of modern, interconnected systems.

As we conclude our exploration of the expansive landscape of Java frameworks in business-oriented software development, it becomes evident that these tools are not merely coding conveniences but strategic assets that drive efficiency, reliability, and scalability. The dual nature of reusable components, thriving within organizational boundaries through inner-source practices and extending across companies through versatile Java frameworks, underscores the dynamic and collaborative spirit of modern software engineering.

In our next section, we will delve into the crucial realm of metadata within Java, a cornerstone that enhances code expressiveness and functionality. Understanding how metadata and annotations operate in the context of Java frameworks is pivotal for navigating the intricate architecture of these tools. We will unravel the layers of information encapsulated within metadata, exploring its role in shaping flexible and extensible frameworks. Join us as we embark on a journey into the nuanced world of metadata, bridging the gap between theory and practical application in the context of Java's rich framework ecosystem.

Java metadata

In the dynamic landscape of Java programming, metadata emerges as a powerful tool, quietly working behind the scenes to bridge gaps between disparate paradigms and streamline conversion processes that define modern software development. But why do we have metadata in Java, and what role does it play in simplifying complex tasks, particularly in scenarios such as conversion or mapping operations?

At its core, metadata in Java is a critical facilitator, significantly easing the intricacies of processes such as converting Java entities to XML files or databases. The essence lies in its ability to decrease impedance between different paradigms, particularly when navigating the nuanced space between relational databases and Java objects.

Consider the scenario where Java, following its convention of camelCase (for example, `clientId`) collaborates with a relational database, which adheres to the `snake_case` convention, for example, `client_id`. This misalignment in naming conventions can pose challenges, creating a disconnect between the two paradigms. Enter metadata — the unsung hero that enables seamless communication and relationship building between a Java class and a database. By encapsulating essential information about the data's structure, properties, and relationships, metadata serves as a linchpin in harmonizing the syntax and semantics of these diverse worlds.

The strategic use of metadata is not just a mere workaround; it is a deliberate approach to enhance interoperability, reduce development friction, and uphold best practices in software engineering. Join us as we unravel the metadata layers in Java, exploring how these silent enablers play a pivotal role in minimizing the distance between paradigms and fostering a more cohesive and efficient development experience. From relational databases to Java objects, we will uncover the mechanisms by which metadata ensures that the intricate dance of data conversion and mapping unfolds seamlessly in the complex choreography of modern software development.

Behold the synergy between a Java file and a relational database, harmonized by a silent influencer – metadata. This visual snapshot captures the seamless communication facilitated by metadata, transcending the naming conventions divergence between Java's camelCase and the database's `snake_case`. In the intricate dance of data conversion and mapping, metadata emerges as the unseen orchestrator, reducing impedance and fostering interoperability. This diagram encapsulates the pivotal role of metadata, transforming potential friction into a fluid exchange that underlies the creation of robust and adaptable software solutions:

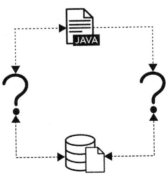

Figure 9.1: The Java application communicates with the database using metadata

Continuing the journey through metadata history in Java, early endeavors in metadata management leaned on XML, a practice notably exemplified in the **Java Persistence API (JPA)**. Taking the `Person` entity as an example, defined in Java code, the subsequent step involved crafting an XML file to articulate the intricate relationship between this Java class and corresponding database mapping statements. This XML file, dynamically interpreted at runtime, played a dual role — not only serving as a blueprint for the association between the `Person` class and the database but also functioning as a conduit for generating real-time metadata. The provided XML snippet illustrates this crucial link, outlining the attributes, tables, and their respective mappings, marking a significant chapter in the evolution of Java's metadata-handling capabilities.

The provided Java code defines a `Person` class with three private fields: `id`, `name`, and `age`. This class encapsulates data related to an individual and includes the necessary getter and setter methods for each attribute. The intent is to represent a person with identifiable characteristics in a Java application:

```java
public class Person {
    private String id;
    private String name;
    private Integer age;
    //getter and setter
}
```

Consider the accompanying XML metadata snippet designed for JPA. This XML file serves as a declarative mapping configuration, establishing a crucial link between the `Person` class and its representation in a relational database. The `<entity>` element denotes the mapping for the `Person` class, specifying its Java class and name. The `<table>` element defines the table name in the database associated with this entity:

```xml
<entity class="entity.Person" name="Person">
    <table name="Person"/>
    <attributes>
        <id name="id"/>
        <basic name="name">
            <column name="NAME" length="100"/>
        </basic>
        <basic name="age"/>
    </attributes>
</entity>
```

Within the `<attributes>` section, the XML delineates individual attributes of the `Person` class. The `<id>` element signifies the primary key attribute, specifying the corresponding field (`id`). Additionally, two `<basic>` elements for the `name` and `age` attributes indicate simple, non-composite attributes. The `<column>` elements nested within the `name` attribute provide further details for database mapping, specifying the column name (`NAME`) and its maximum length.

This XML metadata is a configuration blueprint, establishing relationships between Java objects and their database representations. It not only defines the structure and characteristics of the `Person` class but also guides the runtime generation of metadata, facilitating seamless interaction between the Java application and the underlying database. This robust connection is a fundamental aspect of Java's metadata-handling capabilities, contributing to the efficiency and coherence of data management in Java applications.

Frameworks such as Spring and Jakarta EE offer a more code-centric approach to defining metadata. For example, annotations such as @Entity, @Table(name = "tutorial"), and @Column(name = "title") serve as a simplified alternative to XML configuration files. Here's a code sample using annotations:

```java
@Entity
@Table(name = "tutorial")
public class Tutorial {
    @Id
    @GeneratedValue(strategy = GenerationType.IDENTITY)
    @Column(name = "tutorial_id")
    private Long id;

    @Column(name = "title")
    private String title;

    // Constructors, getters, and setters
}
```

Conversely, in XML-based configuration, the same metadata can be defined as follows:

```xml
<entity class="com.example.Tutorial">
    <table name="tutorial"/>
    <attributes>
        <id name="id">
            <generated-value strategy="IDENTITY"/>
            <column name="tutorial_id"/>
        </id>
        <basic name="title">
            <column name="title"/>
        </basic>
    </attributes>
</entity>
```

Both approaches achieve the same result, with annotations providing a more concise and code-centric way to specify metadata, while XML offers a more externalized and customizable configuration option.

Step into the visual narrative of seamless database integration, where the synergy between a Java file and an XML configuration file unfolds with remarkable cohesion. This captivating diagram captures the intricate dance of integration, showcasing a Java file representing a Person class harmonizing effortlessly with an XML file crafted for JPA. As the framework combines these two entities, Java and XML, a symbiotic relationship emerges, paving the way for streamlined data integration into the database. This visual depiction encapsulates how, through careful coordination of Java code and XML metadata, the framework facilitates a seamless bridge between the application's logic and the database structure. It is a compelling snapshot of the dynamic interplay between code and configuration, demonstrating the powerful capabilities of Java frameworks in orchestrating cohesive and efficient database integration:

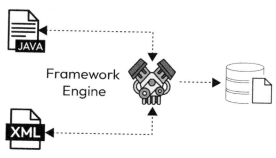

Figure 9.2: The Java application communicates with the database using metadata

The evolution of the Java language and its ecosystem revealed to developers that maintaining generated metadata separately from the code, as was conventionally done with XML files, presented challenges in intuitiveness and, notably, increased complexity during maintenance – updating a field required alterations in both the Java class and the corresponding database configuration, leading to potential discrepancies and inefficiencies.

In a pivotal move to enhance developer experience and streamline this process, Java 5, introduced in mid-2004, ushered in the metadata facility for Java through **Java Specification Request (JSR)** *175*, affectionately known as **Java annotations**. This innovation eliminated the need for a separate configuration file, offering a unified solution where all essential information could reside within the Java class. It simplified the development workflow and significantly improved the maintainability of code and associated metadata, marking a transformative moment in the evolution of Java's metadata-handling capabilities.

In Java annotations, developers can read and process annotations in two distinct phases: dynamically at runtime using reflection or statically at build time utilizing a dedicated tool, such as a Java annotation processor.

The runtime approach, leveraging reflection, involves inspecting and interpreting annotations while executing the program. This method allows for dynamic decision-making based on the presence or values of annotations within the code. However, it comes with some runtime performance overhead as the annotations are introspected during program execution.

On the other hand, the build-time approach utilizes annotation processors, tools that operate during the compilation phase. Annotation processors analyze and manipulate annotated elements of the source code before the actual compilation occurs. This approach is beneficial for tasks determined at compile time, such as code generation, validation, or resource preparation. It offers the advantage of catching potential issues early in development and contributes to more efficient and optimized code.

Ultimately, the choice between runtime reflection and build-time annotation processing depends on the specific requirements of the task at hand. Runtime reflection suits scenarios where decisions must be made dynamically during program execution. At the same time, build-time processing is preferable for tasks that can be resolved at compile time, promoting efficiency and early error detection.

In conclusion, the evolution of metadata handling in Java, transitioning from XML-based configurations to the innovative realm of Java annotations, has marked a transformative phase in software development. The move toward annotations within the Java ecosystem, introduced through JSR 175, simplified metadata integration with code and significantly enhanced maintainability. As we navigate the landscape of Java annotations, we find ourselves at a crossroads where choices between runtime reflection and build-time annotation processing present distinct trade-offs. Potential performance implications counterbalance the dynamic adaptability of runtime reflection, while the efficiency of build-time processing comes at the cost of static decision-making. Join us in the next section as we delve into the nuanced world of trade-offs in Java development, exploring the delicate balance between flexibility and performance when making crucial architectural decisions.

Trade-offs in framework adoption

As developers venture into software architecture, the decision to incorporate a framework introduces many considerations, each laden with trade-offs that profoundly impact the development process. Embracing a framework, be it for Java or any other language, entails a delicate balancing act between the conveniences it offers and the potential drawbacks it may introduce.

One crucial trade-off revolves around the allure of rapid development facilitated by frameworks versus their imposed constraints. Frameworks often expedite the coding process, providing pre-built components and established conventions. However, this acceleration can come at the cost of flexibility, as developers may find themselves confined by the framework's prescribed structure and paradigms.

Furthermore, the trade-off extends to the learning curve of adopting a new framework. While frameworks aim to simplify development, there's an inherent investment in time and effort required for developers to become proficient. This initial learning phase may be perceived as a hurdle, especially in fast-paced development environments.

In this section, we will dissect these trade-offs and explore the nuanced decisions developers face when embracing a framework. From the promise of accelerated development to potential constraints and learning curves, understanding the intricate trade-offs involved is essential for making informed architectural choices. Join us as we navigate the delicate balance between the conveniences and constraints of framework adoption in the dynamic software development landscape.

The decision between adopting an existing framework and creating a custom one constitutes a significant trade-off in software development, each path laden with its considerations. Opting for a well-established framework from the market offers immediate advantages such as proven reliability, community support, and often a wealth of pre-built components. It accelerates development, reduces the need for reinventing the wheel, and taps into the collective knowledge of a user community. However, the trade-off here lies in a potential need for more customization and the risk of being constrained by design choices and opinions embedded in the chosen framework.

Conversely, creating a custom framework provides the freedom to tailor solutions precisely to the project's unique requirements. This approach offers unparalleled flexibility, allowing developers to craft a framework that perfectly aligns with the project's goals and architecture. Yet, this freedom comes at a cost – the investment of time and resources to design, implement, and maintain a bespoke framework. Additionally, the absence of a proven track record may lead to unforeseen challenges and the need for extensive testing and refinement. It's essential to consider whether creating *another framework* aligns with the project's specific needs and goals. While it can offer benefits in terms of customization, it should be a well-considered decision to avoid unnecessary complexity and fragmentation.

Ultimately, the trade-off involves weighing an existing framework's immediate benefits and conveniences against the long-term advantages and potential pitfalls of creating a custom solution. The decision hinges on project requirements, timeline, team expertise, and the strategic vision for the software's evolution. Striking the right balance between leveraging existing solutions and crafting tailored frameworks is a delicate yet pivotal decision in the dynamic landscape of software development.

The trade-off between adopting an existing framework and creating a custom one in software development introduces a pivotal decision-making process. While established frameworks offer immediate benefits and community support, they may constrain flexibility. Conversely, crafting a bespoke framework provides tailored solutions but demands significant time and resources. As we transition to the next section, *Java framework principles*, we will delve into foundational principles guiding the design and development of frameworks. Recognizing how these principles shape intricate choices between leveraging existing solutions and crafting custom frameworks is essential for navigating the dynamic landscape of software development. Join us as we unravel the principles that underpin effective frameworks and illuminate their influence on trade-offs inherent in developers' decisions.

Java framework principles

A nuanced understanding of key principles is paramount for architects and developers in Java framework development. The first crucial aspect to consider is API design, which significantly influences the framework's usability and adoption. Choosing between a declarative and an imperative API design is pivotal. Declarative APIs emphasize expressing the desired outcome, promoting readability and conciseness, while imperative APIs provide a step-by-step approach, offering more explicit control. Striking the right balance between these approaches is vital to ensure not only ease of use but also the long-term maintainability of the framework.

Another critical principle is executability, where careful consideration of reflection becomes pivotal. Reflection can offer dynamic capabilities, enabling examining and manipulating classes, methods, and fields at runtime. However, this flexibility comes with a performance cost. Alternatively, frameworks can opt for solutions that eschew reflection, promoting efficiency within the JVM. Additionally, the advent of technologies allowing the execution of Java code outside the JVM, such as building native images, introduces new dimensions to the executability principle. Navigating these choices demands understanding trade-offs between flexibility, performance, and resource efficiency.

API design is a critical aspect of Java framework development, presenting developers with a choice between two fundamental styles: declarative and imperative. Each approach carries its trade-offs, and the decision between them hinges on factors such as readability, expressiveness, and the level of control developers desire.

A declarative API emphasizes expressing the desired outcome or end state, allowing developers to specify what they want to achieve without dictating the step-by-step process. This style promotes concise and expressive code, making it more readable and often easier to understand. Declarative APIs are particularly beneficial in scenarios focusing on higher-level abstractions and where a more intuitive, natural language-like syntax enhances code comprehension.

On the other hand, imperative APIs adopt a more step-by-step or procedural approach, requiring developers to define each action and control flow explicitly. While this style provides a more granular level of control, it may result in more verbose and boilerplate code. Imperative APIs shine when precise control over the execution flow is paramount, especially when developers need to manage intricate details or handle complex branching logic.

The trade-off between declarative and imperative API design often concerns the balance between expressiveness and control. Declarative APIs are favored for their readability and conciseness, enhancing collaboration and reducing cognitive load on developers. However, they might be less suitable for scenarios demanding fine-grained control. In contrast, imperative APIs offer more explicit control but can be verbose and may require a deeper understanding of the underlying logic.

Choosing between declarative and imperative API design should be informed by the framework's specific requirements and the development team's preferences. Striking the right balance is crucial, and in many cases, a hybrid approach that combines elements of both styles may offer the best of both worlds, providing expressiveness and control where needed.

The executability of a Java framework encompasses the mechanisms by which the framework's code is executed within the JVM. This aspect involves crucial trade-offs, particularly when considering the use of reflection, avoiding reflection, and exploring options such as building native images.

Reflection, a dynamic feature in Java, enables the inspection and manipulation of classes, methods, and fields at runtime. While powerful, reflection comes with a performance cost, often resulting in slower execution times due to its dynamic nature. Additionally, reflection can reduce code safety, as errors might only be discovered during runtime. The trade-off here involves the flexibility and convenience offered by reflection versus potential performance drawbacks and the deferred nature of error detection.

Frameworks can opt for approaches that avoid reflection, relying on more static and compile-time mechanisms. It promotes improved performance and early error detection but may require more explicit configuration and code generation. The decision to forego reflection often hinges on the framework's specific needs, the desired performance level, and the trade-off between dynamism and static analysis.

In recent developments, the concept of building native images has gained traction. Technologies such as GraalVM enable the compilation of Java code into native machine code, bypassing the need for the JVM during execution. This approach offers potential benefits regarding startup time, reduced memory footprint, and enhanced overall performance. However, it introduces trade-offs related to increased build complexity, potential compatibility issues, and the loss of some runtime features provided by the JVM.

Ultimately, the choice of executability strategy involves careful consideration of the specific requirements of the framework, performance goals, and trade-offs between flexibility, convenience, and the overhead associated with reflection or native image compilation. Striking the right balance is crucial for achieving optimal performance while maintaining the desired level of dynamism and ease of development within the framework.

Indeed, in the landscape of Java framework principles and broader software development, several fundamental principles significantly influence the design and usability of frameworks. **Convention over configuration** is a pivotal principle emphasizing default conventions, reducing the need for explicit configuration when developers adhere to established patterns. It simplifies the framework's usage, making it more intuitive and user-friendly.

The creation of components follows the principle of modularity, encouraging the development of independent, reusable units that contribute to maintainability and scalability. Adhering to Java standards, such as coding conventions and design patterns, ensures consistency and interoperability within the Java ecosystem.

Documentation and testing play indispensable roles in the success of a framework. Comprehensive and well-structured documentation enables users to understand the framework's functionality, aiding its adoption and reducing the learning curve. Thorough testing ensures the reliability and robustness of the framework, instilling confidence in developers.

Furthermore, the **Service Provider (SP)** approach introduces a plugin-like architecture, allowing developers to extend or modify the behavior of a framework seamlessly. This principle fosters a **plug-and-play (PnP)** effect, enabling users to incorporate additional functionalities or customize the framework without altering its core code base.

Collectively, these principles contribute to creating effective and user-friendly frameworks in the Java ecosystem. They emphasize conventions, modularity, adherence to standards, robust documentation, testing rigor, and extensibility through SPs, fostering a holistic approach to framework design and development. Embracing these principles ensures that frameworks not only meet the immediate needs of developers but also stand the test of time as reliable and adaptable tools in the dynamic world of software development.

Summary

In concluding our exploration of Java framework principles and broader software development tenets, we've uncovered a tapestry of considerations—from API design and executability to convention over configuration and the significance of documentation and testing. These principles collectively guide the creation of robust, user-friendly frameworks that align with Java standards and embrace modularity. As we transition to the next chapter focused on Java reflection, we delve into a critical aspect of executability, unraveling dynamic capabilities and potential trade-offs inherent in the reflective nature of Java. Join us in this exploration as we navigate the intricacies of reflection, unlocking its power and understanding how it shapes the landscape of dynamic Java programming.

Questions

Answer the following questions to test your knowledge of this chapter:

1. What is a key consideration when deciding between a declarative and an imperative API design in a Java framework?

    A. Code verbosity

    B. Compilation speed

    C. Memory consumption

    D. Database compatibility

2. Which principle emphasizes reducing the need for explicit configuration by relying on established patterns and defaults?

    A. Concurrency control

    B. Convention over configuration

    C. **Dependency injection (DI)**

    D. Modularization

3. Why is comprehensive documentation crucial for a Java framework?

    A. To increase development complexity

    B. To deter users from adopting the framework

    C. To reduce the learning curve for users

    D. To limit the framework's capabilities

4. What approach enables a plugin-like architecture, allowing developers to extend or modify the behavior of a framework seamlessly?

    A. **Aspect-oriented programming (AOP)**

    B. **Model-View-Controller (MVC)**

    C. Observer pattern

    D. SP approach

Answers

Here are the answers to this chapter's questions:

1. A. Code verbosity

2. B. Convention over configuration

3. C. To reduce the learning curve for users

4. D. SP approach

10
Reflection

The Reflection API is a powerful and versatile tool that enables developers to access the inner workings of Java programs. In this chapter, we will explore the various capabilities of reflection, such as field access, method invocation, and proxy usage. Reflection allows developers to inspect and manipulate classes and objects at runtime, providing a dynamic gateway into JVM internals. Throughout this chapter, we will delve into the nuances of reflective field interactions, the intricacies of dynamically invoking methods, and the strategic deployment of proxies to enhance code flexibility. Join us on a journey into the heart of Java's reflective capabilities, where the seemingly unchangeable becomes adaptable, and the boundaries of static code are stretched to accommodate the dynamic requirements of advanced applications.

In this chapter, we'll explore the following topics:

- Overview of reflection

- Exploring practical reflection

- Proxy

Technical requirements

To follow along with this chapter, you will require the following:

- Java 21

- Git

- Maven

- Any preferred IDE

- This chapter's GitHub repository, found at https://github.com/PacktPublishing/Mastering-the-Java-Virtual-Machine/tree/main/chapter-10

Overview of reflection

Reflection, a fundamental feature of the Java programming language, bestows upon developers the ability to inspect and manipulate the structure, behavior, and metadata of classes and objects at runtime. This dynamic capability might open a Pandora's box of possibilities, allowing programmers to transcend the confines of static code and respond to the evolving needs of their applications. Why is reflection so crucial to Java development?

Reflection in Java finds practical use in specialized scenarios, such as framework and library development, empowering developers to create flexible and extensible code. It plays a pivotal role in **dependency injection (DI)** containers, **object-relational mapping (ORM)** frameworks, and testing frameworks, enabling dynamic class instantiation and configuration. Reflection is also essential in serialization and deserialization libraries, GUI development tools, and Java's core libraries, contributing to the dynamic loading and manipulation of objects and classes. While it may not be a daily tool for most developers, reflection proves its worth in enhancing code reusability and adaptability in specific domains, making it an invaluable asset in the Java ecosystem.

At its core, reflection plays a pivotal role in achieving introspection, enabling programs to examine and adapt to their structure. It becomes particularly valuable when dealing with frameworks, libraries, and tools that must operate generically and flexibly, accommodating various types and structures dynamically. Reflection facilitates the retrieval of class information, method signatures, and field details, offering a level of dynamism essential for scenarios where a deep understanding of the code base at runtime is paramount.

Moreover, reflection fuels the development of tools such as IDEs, debuggers, and application servers, providing them with the means to analyze and manipulate Java code in a manner that transcends the constraints of compile-time knowledge. By offering a programmatic interface to class information and facilitating dynamic instantiation, reflection lays the groundwork for sophisticated frameworks and runtime environments.

While reflection is a distinctive feature of Java, similar concepts exist in other programming languages. For example, languages such as Python, C#, and Ruby also embrace reflective capabilities to varying extents. In Python, the `inspect` module allows for runtime introspection, while C# incorporates reflection for dynamic type discovery and invocation. Understanding reflection in the broader context of programming languages provides developers with a versatile skill set that can be applied across different technological landscapes. As we delve deeper into this chapter, we will unravel the intricacies of Java's Reflection API, exploring its nuances and applications that make it a cornerstone of dynamic and adaptable programming.

While the Java Reflection API empowers developers with dynamic capabilities, it has a set of trade-offs that should be carefully considered. Understanding these trade-offs is crucial for making informed decisions about when to leverage reflection and when to seek alternative approaches:

- **Performance overhead**: One of the primary trade-offs associated with reflection is its performance overhead. Reflective operations, such as accessing fields, invoking methods, or creating instances dynamically, are generally slower than their non-reflective counterparts. Reflection involves runtime type checking and method resolution, which can incur additional computational costs. Consequently, in performance-critical applications or situations where rapid execution is paramount, relying excessively on reflection may lead to suboptimal performance.

- **Compile-time safety**: Reflection bypasses some of Java's compile-time checks. Since reflection allows for dynamic access to classes, fields, and methods, the compiler cannot catch certain errors until runtime. This lack of compile-time safety increases the likelihood of runtime exceptions, making the code more error-prone. When using reflection, developers must be vigilant in handling potential issues such as missing classes, methods, or type mismatches.

- **Code readability and maintenance**: Reflective code can be more challenging to read and maintain. The absence of explicit type information in reflective operations makes the code less self-documenting, and it may be harder for developers to understand the program's structure and behavior. It can increase complexity and reduce maintainability, especially in larger code bases where reflection is pervasive.

- **Security concerns**: Reflection can introduce security risks, especially in environments where security is a top priority, such as web applications. By dynamically accessing and manipulating classes and methods, reflective code can potentially violate access controls and security constraints. Careful consideration and validation are necessary to ensure that reflective operations do not compromise the integrity and security of the application.

- **Platform dependence**: Reflection might be platform-dependent, and certain reflective operations may behave differently on different JVM implementations. It can introduce challenges in writing portable and cross-platform code. Developers should be cautious when relying on reflection in scenarios where platform independence is a critical requirement.

While reflection provides powerful mechanisms for dynamic code manipulation, developers should weigh its advantages against these trade-offs. It is essential to use review judiciously, considering factors such as performance requirements, code maintainability, and security implications to balance flexibility and the potential drawbacks associated with reflective programming.

From a framework perspective, reflection is often intertwined with a broader set of processes to dynamically understand and interact with the structure of Java classes and objects. Let's break down the reflection process within a framework, considering a hypothetical scenario illustrated in this step-by-step:

1. **Framework initialization and reflection engine loading**: The process begins with the initialization of the framework. At this stage, the framework's core components, including the reflection engine, are loaded into the runtime environment (Ruime). The reflection engine is how the framework dynamically interacts with and manipulates classes and objects.

2. **Code compilation and annotation processing**: Developers write code that includes annotations and reflection-related elements. This code undergoes the standard Java compilation process. During compilation, the Java compiler reads the source code, processes annotations, and generates bytecode.

3. **Loading classes into Ruime**: Ruime, the runtime environment, is responsible for loading the compiled classes into memory. As part of this process, the reflection engine within Ruime gains awareness of the available classes and their structure.

4. **Reflection engine reads annotations**: The reflection engine, now aware of the loaded classes, begins to scan for annotations within these classes. Annotations are metadata that provides additional information about the code and plays a crucial role in reflective frameworks. The reflection engine reads and interprets these annotations to dynamically understand how to interact with the annotated elements.

5. **Dependency tree generation**: The reflection engine generates a dependency tree based on information gathered from annotations and other reflective elements. This tree outlines the relationships between classes, methods, and fields, providing a dynamic blueprint of the program's structure. The tree serves as a guide for the framework to navigate and manipulate the code at runtime.

6. **Execution of dynamic code**: The framework can now dynamically execute code with the dependency tree in place. It could involve creating instances of classes, invoking methods, or accessing fields based on runtime information gathered through reflection. The framework leverages the reflective capabilities to adapt its behavior dynamically, responding to the specific conditions encountered during runtime.

As JVM initializes, the reflection engine loads, setting the stage for a code compilation ballet. Annotations, the silent choreographers, guide the reflection engine through loaded classes. In JVM memory, a dependency tree emerges, a blueprint of the runtime structure. This ethereal map becomes the key to dynamic execution, where the framework adapts in real time. Arrows trace the fluid path from class loading to execution, encapsulating the transformative essence of reflective frameworks. Behold the graphic ode to dynamic prowess:

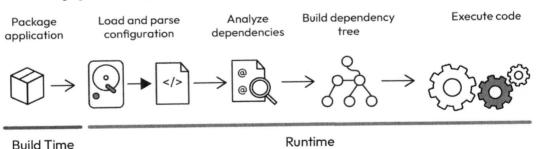

Figure 10.1: The Java perspective using reflection

As we conclude this part, the intricacies of reflection within a framework unfold like a well-choreographed performance. The journey from framework initialization to dynamic code execution, guided by the reflection engine and annotated insights, paints a vivid picture of adaptability and versatility. Now, armed with an understanding of reflection's role in shaping runtime dynamics, we transition seamlessly into the next section, where theory transforms into practice. Brace yourself for a hands-on exploration of the Reflection API, where we will delve into real-world scenarios, demonstrating how to leverage reflection for field access, method invocation, and the strategic use of proxies. Through practical examples, we will bridge the conceptual foundations laid in this chapter with tangible applications, empowering you to wield reflection as a powerful tool in your Java development arsenal. Get ready to witness the Reflection API in action, breathing life into the theoretical constructs we've explored thus far.

Exploring practical reflection

In this hands-on section, we delve into the practical application of Java's Reflection API by creating a versatile `Mapper` interface. We aim to implement methods that dynamically convert objects of a given class to and from `Map<String, Object>`. The `Mapper` interface serves as a blueprint for a generic solution, allowing us to flex the muscles of reflection in a real-world scenario.

Let's begin with the `Mapper` interface:

```
public interface Mapper {

    <T> Map<String, Object> toMap(T entity);

    <T> T toEntity(Map<String, Object> map);
}
```

The `toMap` method is designed to convert an object of type `T` into a map, where each key-value pair represents a field name and its corresponding value. Conversely, the `toEntity` method reverses this process, reconstructing an object of type `T` from a given map.

Now, armed with the theory from the previous part, we'll put reflection into practice to implement these methods. Our journey will involve dynamically inspecting class structures, accessing fields, and creating instances at runtime. Through hands-on coding exercises, we aim to demystify the power of reflection and showcase its practical utility in building flexible and adaptable solutions.

So, buckle up for an engaging session where we bridge the gap between theory and application, crafting a dynamic `Mapper` interface that transforms objects into maps and back again using the magic of reflection. Let's dive into the fascinating world of practical reflection and witness the code in action!

In the ever-evolving landscape of technology, seamless migration between different paradigms often requires bridging conventions. A common challenge arises with varying naming conventions, such as Java's camel case and certain databases' snake case preferences. To tackle this, we introduce the `Column` annotation, allowing developers to define custom column names during object-to-map conversion.

Let's take a closer look at the `Column` annotation:

```
@Retention(RetentionPolicy.RUNTIME)
@Target(ElementType.FIELD)
public @interface Column {
    String value() default "";
}
```

This annotation, applicable to fields (`ElementType.FIELD`), carries a `value` attribute. If provided, this attribute allows developers to specify a custom column name; otherwise, the field name is used by default. This flexibility enables a seamless mapping between Java objects and database structures, accommodating diverse naming conventions.

Additionally, to mark a class as eligible for parsing, we introduce the `Entity` annotation:

```
@Retention(RetentionPolicy.RUNTIME)
@Target(ElementType.TYPE)
public @interface Entity {
}
```

Applied to the class level (`ElementType.TYPE`), this annotation signals that the class can undergo parsing operations. These annotations, when combined, empower developers to annotate their Java classes selectively, tailoring the conversion process based on the specific requirements of each class.

We introduce the `Appends` annotation to enhance flexibility and customization within our `Mapper` framework. This annotation, along with its companion `Append` annotation, provides a means to define default values for entities, enriching the object-to-map conversion process.

Let's delve into the definitions of these annotations:

```
@Retention(RetentionPolicy.RUNTIME)
@Target(ElementType.TYPE)
public @interface Appends {
    Append[] value();
}

@Retention(RetentionPolicy.RUNTIME)
@Target(ElementType.TYPE)
@Repeatable(Appends.class)
public @interface Append {
    String key();
    String value();
}
```

The Appends annotation, applied at the class level (ElementType.TYPE), holds an array of Append annotations. Each Append annotation, in turn, allows developers to specify a key-value pair, indicating the default values to be appended during the object-to-map conversion process.

The Append annotation is marked as repeatable (@Repeatable(Appends.class)) to simplify the specification of multiple append values on a single entity.

In the dynamic landscape of Java development, seamlessly converting objects to maps and vice versa is a powerful feature, especially when navigating diverse naming conventions or dealing with data migration scenarios. Implementing the toEntity method within the ReflectionMapper class marks a pivotal point in our journey through reflection-driven mapping.

This method bridges the map representation of an object and its reconstitution as a fully realized entity. Through the lens of Java reflection, we embark on a step-by-step exploration, unraveling the intricacies of reconstructing an object from a map of its properties. The following code shows the implementation of toEntity:

```java
@Override
public <T> T toEntity(Map<String, Object> map) {
    Objects.requireNonNull(map, "map is required");

    // Step 1: Obtain the fully qualified class name from the map
    T entity = getEntity(map.get(ENTITY_ENTRY).toString());

    // Step 2: Retrieve the class type of the entity
    Class<?> type = entity.getClass();

    // Step 3: Iterate over the declared fields of the class
    for (Field field : type.getDeclaredFields()) {
        // Step 4: Determine the key associated with the field using
        // @Column annotation
        String key = Optional.ofNullable(field.getAnnotation(Column.
          class))
                .map(Column::value)
                .filter(Predicate.not(String::isBlank))
                .orElse(field.getName());

        // Step 5: Retrieve the corresponding value from the map
        Optional<Object> value = Optional.ofNullable(map.get(key));

        // Step 6: Set the value in the object using reflection
        value.ifPresent(v -> setValue(entity, field, v));
    }
```

```
    // Step 7: Return the reconstructed entity
    return entity;
}
```

The `toEntity` method reconstructs an entity from a map, dynamically mapping fields using reflection. It ensures a non-null map, instantiates the entity using the provided class name, and iterates through the fields. Key determination involves `@Column` annotations or field names. Values are retrieved from the map and set in the object using reflection. The method returns the reconstructed entity, exemplifying a concise and dynamic object restoration process.

Here's an explanation:

- **Map validation**:

  ```
  Objects.requireNonNull(map, "map is required");
  ```

  The method begins by ensuring that the input `map` instance is not null, throwing a `NullPointerException` exception with the specified error message if it is.

- **Entity instantiation**:

  ```
  T entity = getEntity(map.get(ENTITY_ENTRY).toString());
  ```

  Using the fully qualified class name stored in the map, the `getEntity` method is called to dynamically instantiate an object of type `T` (the entity).

- **Class-type retrieval**:

  ```
  Class<?> type = entity.getClass();
  ```

  The `getClass` method is employed to obtain the runtime class of the entity.

- **Field iteration**:

  ```
  for (Field field : type.getDeclaredFields()) {
  ```

  The method iterates over the declared fields of the class.

- **Column key determination**:

  ```
  String key = Optional.ofNullable(field.getAnnotation(Column.
  class))
          .map(Column::value)
          .filter(Predicate.not(String::isBlank))
          .orElse(field.getName());
  ```

  For each field, it determines the key associated with it. If the `Column` annotation is present, it uses the specified column name; otherwise, it defaults to the field name.

- **Value retrieval and assignment**:

```
Optional<Object> value = Optional.ofNullable(map.get(key));
value.ifPresent(v -> setValue(entity, field, v));
```

It retrieves the corresponding value from the map using the determined key. If a value is present, it utilizes the `setValue` method to set the value in the object using reflection.

- **Reconstructed entity**:

```
return entity;
```

Finally, the reconstructed entity is returned, now populated with values from the map based on the reflection process.

This method demonstrates the dynamic reconstruction of an object using reflection, considering the custom annotations (`@Column`) for field-to-key mapping. It showcases the flexibility of `ReflectionMapper` in adapting to diverse class structures during the object-to-map conversion reversal.

The `toMap` method within the `ReflectionMapper` class is critical in exploring dynamic mapping using Java reflection. This method takes an object of type `T` as input and dynamically converts it into a `Map<String, Object>` instance. Let's unravel the intricacies of this method step by step:

```java
@Override
public <T> Map<String, Object> toMap(T entity) {
    Objects.requireNonNull(entity, "entity is required");

    // Step 1: Initialize the map to store key-value pairs
    Map<String, Object> map = new HashMap<>();

    // Step 2: Retrieve the class type of the entity
    Class<?> type = entity.getClass();
    map.put(ENTITY_ENTRY, type.getName());

    // Step 3: Iterate over the declared fields of the class
    for (Field field : type.getDeclaredFields()) {
        // Step 4: Set accessibility to true to allow access to
        // private fields
        field.setAccessible(true);

        // Step 5: Check for the presence of the @Column annotation
        Optional<Column> column = Optional.ofNullable(field.
          getAnnotation(Column.class));
        if (column.isPresent()) {
            // Step 6: Determine the key associated with the field
            // using @Column annotation
            String key = column.map(Column::value)
```

```
              .filter(Predicate.not(String::isBlank))
              .orElse(field.getName());

         // Step 7: Retrieve the field value using reflection and
         // add it to the map
         Object value = getValue(entity, field);
         map.put(key, value);
      }
   }

   // Step 8: Process @Append annotations at the class level and add
   // default values to the map
   Append[] appends = type.getAnnotationsByType(Append.class);
   for (Append append : appends) {
      map.put(append.key(), append.value());
   }

   // Step 9: Return the resulting map
   return map;
}
```

- **Explanation**:

  The `toMap` method utilizes reflection to dynamically convert Java objects into `Map<String, Object>`. It ensures non-null input, explores fields with `@Column` annotations, and maps their values. Class-level `@Append` annotations contribute default key-value pairs. This concise method exemplifies the efficiency of reflection for dynamic object-to-map transformations.

- **Input validation**:

  ```
  Objects.requireNonNull(entity, "entity is required");
  ```

  The method begins by ensuring that the input `entity` instance is not null, throwing a `NullPointerException` exception with the specified error message if it is.

- **Map initialization**:

  ```
  Map<String, Object> map = new HashMap<>();
  ```

  A `HashMap` instance is initialized to store the key-value pairs representing the properties of the object.

- **Class-type retrieval**:

  ```
  Class<?> type = entity.getClass();
  map.put(ENTITY_ENTRY, type.getName());
  ```

The method retrieves the runtime class of the entity and stores its fully qualified name in the map using the ENTITY_ENTRY key.

- **Field iteration**:

```
for (Field field : type.getDeclaredFields()) {
```

The method iterates over the declared fields of the class.

- **Accessibility setting**:

```
field.setAccessible(true);
```

The accessibility of the field is set to true, enabling access to private fields.

- **Column annotation check**:

```
Optional<Column> column = Optional.ofNullable(field.
getAnnotation(Column.class));
if (column.isPresent()) {
```

For each field, it checks for the presence of the Column annotation.

- **Column key determination**:

```
String key = column.map(Column::value)
        .filter(Predicate.not(String::isBlank))
        .orElse(field.getName());
```

If the Column annotation is present, it determines the key associated with the field. It uses the specified column name or defaults to the field name.

- **Value retrieval and assignment**:

```
Object value = getValue(entity, field);
map.put(key, value);
```

It retrieves the field value using the getValue method and adds the key-value pair to the map.

- **@Append annotation processing**:

```
Append[] appends = type.getAnnotationsByType(Append.class);
for (Append append : appends) {
    map.put(append.key(), append.value());
}
```

It processes @Append annotations at the class level, adding default key-value pairs to the map.

- **Resulting map**:

```
return map;
```

Finally, the resulting map, representing the object's properties, is returned.

This `toMap` method exemplifies the adaptability of reflection in dynamically mapping object properties to a map. It showcases how annotations and field-level details are harnessed to create a versatile and extensible mapping mechanism within the `ReflectionMapper` class.

In our exploration of reflection-based mapping techniques, we'll turn our attention to practical examples using two distinct entities: `Pet` and `Fruit`. These entities are adorned with annotations that provide valuable insights into the dynamic capabilities of `ReflectionMapper`. Let's delve into each entity, examining their structures and the annotations that will guide our mapping journey:

```
@Entity
public class Pet {

    @Column
    private String name;

    @Column
    private int age;

    // Constructors, getters, and setters...
}
```

The Pet entity is a simple **Plain Old Java Object** (**POJO**) representing a pet. It's marked with the `@Entity` annotation, signifying its eligibility for reflection-based mapping. Each field, such as `name` and `age`, is tagged with `@Column`, indicating their inclusion in the mapping process. This straightforward structure serves as an excellent starting point for understanding how the `ReflectionMapper` class dynamically handles object-to-map conversion and vice versa.

The next step is the `Fruit` entity which has additional settings than the previous class:

```
@Entity
@Append(key = "type", value = "Fruit")
@Append(key = "category", value = "Natural")
public class Fruit {

    @Column
    private String name;

    public Fruit(String name) {
        this.name = name;
    }

    @Deprecated
    public Fruit() {
    }

    public String name() {
```

```
        return name;
    }

    // Additional methods...
}
```

The Fruit entity, on the other hand, not only carries the @Entity annotation but also leverages the @Append annotation at the class level. This introduces default key-value pairs ("type": "Fruit" and "category": "Natural") during the mapping process. The class showcases flexibility by including both a deprecated and non-deprecated constructor, highlighting how the ReflectionMapper class adapts to different entity structures.

In the upcoming sections, we will execute the ReflectionMapper class on instances of these entities, unveiling the power of reflection in handling diverse class structures and annotations. Through this practical application, we aim to provide a comprehensive understanding of how reflection can be harnessed for dynamic object-to-map conversion and reconstruction. Let the mapping journey with Pet and Fruit commence!

To validate the practical application of the ReflectionMapper class on our diverse entities, we've devised a comprehensive MapperTest class. This series of tests demonstrates the mapper's ability to seamlessly convert entities to maps and reconstruct entities from maps, showcasing the flexibility and adaptability of reflection in dynamic mapping scenarios:

```
class MapperTest {

    private Mapper mapper;

    @BeforeEach
    public void setUp() {
        this.mapper = new ReflectionMapper();
    }

    @Test
    public void shouldConvertToMap() {
        // Test for converting Pet entity to map
        Pet ada = Pet.of("Ada", 8);
        Map<String, Object> map = mapper.toMap(ada);

        assertThat(map)
                .isNotNull()
                .isNotEmpty()
                .containsKeys("_entity", "name", "age")
                .containsEntry("name", "Ada")
                .containsEntry("age", 8)
```

```
                        .containsEntry("_entity", Pet.class.getName());
    }

    @Test
    public void shouldConvertEntity() {
        // Test for converting map to Pet entity
        Map<String, Object> map = Map.of("_entity", Pet.class.
          getName() , "name", "Ada", "age", 8);

        Pet pet = mapper.toEntity(map);

        assertThat(pet).isNotNull()
                .isInstanceOf(Pet.class)
                .matches(p -> p.name().equals("Ada"))
                .matches(p -> p.age() == 8);
    }

    @Test
    public void shouldConvertEntityRepeatable() {
        // Test for converting Fruit entity with repeatable
        // annotations to map
        Fruit fruit = new Fruit("Banana");
        Map<String, Object> map = this.mapper.toMap(fruit);

        assertThat(map).isNotNull().isNotEmpty()
                .containsEntry("type", "Fruit")
                .containsEntry("category", "Natural")
                .containsEntry("name", "Banana")
                .containsEntry("_entity", Fruit.class.getName());
    }
}
```

- **shouldConvertToMap**:

  - This test ensures that the ReflectionMapper class can successfully convert a Pet entity into a map

  - It verifies specific keys' presence and corresponding values in the generated map

- **shouldConvertEntity**:

  - In this test, a map representing a Pet entity is converted back into the original entity using ReflectionMapper

  - Assertions validate the correctness of the reconstructed Pet object

- **shouldConvertEntityRepeatable**:

  - This test focuses on converting a `Fruit` entity, which includes repeatable annotations, into a map

  - It verifies the presence of default key-value pairs and entity-specific values in the resulting map

Through these tests, we aim to illustrate how the `ReflectionMapper` class seamlessly handles various entities, annotations, and object-to-map conversions, emphasizing the practical utility of reflection in dynamic mapping scenarios. Let the testing commence, revealing the prowess of reflection in action!

In this section, we delved deep into the intricate world of reflection, unraveling its potential in dynamic object-to-map conversions through the lens of the `ReflectionMapper` class. We explored the reflection's flexibility and adaptability, showcasing its prowess in handling diverse entity structures and annotations. As we conclude this segment, we stand at the threshold of another fascinating realm— dynamic proxies. The upcoming section will usher us into the world of `MapperRepository`, where we will harness the power of dynamic proxies to switch between entities and their map representations seamlessly. Brace yourself for exploring the dynamic and versatile landscape of proxies as we unveil their role in enhancing reflection capabilities.

Proxy

Dynamic proxies in Java are indispensable tools that enable the creation of objects at runtime, implementing one or more interfaces, and intercepting method invocations. The `MapperRepository` class introduces us to the profound utility of dynamic proxies, where their application becomes paramount in seamlessly switching between entities and their corresponding map representations.

Dynamic proxies stand as veritable champions in the arsenal of Java's runtime capabilities, offering a trove of advantages that elevate code's adaptability, flexibility, and conciseness. Their inherent adaptability allows for creating proxy instances on the fly, accommodating diverse interfaces at runtime, and facilitating seamless integration in scenarios where object structures are only known at runtime. The ability to intercept method invocations empowers dynamic proxies to inject custom logic seamlessly, enhancing functionalities without compromising the integrity of core operations. This interception mechanism enables cleaner **separation of concerns** (**SoC**) and contributes to reduced boilerplate code, promoting maintainability. In the forthcoming exploration of `MapperRepository`, dynamic proxies emerge as the linchpin, embodying the ethos of adaptability and efficiency in the dynamic mapping landscape:

- **Adaptability and flexibility**: Dynamic proxies offer unparalleled adaptability, allowing us to create proxy instances for diverse interfaces at runtime. This adaptability becomes crucial when dealing with scenarios where the structure of objects or interfaces is not known until runtime. In the context of `MapperRepository`, dynamic proxies empower us to handle multiple entity types without a priori knowledge, fostering a more flexible and extensible design.

- **Interception of method invocations**: One of the key advantages of dynamic proxies is their ability to intercept method calls. This interception mechanism allows one to perform actions before and after method execution. In the realm of mapping entities to maps and vice versa, this interception becomes instrumental. It enables us to seamlessly inject conversion logic, enhancing the mapping process without altering the core logic of entities.

- **Reduced boilerplate code**: Dynamic proxies significantly reduce the need for boilerplate code. They allow us to centralize cross-cutting concerns, such as logging or validation, by encapsulating these concerns within the proxy. In the context of `MapperRepository`, this leads to cleaner, more concise code for the conversion between entities and maps, promoting maintainability and readability.

However powerful, the utilization of dynamic proxies in Java does not come without its set of considerations and trade-offs. One of the primary trade-offs lies in the performance overhead incurred by the dynamic nature of proxies, as the interception of method calls and the runtime creation of proxy instances can introduce a slight execution delay compared to direct method calls. Additionally, reliance on interface-based proxies restricts their application to scenarios involving interfaces, posing limitations in scenarios where class-based proxies may be more fitting. Recognizing these trade-offs is paramount, as it allows for informed decision-making when implementing dynamic proxies, especially in performance-sensitive contexts. Despite these considerations, the benefits offered by dynamic proxies, such as enhanced flexibility and reduced boilerplate code, often outweigh these trade-offs, reinforcing their indispensable role in dynamic and adaptable Java applications.

- **Performance overhead**: While dynamic proxies provide immense flexibility, their dynamic nature introduces a performance overhead. The interception of method calls and the creation of proxy instances at runtime can lead to slightly slower execution compared to direct method calls. Careful consideration is required when applying dynamic proxies in performance-critical scenarios.

- **Limitations on class-based proxies**: Dynamic proxies in Java are interface-based, limiting their application to scenarios involving interfaces. Class-based proxies are not as prevalent, and certain scenarios may require alternative solutions or compromises. Understanding these limitations is crucial for making informed decisions in design and implementation.

In the ever-evolving landscape of Java, `MapperRepository` emerges as a pivotal interface, seamlessly intertwining the capabilities of reflection and dynamic proxies. This interface serves as a gateway to the dynamic world of object-to-map conversions and vice versa, harnessing the intrinsic power of reflection to navigate and manipulate entities at runtime:

```java
public interface MapperRepository {

    <T> T entity(Map<String, Object> map);

    <T> Map<String, Object> map(T entity);
}
```

Interface description:

- `entity`: This method takes a map representing an object's properties and dynamically reconstructs an object of type T at runtime. Leveraging reflection, it navigates through the map, creating a dynamic proxy entity that adapts to the structure of the provided map.

- `map`: Conversely, the map method accepts an entity of type T and dynamically generates a map representing its properties. Through reflection and dynamic proxies, this method navigates the entity's structure, creating a map that encapsulates the key-value pairs of its properties.

The true prowess of `MapperRepository` lies in its symbiotic relationship with reflection. When reconstructing entities from maps, reflection allows the dynamic exploration of the object's structure, identifying fields, methods, and annotations. This exploration and dynamic proxies enable seamless adaptation to varying entity types, rendering `MapperRepository` a versatile tool for dynamic mappings.

On the reverse journey, when converting entities to maps, reflection plays a pivotal role in introspecting the object's structure. Information gleaned through reflection guides the creation of a map that accurately represents the object's properties. Dynamic proxies enhance this process by intercepting method invocations, allowing for custom logic injection, and providing a dynamic approach to object-to-map conversion.

As our journey into dynamic proxies and reflection with `MapperRepository` unfolds, we step into the implementation arena by introducing the `MapperInvocationHandler` class. This implementation, serving as the `InvocationHandler` class for dynamic proxies, bridges the abstract realm of dynamic mappings defined in `MapperRepository` to the concrete operations facilitated by the underlying `ReflectionMapper` class. Let's delve into the simplicity and power encapsulated within this handler, unlocking the potential for robust, customizable dynamic mappings:

```
public class MapperInvocationHandler implements InvocationHandler {

    private Mapper mapper = new ReflectionMapper();

    @Override
    public Object invoke(Object proxy, Method method, Object[] params)
      throws Throwable {
        String name = method.getName();
        switch (name) {
            case "entity":
                Map<String, Object> map = (Map<String, Object>)
                    params[0];
                Objects.requireNonNull(map, "map is required");
                return mapper.toEntity(map);
            case "map":
                Object entity = params[0];
```

```
                    Objects.requireNonNull(entity, "entity is required");
                    return mapper.toMap(entity);
            }
        if(method.isDefault()) {
            return InvocationHandler.invokeDefault(proxy, method,
                params);
        }
        throw new UnsupportedOperationException("The proxy is not
            supported for the method: " + method);
    }
}
```

The MapperInvocationHandler class, implementing InvocationHandler, mediates dynamic mappings. It uses a ReflectionMapper instance to convert maps to entities or entities to maps based on method calls. The handler supports default methods and ensures a smooth connection between dynamic proxies and the underlying mapping logic:

- **Dynamic method routing**: The invoke method dynamically routes method calls based on their names. For the entity method, it extracts the map from the provided parameters and delegates the operation to ReflectionMapper for entity reconstruction. Conversely, the map method, it extracts the entity and delegates it to ReflectionMapper for map creation.

- **Handling default methods**: The handler accounts for default methods in the MapperRepository interface. If a default method is invoked, it gracefully delegates the call using InvocationHandler.invokeDefault.

- **Exception handling**: In cases where an unsupported method is encountered, an UnsupportedOperationException exception is thrown, providing clear feedback on the limitations of the dynamic proxy in handling certain operations.

One of the standout features of this implementation lies in its potential for customizability. Extending the logic within each method case makes it feasible to check annotation parameters, opening the door to many customization possibilities. This approach transforms MapperRepository into a robust and adaptable tool, ready to cater to diverse mapping scenarios through the lens of reflection.

In exploring dynamic proxies and reflection within the realm of MapperRepository, MapperInvocationHandler emerges as a linchpin, seamlessly connecting abstract mappings to concrete operations. Its dynamic method routing and the ability to handle default methods make it a powerful orchestrator of dynamic mappings. The simplicity of the implementation belies its potential for customization, offering a pathway to inspect annotation parameters and tailor the mapping process to diverse scenarios. As we conclude this chapter, MapperInvocationHandler is a testament to the symbiotic relationship between dynamic proxies and reflection, showcasing their combined might in creating adaptable, customizable, and dynamic mapping solutions in Java. The upcoming practical application will illuminate how this implementation transforms abstract concepts into a toolset that empowers developers to navigate the intricate landscape of dynamic mappings easily.

Summary

On our exploration of dynamic proxies and reflection, amalgamating these powerful Java features as `MapperInvocationHandler` marks a pivotal moment in our journey. The ability to dynamically route method calls and the potential for customization through annotation parameters underscore the versatility encapsulated within this implementation. Yet, this is merely a precursor to the next chapter, where we dive into the sophisticated realm of Java annotation processing. Building upon the foundation of dynamic mappings, the annotation processor promises to elevate our capabilities further, offering a structured and compile-time approach to harnessing metadata within our code. Join us in the upcoming chapter as we unveil the intricate world of Java annotation processing, where compile-time reflection becomes a cornerstone in crafting efficient, robust, and intelligently processed Java applications.

Questions

Answer the following questions to test your knowledge of this chapter:

1. What is the primary purpose of the MapperInvocationHandler class in the context of dynamic proxies?

   A. Handling database connections

   B. Routing method calls for dynamic mappings

   C. Implementing complex business logic

   D. Parsing XML configurations

2. Which feature makes dynamic proxies adaptable in scenarios where object structures are not known until runtime?

   A. Method overloading

   B. Interface-based implementation

   C. Dynamic method routing

   D. Static method invocation

3. How does the `MapperInvocationHandler` class demonstrate customizability in the dynamic mapping process?

   A. It uses hardcoded values for method calls.

   B. It leverages external libraries for mapping.

   C. It inspects annotation parameters and adapts the mapping logic.

   D. It enforces strict immutability in mapped entities.

4. What is the primary purpose of reflection in Java?

    A. Compile-time code optimization

    B. Dynamic exploration and manipulation of object structures

    C. Secure encryption of sensitive data

    D. Asynchronous event handling

5. In the context of the `MapperRepository` interface, how does reflection contribute to dynamic mappings?

    A. It ensures type safety in method calls.

    B. It provides a secure encryption mechanism.

    C. It dynamically routes method calls.

    D. It enforces strict immutability in mapped entities.

Answers

Here are the answers to this chapter's questions:

1. B. Routing method calls for dynamic mappings

2. C. Dynamic method routing

3. C. It inspects annotation parameters and adapts the mapping logic.

4. B. Dynamic exploration and manipulation of object structures

5. C. It dynamically routes method calls.

11

Java Annotation Processor

In the dynamic landscape of Java programming, the ability to introspect and analyze code at runtime has long been facilitated by reflection. While reflection offers a powerful mechanism for inspecting and manipulating classes, fields, and methods, it comes with its trade-offs, such as performance overhead and the potential for runtime errors. Recognizing these challenges, a compelling alternative arises—shifting the focus from runtime to build time using Java Annotation Processors.

This chapter delves into the world of Java Annotation Processors, offering insights into their role as a robust tool for harnessing metadata during the compilation phase. By doing so, developers can sidestep the pitfalls associated with runtime reflection, understanding how to leverage annotation processors for enhanced code generation and manipulation. Through practical examples and hands-on exploration, you will discover the intricacies of integrating annotation processors into your development workflow, ultimately empowering you to optimize your codebase and balance flexibility and performance. Join us on this journey to unlock the full potential of Java annotation processors and transform how you approach metadata processing in your projects.

In this chapter, we'll explore the topics:

- Overview of Java Annotation Processor
- Exploring Practical Java Annotation Processor

Technical requirements

For this chapter, you will require the following:

- Java 21
- Git
- Maven
- Any preferred IDE
- This chapter's GitHub repository, found at - `https://github.com/PacktPublishing/Mastering-the-Java-Virtual-Machine/tree/main/chapter-11`

Overview of Java Annotation Processor

Developers, here we delve into the capabilities and significance of Java Annotation Processors. In the ever-evolving realm of Java, efficient and optimized code is paramount, and to achieve this, understanding the role of tools such as annotation processors becomes crucial. We'll explore why Java Annotation Processors exist, how they differ from the widely used reflection mechanism, and the trade-offs in making the right choice for your projects.

Java Annotation Processors emerged as a powerful tool to address some challenges runtime reflection poses. While reflection allows dynamic inspection and manipulation of code elements during runtime, it comes with performance overhead and the potential for runtime errors. In contrast, annotation processors operate at compile time, offering a way to analyze and generate code based on annotations present in the source code. This shift from runtime to build time brings significant advantages, including improved performance, early error detection, and enhanced code maintainability.

Distinguishing between Java Annotation Processors and reflection is crucial for optimizing Java development. Reflection, a dynamic runtime mechanism, provides flexibility but incurs a performance cost. In contrast, Java Annotation Processors operate during compilation, offering static analysis for optimizations and early error detection. This section explores these differences, empowering developers to make informed decisions based on their project needs.

Let's delve into a comparative analysis of Java Annotation Processors and reflection. While both mechanisms involve annotations for metadata processing, their execution times and impacts on performance set them apart. Reflection operates dynamically at runtime, allowing for high flexibility but incurring a runtime performance cost. In contrast, annotation processors are used during compilation, enabling optimizations and catching errors before the code runs.

The following table presents a concise comparison between reflection and Java Annotation Processors—two pivotal mechanisms in Java development. This comparison spans crucial aspects such as execution time, flexibility, performance, error detection, code generation capabilities, use cases, debugging implications, and overall usability. By juxtaposing these features, developers can gain valuable insights into when to leverage reflection's dynamic runtime capabilities and opt for the static, compile-time analysis provided by Java Annotation Processors. This table aims to serve as a practical guide, empowering developers to make informed decisions based on the specific requirements of their projects.

Feature	Reflection	Java Annotation Processors
Execution time	Runtime	Compile time
Flexibility	Dynamic; allows runtime code inspection	Static, enforces analysis during compilation

Feature	Reflection	Java Annotation Processors
Performance	May incur runtime overhead	Improved performance due to compile-time optimizations
Error detection	Runtime errors possible	Early error detection during compilation
Code generation	Limited capability for code generation	Robust support for code generation and manipulation
Use cases	Suitable for dynamic scenarios, e.g., frameworks and libraries	Preferred for static analysis, code generation, and project-wide optimizations
Debugging	May complicate debugging due to its dynamic nature	Compile-time analysis aids in cleaner debugging
Usability	Simple to use for basic introspection	Requires understanding of annotation processing and may involve more setup
Examples	`Class.forName()`, `Method.invoke()`	Frameworks such as Lombok, MapStruct, and Android's Dagger use annotation processors extensively

Table 11.1: Comparing reflection versus Java Annotation Processor

This table provides a quick overview of the key differences between reflection and Java Annotation Processors across various aspects, aiding developers in choosing the most suitable approach for their specific use cases.

Delving deeper into the trade-offs between Java Annotation Processors and reflection reveals a nuanced balance that developers must carefully consider. Reflection, with its dynamic nature, grants unparalleled flexibility by enabling runtime code inspection and modification.

Contrastingly, Java Annotation Processors operate during the compilation phase, opting for a static analysis approach. While this sacrifices some runtime flexibility, it introduces several advantages. Early error detection becomes a notable benefit, as potential issues are identified before the code is executed, reducing the likelihood of runtime errors. The trade-off pays dividends in terms of improved performance since optimizations can be applied during compilation, resulting in more efficient and streamlined code execution. Furthermore, the static nature of annotation processors contributes to cleaner and more maintainable codebases, as developers can catch and rectify issues at an earlier stage in the development process.

Ultimately, the choice between Java Annotation Processors and reflection hinges on project requirements and priorities. Developers seeking a dynamic, flexible approach may opt for reflection despite the associated runtime costs. Meanwhile, those prioritizing early error detection, performance optimization, and maintainability may find that the trade-offs of adopting annotation processors align more closely with their project goals. Striking the right balance between runtime flexibility and static analysis is key to crafting robust, efficient, and maintainable Java applications.

In the intricate world of frameworks, the Java Annotation Processor emerges as a game-changer, offering a paradigm shift in code analysis and generation compared to the runtime-centric nature of reflection. This processor operates dynamically during the build phase, providing frameworks with a potent toolset for enhanced performance, code optimization, and systematic project structuring:

- **Load and parse configuration**: During the initial step, the Java Annotation Processor meticulously reads annotations and scrutinizes the project's configuration at build time. This early analysis not only identifies annotations but also scans classes for relevant metadata, laying the foundation for subsequent processing steps.

- **Analyze dependencies**: One of the key strengths lies in the processor's ability to analyze project dependencies based on the loaded classes dynamically. By scrutinizing these dependencies, the framework gains valuable insights into the components needed for seamless functionality, fostering a more efficient and streamlined development process.

- **Build dependency tree**: Armed with insights into project dependencies, the annotation processor constructs a comprehensive dependency tree. Based on loaded classes and their interdependencies, this data structure undergoes pre-processing, enabling the creation of intricate frameworks. The resulting structures serve as a blueprint for the framework's architecture, ensuring that classes are orchestrated coherently and optimally.

- **Package application**: After the annotation processor has diligently created classes and factored in the necessary libraries, the subsequent step involves packaging the application. Following the natural flow of the code, the framework compiles and generates bytecode. This process ensures the absence of reflection, enhances application robustness, and opens avenues for creating native applications, contributing to a more efficient and self-contained end product, as the following figure shows:

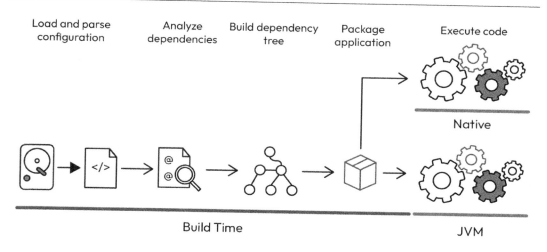

Figure 11.1: The Java perspective using Java Annotation Processor

As we conclude this exploration into Java Annotation Processors, it becomes evident that their integration offers a transformative approach to code analysis, generation, and project structuring. The dichotomy between the reflection's runtime dynamism and the Annotation Processor's compile-time prowess reveals a spectrum of trade-offs, each catering to specific development needs. We've dissected the intricacies of annotation processing from a general and framework-centric standpoint, shedding light on the advantages and sacrifices inherent in this powerful tool.

Empowered with insights into the benefits of early error detection, improved performance, and cleaner, maintainable code, you are now better equipped to navigate the decision-making process in your development projects. Striking a balance between the dynamic capabilities of reflection and the performance optimizations afforded by annotation processors is key to crafting robust, efficient, and maintainable Java applications.

To solidify your understanding, we encourage you to delve into practical exercises. Experiment with incorporating Java Annotation Processors into your projects, explore their code generation capabilities, and witness the advantages of compile-time analysis firsthand. Engage in the hands-on practice provided, and unlock a new dimension of efficiency and reliability in your Java development journey. Let the code speak, and may your exploration of Java Annotation Processors lead you to innovative and optimized solutions in your projects.

Exploring Practical Java Annotation Processor

In this hands-on segment, we'll dive into a practical exercise to reinforce the concepts we've explored regarding Java Annotation Processors. The goal is to revisit a previously examined example that utilized reflection, enabling us to compare solutions and showcase the distinctive features and advantages of employing Java Annotation Processors.

The task at hand involves converting a Map instance to an entity instance and vice versa, adhering to the specifications outlined in the provided interface:

```java
public interface Mapper {

    <T> T toEntity(Map<String, Object> map, Class<T> type);

    <T> Map<String, Object> toMap(T entity);
}
```

By revisiting this familiar scenario, you'll witness firsthand how annotation processors can streamline code generation and manipulation during compile time. As you undertake the practical exercises, consider the trade-offs, efficiencies, and benefits of annotation processors compared to reflection. Let's dive into the code and explore the potential of Java Annotation Processors in this real-world example.

We introduce two additional annotations to augment the functionality in our specific context. The Entity annotation declares a class is mappable, indicating its eligibility for the parsing process. When applied to a class, this annotation communicates to the Java Annotation Processor that instances of the class can be seamlessly converted to and from Map<String, Object>. The added annotation enhances the clarity of the mapping process, ensuring effective communication between the class and the annotation processor during compilation:

```java
@Documented
@Target(ElementType.TYPE)
@Retention(RetentionPolicy.RUNTIME)
public @interface Entity {
    String value() default "";
}
```

The @Entity annotation in Java has three annotations that define its behavior and characteristics: @Documented, @Target(ElementType.TYPE), and @Retention(RetentionPolicy.RUNTIME). The @Documented annotation ensures that its usage and presence are documented in JavaDocs. The @Target(ElementType.TYPE) annotation specifies that the @Entity annotation can only be applied to class declarations, indicating its role at the class level. Finally, the @Retention(RetentionPolicy.RUNTIME) annotation signifies that this annotation will be retained at runtime, allowing for dynamic access and reflection, which is essential for the Java Annotation Processor practice discussed in this chapter. Together, these annotations provide a clear framework for the @Entity annotation, making it well-documented, class-specific, and accessible at runtime, which is pivotal for code generation and metadata creation.

Like the Entity annotation, the Column annotation extends the customization capabilities to the property level. Applied to fields within an annotated class, it allows developers to override default property names during the conversion process. It becomes precious when dealing with diverse naming conventions, such as camel case, snake case, or kebab case, enhancing the adaptability of the class to different paradigms:

```
@Documented
@Target(ElementType.FIELD)
@Retention(RetentionPolicy.RUNTIME)
public @interface Column {
    String value() default "";
}
```

We will kickstart a Maven project that seamlessly incorporates Java and Mustache, empowering us to generate maintainable code dynamically during the build process. To integrate Mustache templates into our Java project, we'll add the Mustache compiler as a dependency. Update the pom.xml file with the following dependency:

```
<dependency>
    <groupId>com.github.spullara.mustache.java</groupId>
    <artifactId>compiler</artifactId>
    <version>0.9.6</version>
</dependency>
```

Mustache is a lightweight and powerful templating engine that developers use to generate dynamic content while keeping code logic and presentation separate. It provides a flexible and structured way to generate textual output, making it ideal for generating code, HTML, or other text-based formats. Mustache templates use placeholders, shown by double curly braces like {{variable}}. During rendering, these placeholders are replaced with real values or content.

In the context of our Maven project, we are incorporating Mustache to automate code generation. Specifically, we use it to create Java classes during the build process. By adding the Mustache compiler as a dependency in the project's pom.xml file, we seamlessly integrate Mustache into our Java project. This integration empowers us to generate maintainable code dynamically, which improves efficiency and reduces the risk of human error when manually writing repetitive or boilerplate code. Mustache templates provide a structured and clean way to define the structure of the generated code, making it easier to maintain and adapt as project requirements evolve. Overall, Mustache plays a crucial role in streamlining code generation in our Java project, enhancing code quality, and developer productivity.

In our journey to harness Java Annotation Processors' power, we now implement the EntityProcessor class. Extending AbstractProcessor, this processor plays a crucial role in scanning and processing classes annotated with the @Entity annotation:

```
@SupportedAnnotationTypes("expert.os.api.Entity")
public class EntityProcessor extends AbstractProcessor {
    // Implementation details will be discussed below
}
```

Now, let's dive into the `process` method, where the magic happens:

```java
@Override
public boolean process(Set<? extends TypeElement> annotations,
                       RoundEnvironment roundEnv) {

    final List<String> entities = new ArrayList<>();
    for (TypeElement annotation : annotations) {
        roundEnv.getElementsAnnotatedWith(annotation)
                .stream().map(e -> new ClassAnalyzer(e,
                    processingEnv))
                .map(ClassAnalyzer::get)
                .filter(IS_NOT_BLANK).forEach(entities::add);
    }

    // Further processing logic can be added here

    return true;
}
```

In this method, we initiate the processing of classes annotated with @Entity. Let's break down the key components:

1. **Scanning annotated elements**: We start by iterating over the set of TypeElement instances representing the annotation types (annotations parameter).

2. **Processing annotated elements**: For each annotation type, we use roundEnv. getElementsAnnotatedWith(annotation) to retrieve all program elements annotated with the specified annotation (in this case, @Entity).

3. **Mapping to ClassAnalyzer**: We convert the annotated elements into a stream and map each element to a ClassAnalyzer instance. ClassAnalyzer is a custom class designed to analyze and extract information from the annotated class.

4. **Filtering blank results**: We then extract the analysis result from each ClassAnalyzer instance using .map(ClassAnalyzer::get). After that, we filter out any blank or null entries from the list using .filter(IS_NOT_BLANK).

5. **Collecting results**: The non-blank results are collected into the entities list using .forEach(entities::add).

6. **Further processing logic**: The method serves as a foundation for any additional processing logic. Developers can extend this part to include custom actions based on the extracted entities.

This `process` method forms the core of our annotation processing logic. It scans, analyzes, and collects information from classes annotated with `@Entity`, providing a flexible and extensible mechanism for code generation and manipulation. Let's continue our exploration and delve into the additional processing steps that can be integrated into this method to tailor it to our project's specific requirements.

In the intricate process of analyzing an entity class annotated with `@Entity`, `ClassAnalyzer` plays a pivotal role. It scrutinizes each field within the class, employing a collaborative effort with `FieldAnalyzer` for a detailed examination:

```java
public class ClassAnalyzer implements Supplier<String> {

    private String analyze(TypeElement typeElement) throws IOException
    {

        // Extracting fields annotated with @Column
        final List<String> fields = processingEnv.getElementUtils()
            .getAllMembers(typeElement).stream()
            .filter(EntityProcessor.IS_FIELD.and(EntityProcessor.
              HAS_ANNOTATION))
            .map(f -> new FieldAnalyzer(f, processingEnv,
              typeElement))
            .map(FieldAnalyzer::get)
            .collect(Collectors.toList());

        // Obtaining metadata for the entity class
        EntityModel metadata = getMetadata(typeElement, fields);

        // Creating the processed class based on metadata
        createClass(entity, metadata);

        // Logging the discovery of fields for the entity class
        LOGGER.info("Found the fields: " + fields + " to the class: "
          + metadata.getQualified());

        // Returning the qualified name of the entity class
        return metadata.getQualified();
    }
}
```

Here, the code is explained in more depth:

1. **Field analysis**: The heart of the `analyze` method lies in extracting fields from the given `TypeElement`. Using `processingEnv.getElementUtils()`, it retrieves all members of the class and filters them to include only fields annotated with `@Column`. `FieldAnalyzer` is instantiated for each field, allowing for detailed analysis.

2. **FieldAnalyzer collaboration**: The creation of `FieldAnalyzer` for each field involves passing the field (`f`), the processing environment (`processingEnv`), and the type element of the entity class (`typeElement`). This collaborative effort with `FieldAnalyzer` enables an in-depth examination of each field.

3. **Metadata extraction**: The `getMetadata` method is then invoked to obtain metadata for the entity class. This metadata likely includes information about the class itself and the fields discovered during the analysis.

4. **Class creation**: The `createClass` method is called, indicating that the Entity class is being generated based on the metadata. This step is crucial for code generation and manipulation based on the analyzed class.

5. **Logging information**: Logging statements, facilitated by the `LOGGER` instance, provide visibility into the discovered fields and their association with the class. It aids in tracking and understanding the analysis process.

6. **Return statement**: The method concludes by returning the qualified name of the analyzed entity class. This information may be useful for further processing or reporting.

This collaborative interaction between `ClassAnalyzer` and `FieldAnalyzer` encapsulates the essence of thorough entity class analysis. As part of the broader annotation processing framework, it sets the stage for subsequent actions, such as code generation, metadata extraction, and logging. As we delve deeper into the book, we'll uncover more intricacies of the analysis process and its impact on the development workflow.

In code generation, the choice of tools can significantly impact the maintainability and flexibility of the generated code. One standout approach embraced in the entity class generation process is the utilization of Mustache templates. Let's explore the virtues of leveraging Mustache for class generation and why it surpasses manual text concatenation:

- **Declarative templating**: Mustache provides a declarative and template-based approach to code generation. Rather than manually concatenating strings to construct classes, developers can define templates using Mustache syntax. This approach aligns with a more intuitive and maintainable way of expressing generated code structure.

- **Readability and maintainability**: Mustache templates enhance the readability of generated code. By separating the template from the actual code, developers can focus on the logical structure of the class without being entangled in intricate string concatenation. This separation improves code maintainability and reduces the chances of introducing errors during manual text manipulation.

- **Dynamic data binding**: Mustache supports dynamic data binding, allowing the injection of data into templates during the generation process. This dynamic nature enables the adaptation of generated code based on varying inputs or metadata obtained during the analysis phase. In contrast, manual concatenation lacks this level of flexibility.

- **Consistency across generations**: Mustache templates provide a standardized and consistent approach to code generation. Templates can be reused across different entities, ensuring a uniform structure for generated classes. This consistency simplifies the maintenance of templates and promotes a cohesive code-generation strategy.

- **Seamless integration with Java**: Mustache has robust support for integration with Java. By incorporating Mustache into the code generation process, developers can seamlessly combine the power of Java logic with the clarity of Mustache templates. This synergy results in a more natural and expressive generation workflow.

- **Avoidance of string manipulation pitfalls**: Manual string concatenation for code generation can introduce pitfalls, such as formatting errors, typos, or unintended variations in code structure. Mustache eliminates these risks by providing a higher-level abstraction that mitigates the need for meticulous string manipulation.

In essence, leveraging Mustache for class generation introduces a paradigm shift in the approach to code generation. It promotes clarity, maintainability, and flexibility, offering a superior alternative to manual text concatenation's error-prone and cumbersome nature. As we progress in our exploration of annotation processing and code generation, the integration of Mustache templates will continue to showcase its prowess in enhancing the efficiency and reliability of our development workflow.

The provided Mustache template, combined with `EntityModel` to generate an entity class, showcases the elegance and clarity Mustache brings to code generation. Let's delve into the key aspects of this template:

```
package {{packageName}};

// (Imports and annotations)

public final class {{className}} implements EntityMetadata {

    private final List<FieldMetadata> fields;

    // Constructor and initialization of fields

    // Implementation of EntityMetadata methods

    // ... Other methods ...

}
```

In this Mustache template, a Java class implementing the `EntityMetadata` interface is dynamically generated. The placeholders `{{packageName}}` and `{{className}}` will be replaced during code generation. The class includes a list of `FieldMetadata` objects representing entity fields, and the constructor initializes these fields. This template streamlines code generation, enhancing clarity and maintainability by automating the creation of metadata classes in Java projects. Here, we explain the template in more depth:

- **Package declaration**: The {{packageName}} placeholder dynamically injects the package name obtained from EntityModel. It ensures that the generated entity class resides in the correct package.

- **Imports and annotations**: The template includes necessary imports and annotations, such as import java.util.List;, import java.util.Map;, and @Generated. The @Generated annotation includes metadata indicating the generator tool and the generation date.

- **Class declaration**: The {{className}} placeholder injects the name of the generated class (EntityModel#getClassName()). The class implements the EntityMetadata interface, ensuring adherence to the specified contract.

- **Fields initialization**: The constructor initializes the fields list with instances of FieldMetadata. The list is populated based on the fields defined in EntityModel. This dynamic initialization ensures that the generated class includes metadata for each field.

- **EntityMetadata implementation**: The template implements various methods defined in the EntityMetadata interface. These methods provide information about the entity class, such as its name, class instance, fields, and mappings.

- **FieldMetadata generation**: The {{#fields}} section dynamically generates code for each field. It creates instances of the corresponding FieldMetadata for each field, adding them to the fields list during class instantiation.

- **Date and generator information**: The @Generated annotation includes information about the generator tool (EntityMetadata Generator) and the date of generation ({{now}}). This metadata aids in tracking the origin and timing of the class generation.

In essence, Mustache allows for creating a clean and maintainable template where placeholders seamlessly integrate with the data provided by EntityModel. This template-driven approach enhances the readability of the generated code and promotes consistency across different entities. As we progress, the flexibility of Mustache will continue to shine, allowing for further customization and adaptation to specific project requirements.

In the fascinating journey of annotation processing and code generation, the pivotal moment arrives when we transform the analyzed entity metadata into tangible Java source code. This crucial step is orchestrated by the createClass method, which seamlessly combines the information from EntityModel with the expressive power of the Mustache template:

```
private void createClass(Element entity, EntityModel metadata) throws
IOException {
    Filer filer = processingEnv.getFiler();
    JavaFileObject fileObject = filer.createSourceFile(metadata.
      getQualified(), entity);
```

```
        try (Writer writer = fileObject.openWriter()) {
            template.execute(writer, metadata);
        }
    }
```

This method, `createClass`, is a pivotal component of the Java Annotation Processor, responsible for generating source code dynamically. It takes `Element`, which represents the annotated class (`entity`), and `EntityModel`, which contains metadata for code generation (`metadata`). Utilizing `Filer` from the processing environment, it creates `JavaFileObject` for the specified qualified name of the generated class. The method then opens a writer for the file and executes the Mustache template (`template`) by passing in the writer and the metadata. Ultimately, this process ensures the generation of source code for the annotated class with the corresponding metadata, contributing to the power and flexibility of the Java Annotation Processor. Here, the code is explained in more depth:

1. **Acquiring the filer**: We obtain the `Filer` instance from the annotation processing environment. `Filer` is our gateway to file creation within the build process.

2. **Creating a source file**: The `filer.createSourceFile(metadata.getQualified(), entity)` line orchestrates the creation of a new source file. The fully qualified name (`metadata.getQualified()`) provides a unique identity for the generated class, and the reference to the original `entity` ensures a connection between the generated and original entities.

3. **Opening a writer**: The code gracefully opens a writer for the newly created source file as we write the generated content. `try (Writer writer = fileObject.openWriter())` automatically closes the writer after its scope is executed.

4. **Mustache magic**: The real magic unfolds with `template.execute(writer, metadata)`. This line triggers the Mustache engine to interpret the template, injecting the data from `EntityModel` (`metadata`) into the placeholders. The result is a dynamically generated entity class.

5. **Automatic Resource Management (ARM)**: Thanks to Java's ARM, the opened writer is automatically closed, mitigating the risk of resource leaks and contributing to cleaner, more robust code.

This method encapsulates the alchemy of transforming metadata into tangible code. The Mustache template acts as a dynamic blueprint, allowing for flexibility and maintainability in code generation. As we progress in our exploration, the generated entity classes will come to life, reflecting the richness of metadata analysis and the efficiency of code generation in our annotation processing adventure.

As we venture into the testing phase of our annotation processor, we find ourselves at the crossroads of dependency management. We will explore two approaches for including the processor in our Maven project: one employs the `provided` scope and the other utilizes the `annotationProcessorPaths` configuration within the Maven Compiler Plugin.

The first option is to use the `provided` scope:

```xml
<dependency>
    <groupId>${project.groupId}</groupId>
    <artifactId>processor</artifactId>
    <version>${project.version}</version>
    <scope>provided</scope>
</dependency>
```

This approach declares the processor dependent on the `provided` scope. It signifies that the processor will be available during compilation but not bundled with the final application. It is a suitable choice when the processor's functionality is strictly needed at compile time and not runtime.

The second option is to leverage `annotationProcessorPaths`:

```xml
<build>
    <plugins>
        <plugin>
            <artifactId>maven-compiler-plugin</artifactId>
            <version>3.11.0</version>
            <configuration>
                <target>${maven.compiler.target}</target>
                <source>${maven.compiler.source}</source>
                <annotationProcessorPaths>
                    <path>
                        <groupId>${project.groupId}</groupId>
                        <artifactId>processor</artifactId>
                        <version>${project.version}</version>
                    </path>
                </annotationProcessorPaths>
            </configuration>
        </plugin>
    </plugins>
</build>
```

Alternatively, we can leverage the `annotationProcessorPaths` configuration within the Maven Compiler Plugin. This approach provides a more direct integration with the compiler, ensuring the processor is available during compilation without being included in the final artifact. It offers a more explicit declaration of the annotation processor's role in the compilation workflow.

Please, once you go to this approach, consider the following:

- Use the `provided` scope when you want the processor for compilation only and not as part of the runtime dependencies

- Utilize `annotationProcessorPaths` when you prefer a configuration-centric approach, directly specifying annotation processors for the compiler plugin

Now, we dive into a practical example of using our annotation processor by annotating a class and witnessing the magic unfold during the build process.

Consider the following `Animal` class adorned with our custom annotations:

```
@Entity("kind")
public class Animal {

    @Id
    private String name;

    @Column
    private String color;
}
```

This simple class represents an animal, with annotations indicating the entity name and specific details about the fields. At the build time, thanks to our Annotation Processor, classes such as `AnimalEntityMetaData`, `AnimalNameFieldMetaData`, and `AnimalColorFieldMetaData` are generated based on the annotated class and its fields.

Let's take a closer look at the generated `AnimalEntityMetaData` class:

```
@Generated(value = "EntityMetadata Generator", date = "2023-11-
23T18:42:27.793291")
public final class AnimalEntityMetaData implements EntityMetadata {

    private final List<FieldMetadata> fields;

    public AnimalEntityMetaData() {
        this.fields = new ArrayList<>();
        this.fields.add(new expert.os.example.
          AnimalNameFieldMetaData());
        this.fields.add(new expert.os.example.
          AnimalColorFieldMetaData());
    }

    // ... Rest of the class ...

}
```

This class serves as metadata for the `Animal` entity, providing information about its name, class, fields, and more. Notably, it includes instances of `FieldMetadata` for each field in the `Animal` class.

Here, we will look at the generated code in more depth:

- **Constructor initialization**: In the constructor, instances of FieldMetadata (such as AnimalNameFieldMetaData and AnimalColorFieldMetaData) are added to the fields list. This initialization captures the metadata for each field defined in the Animal class.

- **Implementation of EntityMetadata Methods**: The generated class implements methods defined in the EntityMetadata interface. These methods enable the retrieval of information such as the entity name, class instance, fields, and more.

- **Annotations for code generation**: The @Generated annotation includes details about the generation process, such as the tool used ("EntityMetadata Generator") and the date of generation.

In the target directory at build time, the generated classes are organized, showcasing the dynamic nature of code generation. Each field in the original `Animal` class contributes to creating a corresponding metadata class as the following figure shows:

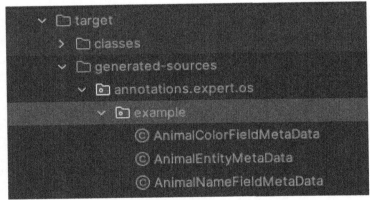

Figure 11.2: The classes generated at build time

In this hands-on exploration of annotation processors, we've witnessed the transformative capabilities they bring to Java development. The practice code exemplifies how, with a sprinkle of annotations, we can orchestrate the generation of intricate metadata, propelling our projects to new heights of efficiency and maintainability.

The annotated `Animal` class served as our canvas, adorned with custom annotations such as `@Entity` and `@Id`. As the build process unfolded, our custom annotation processor worked diligently behind the scenes, crafting a symphony of metadata classes: `AnimalEntityMetaData`, `AnimalNameFieldMetaData`, and `AnimalColorFieldMetaData`.

Here is what we unveiled in this process:

- **Dynamic metadata generation**: The generated metadata classes dynamically adapt to the annotated class's structure, showcasing annotation processors' flexibility and adaptability.

- **Efficient code organization**: Our codebase remains clean and concise by automating metadata generation. Boilerplate code is replaced with dynamically crafted classes, fostering better organization and readability.

- **Build-time magic**: The magic happens at build time. Annotation processors provide a robust mechanism to analyze and generate code before the application runs, enhancing performance and eliminating runtime reflection costs.

- **Customization at scale**: Annotations empower developers to convey intent and customization preferences. Our annotation processor translates this intent into tangible metadata, providing a powerful avenue for large-scale codebase management.

As we reflect on this practice, we've just scratched the surface of the potential annotation processors offer. The journey ahead invites us to explore advanced scenarios, tackle real-world challenges, and harness the full spectrum of customization options. Annotation processors emerge as tools for code generation and catalysts for a paradigm shift in how we architect and maintain our Java projects.

Summary

In concluding our journey through annotation processors, we've explored the art of code generation and the elegance they bring to Java development. From annotated classes to dynamic metadata, we've witnessed the transformative power of automation. As we transition to the final considerations, the next chapter serves as a compass, guiding us through best practices, potential pitfalls, and strategic insights into the broader landscape of Java development.

Our exploration has armed us with the tools to wield annotation processors effectively. Join us in the concluding chapter as we distill vital insights and chart a course for the future. The final considerations encapsulate the essence of our annotation processor odyssey, offering a roadmap for mastering these tools and shaping the trajectory of Java development. Let's embark on this last leg of our journey together.

Questions

Answer the following questions to test your knowledge of this chapter:

1. What is the primary role of the Java Annotation Processor introduced in this chapter?

    A. Dynamic code execution

    B. Code compilation at runtime

    C. Metadata analysis and code generation

    D. User interface design

2. In the context of Java Annotation Processors, what is the purpose of the
    `@SupportedAnnotationTypes` annotation?

    A. Declaring runtime retention

    B. Indicating compiler paths

    C. Specifying supported annotations

    D. Defining annotation inheritance

3. What is the advantage of using Java Annotation Processors over reflection, as discussed in
    the chapter?

    A. Greater runtime flexibility

    B. Improved performance and early error detection

    C. Simplified code inspection

    D. Enhanced debugging capabilities

4. Which Maven scope indicates that a dependency should be available only during compilation
    and not included in the runtime dependencies?

    A. `compile`

    B. `runtime`

    C. `provided`

    D. `annotationProcessor`

5. What is the primary purpose of the Mustache template in the context of the Java Annotation
    Processor practice session?

    A. Generating random code snippets

    B. Creating JavaDoc documentation

    C. Enabling code concatenation

    D. Facilitating maintainable code generation

6. Which Maven configuration allows specifying annotation processors directly for the
    Compiler Plugin?

    A. `<annotationPaths>`

    B. `<annotationProcessors>`

    C. `<annotationProcessorPaths>`

    D. `<compilerAnnotations>`

Answers

Here are the answers to this chapter's questions:

1. C. Metadata analysis and code generation
2. C. Specifying supported annotations
3. B. Improved performance and early error detection
4. C. `provided`
5. D. Facilitating maintainable code generation
6. C. `<annotationProcessorPaths>`

12

Final Considerations

As we conclude our journey through the intricate landscapes of the JVM, it is fitting to reflect upon the wealth of knowledge we have unearthed in the preceding chapters. This book has delved deep into the inner workings of the JVM, unraveling its mysteries and empowering you with a profound understanding of Java's runtime environment. In this final chapter, we aim to provide some overarching considerations, tying together the threads of our exploration and offering insights that transcend the confines of these pages.

Throughout this book, we have strived to equip you with a comprehensive understanding of the JVM, covering topics ranging from memory management and class loading to bytecode execution and garbage collection. As we approach the conclusion, we want to extend our appreciation for your dedication to mastering the intricacies of Java's powerhouse. However, the journey doesn't end here; instead, it serves as a stepping stone for further exploration and growth. In this final chapter, we will guide you toward additional resources and references that can serve as compass points in your ongoing quest for JVM mastery. These recommended readings will extend and deepen your understanding, providing a roadmap for continued learning in the dynamic realm of Java development.

In this chapter, we'll explore the following topics:

- Exploring the JVM landscape
- Navigating the system operation architecture
- Mastering the art of garbage collection
- Platform threads and virtual threads

Exploring the JVM landscape

In our journey through the intricacies of the JVM, we have navigated through diverse terrains, from the nuances of bytecode compilation to the delicate choreography of garbage collection. The beauty of the JVM lies in its adaptability, catering to a wide array of applications and scenarios. As we bring this book to a close, it's essential to recognize the multifaceted nature of JVM implementations.

This chapter serves as a vantage point to survey the landscape we've traversed, reminding us that the JVM ecosystem is far from monolithic. While our discussions have provided a solid foundation, it's crucial to acknowledge the diversity among JVM implementations. Each environment may exhibit unique characteristics and optimizations, adding layers of complexity and depth.

One of the remarkable aspects of the JVM is its adherence to a minimum set of specifications while allowing for specialization. This balance between standardization and adaptability makes the JVM a powerhouse in programming languages. To delve further into the intricacies and specifications governing the JVM, consider exploring *The Java® Virtual Machine Specification* available at `https://docs.oracle.com/javase/specs/jvms/se21/html/index.html`. This detailed resource provides an in-depth look into the inner workings of the JVM, offering insights that extend beyond the scope of this book.

For a comprehensive understanding of the Java programming language itself and its interactions with the JVM, *The Java® Language Specification* at `https://docs.oracle.com/javase/specs/jls/se21/html/index.html` is an invaluable reference. This specification elucidates the rules and semantics that govern the Java language, complementing our exploration of the JVM.

As we conclude our expedition through the JVM, let these resources serve as beacons guiding you to further depths of knowledge. The journey does not end here; it evolves, much like the dynamic landscape of Java development. Embrace the diversity, explore the nuances, and continue to unravel the mysteries of the JVM.

Navigating the system operation architecture

In our exploration of the JVM, we've peeled back the layers of bytecode execution, memory management, and garbage collection. However, a crucial dimension of JVM mastery is understanding its integration with the broader system operation architecture. This section is a gateway to unraveling the intricate dance between the JVM and the underlying operating system, a nexus where efficiency and performance harmonize.

While our journey has primarily focused on the JVM's internal mechanics, delving into the symbiotic relationship between the JVM and the operating system unveils new vistas. The system operation architecture is pivotal in shaping the JVM's behavior, influencing aspects such as thread management, I/O operations, and resource allocation. Understanding this integration is paramount for Java developers aiming to optimize their applications for specific operating environments.

To illuminate the path toward a deeper comprehension of system operation architectures, we recommend exploring *Modern Operating Systems* by Andrew S. Tanenbaum. This seminal work provides an overview of operating systems, offering insights into their design principles, functionalities, and interactions with software applications. By delving into Tanenbaum's expertise, you'll gain a broader perspective on the intricate dance between the JVM and the underlying operating system.

As you embark on this exploration, remember that a well-rounded understanding of the system operation architecture enhances your ability to optimize Java applications. From process scheduling to memory management, the operating system influences the JVM's performance at every turn. Armed with insights from *Modern Operating Systems*, you'll be better equipped to navigate the nuances of system-level interactions, unlocking new possibilities for efficiency and robust application design.

Mastering the art of garbage collection

As we conclude our exploration of the JVM, it's imperative to spotlight a critical aspect that profoundly influences application performance – the Garbage Collector. While we've touched on the principles of garbage collection, the intricacies of this process extend far beyond the scope of a single chapter. To delve deeper into this complex realm, we recommend immersing yourself in dedicated resources, such as *Java Memory Management – a Comprehensive Guide to Garbage Collection and JVM Tuning* by Maaike van Putten and Sean Kenned.

Garbage collection, the unsung hero of memory management, ensures the efficient allocation and deallocation of resources within the JVM. While we've provided foundational insights, *Java Memory Management* delves into the nuances of garbage collection algorithms, tuning strategies, and best practices. This book guides those seeking mastery in optimizing Java applications by fine-tuning the Garbage Collector to align with specific performance requirements.

For a more immersive understanding of the challenges and solutions in Garbage Collector optimization, Bruno Borges' workshop, *Secrets of Performance Tuning Java on Kubernetes*, presented at Devoxx BE, is a treasure trove of insights. In this workshop, Borges elucidates real-world scenarios and common pitfalls encountered in Garbage Collector tuning, especially in Java applications running on Kubernetes. The session provides a practical lens into the dynamic landscape of performance optimization.

As you embark on your quest for Garbage Collector mastery, let these resources be your guiding lights. The journey into the intricate world of memory management is ongoing, and the depth of understanding you seek will contribute to the resilience and efficiency of your Java applications. Remember, the nuances of garbage collection are not merely theoretical – they manifest in the responsiveness and reliability of your software.

Platform threads and virtual threads

In the evolving landscape of Java concurrency, the role of threads takes center stage, influencing the performance and responsiveness of our applications. With the release of version 21, the Java platform introduces a groundbreaking paradigm shift – the coexistence of two distinct thread types, platform threads and the revolutionary virtual threads.

Traditionally, every instance of `java.lang.Thread` in the JDK has been a platform thread. This thread type runs Java code on an underlying OS thread, monopolizing that thread for the entirety of the code's execution. The number of platform threads is limited by the number of available OS threads, leading to potential bottlenecks in resource utilization.

Virtual threads mark a paradigmatic shift in the concurrency landscape. Unlike their platform counterparts, virtual threads run Java code on an underlying OS thread without capturing it for the code's entire lifetime. It means that multiple virtual threads can efficiently share the same OS thread, offering a lightweight and scalable approach to concurrency. In contrast to the limited number of platform threads, the flexibility of virtual threads allows for a much larger pool, making them a powerful tool for optimizing resource usage.

Virtual threads introduce the *M:N* scheduling concept, a departure from the traditional *1:1* scheduling of platform threads. In this new paradigm, a substantial number (*M*) of virtual threads can be scheduled to run on a smaller number (*N*) of OS threads. This approach mirrors the success of user-mode threads in other languages, such as goroutines in Go and processes in Erlang. It harks back to Java's early days when green threads, albeit sharing a single OS thread, laid the foundation for what would later become the virtual threads we have today.

As we navigate the threadscape of the JVM, embracing the synergy of both platform threads and virtual threads becomes pivotal. The efficiency gains and scalability offered by virtual threads are transformative, especially in scenarios where resource optimization is paramount. Whether you're orchestrating complex concurrent operations or aiming for more responsive applications, understanding the nuances of these thread types equips you to make informed choices.

In this dynamic era of Java concurrency, where threads are no longer one-size-fits-all, the ability to leverage both platform and virtual threads empowers developers to navigate the complex terrain of modern application development. As you delve into the intricacies of *M:N* scheduling and lightweight concurrency, seize the opportunity to enhance the responsiveness and efficiency of your Java applications in the era of virtual threads.

Summary

As we draw the final curtain on our exploration of the JVM, we extend our sincere gratitude to your company on this journey. It's been a pleasure delving into the intricate workings of the JVM, from bytecode intricacies to the advent of virtual threads.

We hope this book has been enlightening and empowering, giving you a deeper understanding of the JVM's pivotal role in Java application development. The dynamic landscape of garbage collection, system operations, and the revolutionary era of virtual threads await your continued exploration.

Thank you for investing your time and curiosity in this endeavor. We hope this book has sparked new insights, fueled your passion for Java development, and provided practical knowledge for your coding ventures.

As you venture into the ever-evolving realm of JVM mastery, may your coding endeavors be efficient, your applications resilient, and your curiosity insatiable. Happy coding, and we sincerely hope you enjoyed the journey through the JVM!

Index

V

Z

packtpub.com

Subscribe to our online digital library for full access to over 7,000 books and videos, as well as industry leading tools to help you plan your personal development and advance your career. For more information, please visit our website.

Why subscribe?

- Spend less time learning and more time coding with practical eBooks and Videos from over 4,000 industry professionals

- Improve your learning with Skill Plans built especially for you

- Get a free eBook or video every month

- Fully searchable for easy access to vital information

- Copy and paste, print, and bookmark content

Did you know that Packt offers eBook versions of every book published, with PDF and ePub files available? You can upgrade to the eBook version at packtpub.com and as a print book customer, you are entitled to a discount on the eBook copy. Get in touch with us at customercare@packtpub.com for more details.

At www.packtpub.com, you can also read a collection of free technical articles, sign up for a range of free newsletters, and receive exclusive discounts and offers on Packt books and eBooks.

Other Books You May Enjoy

If you enjoyed this book, you may be interested in these other books by Packt:

Learn Java with Projects

Dr. Seán Kennedy, Maaike van Putten

ISBN: 978-1-83763-718-8

- Get a clear understanding of Java fundamentals such as primitive types, operators, scope, conditional statements, loops, exceptions, and arrays
- Master OOP constructs such as classes, objects, enums, interfaces, and records
- Develop a deep understanding of OOP principles such as polymorphism, inheritance, and encapsulation
- Delve into the advanced topics of generics, collections, lambdas, streams, and concurrency
- Visualize what is happening in memory when you call a method or create an object
- Appreciate how effective learning-by-doing is

Transitioning to Java

Ken Fogel

ISBN: 978-1-80461-401-3

- Gain a solid understanding of the syntax in Java
- Explore the object-oriented programming basics of the Java language
- Discover how to implement functions in Java
- Understand which Java frameworks would be best for solving various problems
- Explore creational, structural, and behavioral patterns in Java
- Get to grips with server-side coding in Java

Packt is searching for authors like you

If you're interested in becoming an author for Packt, please visit `authors.packtpub.com` and apply today. We have worked with thousands of developers and tech professionals, just like you, to help them share their insight with the global tech community. You can make a general application, apply for a specific hot topic that we are recruiting an author for, or submit your own idea.

Share Your Thoughts

Now you've finished *Mastering the Java Virtual Machine*, we'd love to hear your thoughts! Scan the QR code below to go straight to the Amazon review page for this book and share your feedback or leave a review on the site that you purchased it from.

`https://packt.link/r/1835467962`

Your review is important to us and the tech community and will help us make sure we're delivering excellent quality content.

Download a free PDF copy of this book

Thanks for purchasing this book!

Do you like to read on the go but are unable to carry your print books everywhere?

Is your eBook purchase not compatible with the device of your choice?

Don't worry, now with every Packt book you get a DRM-free PDF version of that book at no cost.

Read anywhere, any place, on any device. Search, copy, and paste code from your favorite technical books directly into your application.

The perks don't stop there, you can get exclusive access to discounts, newsletters, and great free content in your inbox daily

Follow these simple steps to get the benefits:

1. Scan the QR code or visit the link below

https://packt.link/free-ebook/9781835467961

2. Submit your proof of purchase

3. That's it! We'll send your free PDF and other benefits to your email directly

Printed in Great Britain
by Amazon

45964690R00130